The Ekphrastic Writer

The Ekphrastic Writer

*Creating Art-Influenced Poetry,
Fiction and Nonfiction*

Janée J. Baugher

McFarland & Company, Inc., Publishers
Jefferson, North Carolina

Library of Congress Cataloguing-in-Publication Data

Names: Baugher, Janée J., author.
Title: The ekphrastic writer : creating art-influenced poetry, fiction and nonfiction / Janée J. Baugher.
Description: Jefferson, North Carolina : McFarland & Company, Inc., Publishers, 2020. | Includes bibliographical references and index.
Identifiers: LCCN 2020020128 | ISBN 9781476679457 (paperback : acid free paper) ∞
ISBN 9781476639611 (ebook)
Subjects: LCSH: Ekphrasis. | Description (Rhetoric) | Creation (Literary, artistic, etc.) | Art and literature.
Classification: LCC PN56.E45 B38 2020 | DDC 808—dc23
LC record available at https://lccn.loc.gov/2020020128

British Library cataloguing data are available

ISBN (print) 978-1-4766-7945-7
ISBN (ebook) 978-1-4766-3961-1

Front cover: Willem van Haecht, *Apelles Painting Campaspe*, oil on panel, 41" × 58.5", c. 1630 (courtesy of the Mauritshuis, The Hague, Netherlands). Printed in the United States of America

Printed in the United States of America

McFarland & Company, Inc., Publishers
Box 611, Jefferson, North Carolina 28640
www.mcfarlandpub.com

For Dad & Mom,
I love you

Table of Contents

Acknowledgments

Much gratitude for your tutelage, your secretarial and editorial assistance, your love, and your professional support: Mom (Kris), Dad (Bob), Karen & Brad Brown, Shawn Baugher, Gerard Wozek, Charles Emerson, Rosemary Adang, Judy Skillman, Jason Bourguignon, Peter Elbow, Jonathan Johnson, Jana Harris, Belle Randall, Michael Hickey Michael J. Grodesky, Jonathan Lampel, Meghan McCandless, Tom C. Hunley, North Cascades Institute Residency, Das River House Artist Residency, and Pacific Beach Lighthouse Writers Residency.

Thank you to the writers who said yes when I asked if they'd be willing to write ekphrastically for this project: Kim Addonizio, Vidhu Aggarwal, Rae Armantrout, Kim Barnes, Grace Bauer, Erin Belieu, Robin Chapman, Marilyn Chin, Nicole Cooley, Peter Cooley, Lynn Crawford, Sayantani Dasgupta, Lucille Lang Day, Rebecca Foust, Peter Grandbois, Hedy Habra, Jana Harris, Didi Jackson, Major Jackson, Jonathan Johnson, Alice Jones, Jeffrey Levine, Laura McCullough, Sandra Meek, Michael Mejia, Judith Skillman, Michael Spence, Cole Swensen, Gerard Wozek, and David Wright.

With gratitude to the following visual artists, galleries, and museums: George Rodriguez; Sandy Skoglund; Kristina J. Baugher; Lo Ch'ing; Etsuko Ichikawa; Sally Mann; Kara Walker; Carmen Herrera; Richard Billingham; Yayoi Kusama; Gagosian Gallery (NYC); Sikkema Jenkins & Co.; Lisson Gallery (London); Saatchi Gallery (London); Museum of Fine Arts, Houston; Fairchild Tropical Botanic Garden, Miami, Florida; Mauritshuis, The Hague (Netherlands); National Portrait Gallery, Smithsonian Institution; New Orleans Auction Galleries; Art Resource, NY; Art Institute of Chicago Public Domain collection; Metropolitan Museum of Art Open Access collection (NY); Philadelphia Museum of Art of New York City Public Domain collection; and J. Paul Getty Museum Open Content program.

With appreciation to the editors at the literary magazines and book press wherein the following ekphrastic writing found an earlier home:

"After Alberto Giacometti's sculptures" by JJB reprinted from Art Access Vol. 29 No. 2 by permission of the author; "After Allison Collins' 2002 painting, Steptoe Butte" by JJB reprinted from Art Access Vol. 29 No. 1 by permission of the author; "After Francisco de Goya's painting, The Third of May 1808 in Madrid: The Execution at Principe Pío" by JJB reprinted from Art Access Vol. 28 No. 6 by permission of the author; "After René Magritte's 1928 painting, The Lovers" by JJB reprinted from Art Access Vol. 29 No. 3 by permission of the author; "After Sandro Botticelli's c. 1475 painting, Spring" by JJB reprinted from Art Access Vol. 28 No. 6 by permission of the author; "The Anatomy Lesson of Dr. Nicolaes Tulp" by Jeffrey Levine from At The Kinnegad Home for the Bewildered, © 2019 , by permission of Salmon Poetry publisher and the author; "Babies at Paradise Pond" by Kim Addonizio reprinted from The American Journal of Poetry Vol. 7 by permission of the author; and "Tia Catrina |||| Uncle Sam" by Michael Mejia reprinted from DIAGRAM Vol. 19 No. 6 by permission of the author.

Preface

The first time I committed ekphrasis was in 1995 at the Guggenheim Museum in New York City. It was a small painting by Georg Baselitz that caused in me the Stendhal Syndrome—floating amid concentric circles painted in reds and browns, a dwarfish man with malformed limbs. Crude sketches of serpents and snakes created a vortex around him. Seemingly bewildered, his eyes were fused open and mouth agape. The painting was entitled *Der Dichter*, German for *the poet*. Although I had not yet been introduced to the term ekphrasis, naïvely I called my poem, "Poet Describing Painting Describing Poet."

Some might wonder, as an aesthetic pursuit, what currency does ekphrastic writing hold? To the literary canon? To the art world? To the general public? Ekphrastic criticism has been treated ad nauseam. It is about time that we finally have a comprehensive guide for creative writers on the mode of ekphrastic writing. My wish was to create a book that I would have wanted when I was a young ekphrasist and also one that I wish I had when I began teaching ekphrasis across genres twenty years ago.

In seventh grade, on the first day of school, our mathematics teacher held up a can of soup and said she could spend the whole term using that one specific object to teach us all that we needed to know. An entire semester's worth of instruction on a soup can? Did it matter if the contents were clam chowder or alphabet? Minestrone or split pea? That proclamation of hers haunted me for decades. "Eureka," I imagine her exclaiming when she was challenged with how to get a gaggle of twelve-year-olds excited about mathematics. How to encapsulate the concepts of radius, circumference, perimeter, area, volume, angles, fractions, and the like in a single, tangible object? Recently, I realized that the spirit of her message was that she had arrived at a portal through which she could teach her passion. Any subject, I now know, can be taught using the visual arts as a starting point.

While *product* is vital to a majority of writers, this book's primary

1

focus is on *process*. This book was designed to be used in the classroom by instructors who are comfortable giving their students artistic freedom in the ideas and assignments presented, as well as by independent writers. This guide, ultimately, is an invitation to marvel in the deep wonderment of the visual arts and to see how that marveling might ignite your writing.

Introduction

Art contains multitudes.

First and foremost, I am optimistic that the artwork I have selected for this book will compel you to write ekphrastically. Even if you do not feel tempted by each image, it is a way to develop your ekphrastic skills, and it's a doable challenge. Second, the artwork here represents images on which contemporary writers created poems and short prose specifically for this book. The pairing of image and companion text will allow you to appreciate the myriad of ekphrastic responses, as well as to become introduced to current practices in ekphrasis.

What is required of someone wishing to write ekphrastically? Ekphrasis is an aesthetic pursuit. So, eyesight and an investigative spirit are required. Who isn't enamored with beauty? When we stimulate the eye, that sight can lead to insight. Do you have a relationship with art? Iconography in your place of worship, artwork in your childhood home, objects d'art in your school, favorite posters in your library, or public art in your neighborhood? What type of art do you find provocative? Realistic, abstract, digital, conceptual, political or installation, photography, graffiti, collage, portraiture, cartoon? Before you can engage verbally with art, you must know the types of art that attract you.

Given any work of art, at the intersection of imagination and fact lives ekphrasis. Jane Hirshfield in *Nine Gates* wrote, "Outer images carry reflective and indirect meanings as well." Ekphrastic writing generally takes one of three stances—subjective, reflective, or objective (131). Keep these three stances in mind as you begin to engage with the artwork presented in this book.

Excerpt of Ekphrastic Fiction: Responding to art can result in a simple description. For example, here is one sentence from Susan Vreeland's novel *Girl in Hyacinth Blue*, in which the character is captivated by Johannes Vermeer's painting of the same name: "A most extraordinary painting in which a young girl wearing a short blue smock over a rust-colored skirt sat in profile at a table by an open window" (4).

Let's get started by looking at the cover art. In Willem van Haecht's 1630 painting *Apelles Painting Campaspe,* the art room (*kunstkammer*) is filled with paintings and sculptures, as well as the artist at work. Did you notice Apelles painting a portrait of Alexander the Great's love, Campaspe? While the inclusion of art within art is striking, you will perhaps be impressed to learn that the artwork adorning the walls and lining the halls are indeed facsimiles of actual Flemish, German, and Italian artwork. In the bottom right-hand corner, for example, is a stunning mini-reproduction of Quentin Metsys' 1466 painting of a money-lender weighing his gold coins while his wife reads the Bible. In the words of John Hollander in *The Gazer's Spirit, Apelles Painting Campaspe* is indeed an "imaginary gallery with real paintings in it" (43).

Cover Art: Here are some suggestions for engagement: What is your aesthetic response? Begin your writing with, "I see." What is included in the artwork as compared to what is missing? Begin with, "I do not see." What is your emotional response? Begin with, "I feel." Locate a point at which the art defies expectation, and begin, "I wonder." See from the artist's perspective, and begin, "The artist...."

Questions: Is the style more realistic or abstract? Did the artist use color? What is the overall shape and size? What is the significance of its shape and size? How is the artist using scale? What topics is the artist treating? What are the compositional elements? Where is the viewer's attention directed? What do you see when you divide the image on the horizontal, vertical, or diagonal? What shapes are used? What symbols are used? What is the quality of the lines? How is the artist negating or conveying depth (perspective)? What is in the foreground? What is in the background? If there is a middle ground, what is included? Where is the source of light, and how is that creating shadows? What textures exist? What patterns exist (visual rhythm)? What surprises you? What juxtapositions exist? What is beautiful in this artwork? What is the relationship between the subject and the way the subject is depicted? Why was it created? Are the subjects partaking in activities you find relatable? What are the connotations? Can you sense a story?

Literal Description: Here is an exercise for your attentive eyes: Using concrete language only, describe the features of the artwork—the objects, the subjects, the colors. Write only what you literally see, not what you imagine, interpret, or surmise.

Figurative Description: Once you have reported on what you actually see, spend more time imagining. Here, you are welcome to use abstraction. For example, if you noted "in the background is a grand hall with high ceilings and stone arches," in this exercise, you are free to assume, "afterward, the artist will escort his entourage to the feast that awaits." Let your writing leap into figurative language.

Associative Leaps: Once you have written what you actually see, as well as what you have interpreted, see where association might take you. Wander and wonder. In other words, does the entire scene remind you of something? Does an object or figure spark a personal association? Be open to the possibilities of being cast from the artwork into your own set of experiences. What general mood is aroused? Does the artwork express feelings about life or nature? In what ways do you feel moved?

Formal Assessment: Include specifics such as the title, the artist's name, country of origin, and the year the artwork was produced. What materials were used and why? What are the main visual elements? How is the work composed and why? Is the artist's palette built on harmony or contrast? What are the effects of the palette the artist chose? What is the subject matter? What is the perspective of the artist? What is the perspective of the viewer? How are the objects and figures portrayed (e.g., realistically, exaggerated, over-simplified)?

Meaning: In "On the Relation of Analytical Psychology to Poetry," psychoanalyst Carl Gustav Jung asks, Does art have meaning? Or, "is it like nature in that it just *is* and 'means' absolutely nothing beyond that" (Campbell 316)? Lastly, look *into* the artwork and find meaning in details you see. Coupled with your suppositions, you might also choose to embark on scholarly research. Does the artwork have historical implications? Is there an underlying message? An allegory? An allusion? Is the artwork a reflection or an antithesis of the time in which it was produced? What is the artist's background, and how does that relate to this specific painting? What is the model's story? Is the artwork a personal statement? Is the artwork a political statement? What influence did the artwork have on society at the time it was produced?

This book has three sequential areas of focus: *ekphrasis*, with an overview of the mode of ekphrastic writing; *the visual arts*, with chapters offering an overview of the tools and techniques of artists; and *creative writing*, which covers the creative process, three genres, and ideas for collaborators and teachers. My wish is that this book inspire you to create your own writing exercises, as well as being motivated to discover new artists. This book includes drawings, paintings (including watercolors), prints, sculpture, and photography, with a general overview of abstract art, conceptual art, assemblage art, mixed media, performance art, and installation art. Conduct research if your interest lies elsewhere (for example, film, video, graphic design, fiber arts, architecture, glass art, woodworking, mosaics, digital art, multimedia, or other types of art).

The aim of *The Ekphrastic Writer: Creating Art-Influenced Poetry, Fiction and Nonfiction* is to guide the reader to learning about the visual arts (through a historical overview of periods and movements and specific instructions on how to *read* different types of visual art), engaging cerebrally with art (through learning about schools of criticism, ekphrastic conventions, and artists' techniques), and making creative use of visual stimulation. Given that engaging in art is a bio-psycho-social experience, these questions will be considered: What are the psychological arguments for ekphrasis? What are the anatomical and physiological processes of seeing and assigning language? Why do some creative writers choose to engage with artwork? What are the perils and pleasures of using art as a launching point for a poem, essay, or story? What are the historical and political implications of art in a certain milieu? Finally, this book is for writers of any genre who are open to using artwork to influence, drive, and otherwise inform their creative writing.

Excerpts of Ekphrastic Poetry, Nonfiction, Fiction: The excerpts included are from poems, stories, novels, essays, and memoir, that in some way treat at least one piece of visual art. Very few prose works (compared to poems) are entirely driven by ekphrasis. Hence, my excerpting of those specific and relevant ekphrastic moments.

Ekphrastic Freewriting: To give you an idea about how a writer could begin to engage with artwork, I have included examples of my own freewriting. As with all freewrites, those presented here are rough, fragmented, and non-sequitur. Most of the freewrites I'm sharing with you were eventually revised and included in my ekphrastic poetry collections.

Writing Invitations: Because this book is intended for writers of all genres, for the most part, the writing invitations do not specify a genre. I have created open-ended prompts and ones that could be easily modified to suit your particular needs and interests. While I sometimes invite you to "freewrite," you're welcome to take other approaches, such as brainstorming (free-associating by creating lists), clustering/ballooning (begin free-associating by placing a single word on the page and riffing off that word, and then riffing off the words that that word sparked, and so forth), or even free-drawing your responses. Write in the spirit of discovery.

Creative Writing Genres: While I have used the typical genre designations of "poetry," "creative nonfiction," and "fiction," I recommend that you see the naming of a genre as relatively loose. I suggest you embrace the current fluidity of genres and be open to all sections of the book, even if a term for a genre you do not normally adopt is noted. We live in a time of transgenre writing, in which writers are free to reject the limitations of categories. Having said that, I do want to offer a suggestion for a companion bibliography for this textbook: Robert Denham's *Poets on Painting*, which lists thousands of ekphrastic poems, the art and artist that influenced the work, as well as the literary journals, poetry collections, and anthologies where these pieces have been published. Writers of all genres can learn from each other.

Suggested Viewing: Throughout the book I offer suggestions for you to view other artwork. Most of my suggestions pertain directly to corresponding writing invitations.

Curated Poems and Prose: The assignment I gave to the thirty poets and prose writers appearing in this book was "write an ekphrastic piece." A one-page poem or a half-page prose piece was the length limit. I provided each person with links to over forty images of the artwork I had curated, and the writers got to choose which artwork they would engage with. There were no other mandates, suggestions, or hints. No one was instructed on my working definition of "ekphrasis," and they had no direct information about the layout or design of the book or whether or not the images would be part of the reading experience.

I have honored the titling and epigraphic decisions of each of the writers. Some chose to offer specific information about the artwork—naming it, the artist, and/or using a quote. Some writers simply used the artwork's title as their title, and some writers chose not to mention the artwork or artist at all.

Curated Art: The art I curated for this project is work that I think will be provocative for creative writers; it was through that filter I chose certain artists, periods, techniques, and subject matter. The artwork that I selected, as well as those listed in "suggested viewing," are widely accessible—pieces you can find in museums and online. In this digital generation, we can enjoy the global accessibility of images that until now were sequestered in museums (as well as art from underrepresented artists). After making my selections, securing permissions, evaluating the work's reproduction quality, given the color and size constraints, I am pleased to present these thirty-four images. The years of composition span 1460 to 2019, and the works represented include a drawing, a watercolor, an engraving, a woodblock, paintings, sculptures, photographs, silk on linen (fiber arts), installation, and public art. I was tasked with determining which images would be translated reasonably well in black in white, though we ultimately decided to print the images in color. My first priority, though, was always what would appeal to ekphrastic writers.

In general, absent seeing art in real life, the next best option is to find an art book produced within the last few decades. Keep in mind that any image of the artwork (digital or otherwise) will be an inferior reproduction. Regarding viewing art online, museum websites will offer the best reproductions. If it is available, take a virtual museum tour, which can give you a sense of the art-viewing experience.

You will notice the emphasis is on the artwork, not the artists. Scarcely any biographical information is included. Why? It is easy to get loaded down with a biography and forget about art as an aesthetic experience. Art transcends time and space, as well as its maker. But if this New Criticism approach does not suit you, there is plenty of research you can do to augment your experience of art.

Image/Text placement: Since each image and curated writing can illustrate a myriad of ideas related to ekphrasis (such as artists' techniques and elements of craft), you will find that not all images and their companion pieces are in close proximity to each other.

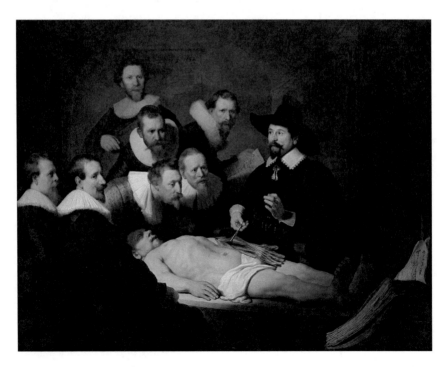

Rembrandt van Rijn's 1632 painting, *The Anatomy Lesson of Dr. Nicolaes Tulp* **(courtesy Mauritshuis, The Hague).**

Glossary of Terms: To simplify things, here are some terms and meanings I've employed: "art" for visual arts; "artist" for those who create visual art; "artwork" for any type of fine art; "writing" for any literary genre; "poetry" for that specific discipline, although most of what's said about poetry can apply to other genres of writing.

Finally, do not overlook two obvious uses for this book: I encourage you to make creative use of the images as a springboard for your writing, while also learning from the curated ekphrastic writing in terms of the topics, conventions, and craft.

The Rembrandt painting on the facing page was commissioned by the Amsterdam Surgeons' Guild. What do you make of this interior? Is there anatomic realism to the corpse? Is there a contrast between the dead and the living? In the companion poem, the speaker moves beyond the exterior and engages the artist himself:

The Anatomy Lesson of Dr. Nicolaes Tulp
(in conversation with Rembrandt)
by Jeffrey Levine

Everything perishes under the paintbrush as stony
contemplation tears at the canvas, and he must paint
without hoping to reach what he hoped.

The soul of painting lay in the fatal desire to conquer.
He breathes rage. Disgust for wisdom,
the urgent need to seize the sky by its hair,

the gods by their feet, to unseal the sun, to drag
the whole of nature along in his triumphal procession.
At any price, to paint the forbidden,

crammed full with scented absence.
And the truth, if found: he would go so far
as to slaughter in order to contemplate

more deeply still. "The world is a chest,
and I want to paint the living heart," he said.
"And in order to paint the world's heart,

one must paint with one's own heart
equally naked," Rembrandt's horrible joy
before his canvas, his agony visible:

Silence bursting with all its might, for he was painting
with all his might, every nerve ending, bough,
rib, drawn arched stretched to breaking,

a consecration of the house of organs,
awful body vibrating under the massive weight,
and Rembrandt keeping a mad fool's silence about his madness

in a breathless hand-to-hand battle—
legs shackled, gripping himself with each brushstroke,
wrenching his arm from his arm, his chest crushed

by his chest, himself turned against himself,
painting beyond painting, bloody, skinned, his teeth
clenched upon the cry, painting his prey, painting astride

a foaming horse, pursuing an army in retreat,
and in the end racing over the body of Aris Kindt fast
becoming a famous canvas beneath his feet.

He burst out laughing, drunk with his own genius.
"I conquered Rembrandt," he told his wife,
"and I led him to victory."

One day, he murmured at dinner, I'll end up
painting astride my own corpse.
The studio behind the door seemed inaccessible

even to Rembrandt. A dream. No one would see
what he had painted. Not even himself.
He had a cramp in his calf.

The true Rembrandt, he could have wept from it.
At night, eyes open in the dark, lying
in his boat, he wondered who, at daybreak,

would come ashore.
Awaiting with a dead man's impotence
his resurrection.

If it ever comes about, he thought, I will paint
a self-portrait, I will paint all, I will tell all,
I will make my secret shine, I will dazzle

the whole world with horror.
And if I cannot do it directly, from the very first stroke,
then I will approach it sideways.

I'll start by painting an ox of manganese
to sell for fifty-seven oboes—and the echo
of galloping stars to listen for

when the cave wall fades into a picture,
and the picture into that trembling
the morning before the world began.

Ekphrasis
History, Criticism, Conventions

As a child, did you ever lie in the grass, staring up at the passing clouds, and attempt to make meaning of the shapes? Partaking in ekphrasis is a type of play that provides a framework for the imagination.

Early Art Engagement

Inherently, it seems, we can see in pictures things beyond our immediate awareness. Children know this well. In adulthood, we tend to lose that sense of wonderment and the notion that the world's a wild place for our pleasure.

Have we forgotten those pivotal moments that helped to cultivate our creative minds? In this companion poem to Etsuko Ichikawa's installation art, childhood and play are considered:

Hakoniwa
by Alice Jones

Wave goodbye now
   the child is dreaming
      inside the nest

enclaved cat's eye, crystal, mudra, sign,
   the moving finger
      points elsewhere

globes etched with image
   the vitreous eye
      between sky and sea

a small hand juxtaposes claw and trowel
   bucketing wet slush
      its refractile grains

11

slipping through fingers'
   whorled prints
      forming and unforming

a Ryaon-ji field of no sand, kernels
   of texture woven with water
      direction erased

venture a chance arrangement
   river stones, snake and planet,
      dinosaur egg, stacked cairns

explode—shape becomes molten,
   aquatic waves-forms
      of silica and flesh

glass is liquid too, on-flowing
   atomized ocean, salt spray
      the same salt inside our cells

droplets touching your cheek
   carry the squid's spit,
      shark ova, whale pee

there is a landscape to the mind
   its mineral rilles, moon terraces
      chalk stone, a cat's face, bird sign

a child has no purpose
   play is dream
      without words

Poet's Comments

In Japanese, the word *Hakoniwa* means a miniature garden. It has also been used to describe Sandtray psychotherapy in which a child arranges objects to create a landscape that is both interior and exterior, real and dream. As a psychoanalyst, I was drawn to the artist Etsuko Ichikawa whose body of work creates an in-between space to reflect on the intersection of the human with elemental nature. Through her images and objects, she brings in the transformative effects of fire, as in creating glass, as well as its destructive power in nuclear and environmental traumas (Alice Jones).

The aptitude that children have for looking is admirable. The adult might render taking time for deep-looking frivolous, while the child, in the spirit of play, relishes and marvels looking irrespective of the passage of time.

Coloring books—A pre-drawn shape in which we can freely introduce color? First, our introduction of whichever color is a chaos of lines that appear as if we had held a crayon in our fist and went back and forth in the general vicinity of the shape. As we age, the way we handle the crayon changes, and our hitting the target area becomes more precise. Later, we are able to intellectualize the decision of which color for which section of the drawing and are mindful to stay within the lines. Before we are taught what is a "wrong" color for the sky and grass, for example, we pick and apply colors freely.

I once overheard a parent indelicately directing the selection of colors to her two-year-old: "No, purple is not the color for trees. Here, use this crayon. Color inside the lines carefully." It is fascinating to consider the moments in our past that could have tipped us toward or away from creative autonomy. Imagine a world in which there were no purple trees.

Most school children are introduced to art before they can read or write. We are introduced to picture books and paints and construction paper and cutouts and Play-Doh whereon we make our marks and then tote those artworks home for full display around the house. Even if you do not have memories of those early art-making activities, perhaps you have had the privilege of seeing some of your early masterpieces: finger paintings, pinch pots and ashtrays made of clay, a burlap bag embroidered with thick yarn, and a turkey made of your handprint with your fingers as erect feathers.

While many books for children have didactic purposes, it is revealing to learn about how we were shaped by enjoying those early image/word relationships. Why did we find picture books irresistible? Because they represented a participatory experience—not only by inviting us to engage with pictures to tell a story in our own words but also because those moments were typically spent with an adult we loved.

Assuming there were adults in your life who introduced you to the fun of first books, it is not difficult to plot your personal history with images/words. Examine the language we use: To a piece of writing, we instruct someone "read this." To art, we instruct someone to "look at this." However, with children's picture books, the spirit is "experience this."

How do images and words in picture books intersect to form meaning? Picture books use dual narrative forms of media—illustrations and words. Within the constructs of that one object, you have two modes of narration intersecting towards a singular goal. The marriage between image and words our childhood books extends into our proclivity for ekphrasis as adults. As adults though, it can take effort to cultivate those image/word associations in a playful and creatively fecund way. Revisiting favorite illustrated books from your childhood can be a useful exercise. Which picture books do you remember? Why have those books had a lasting impression on you?

In the case of illustrated books, there are some visual limitations. Dana Arnold in *Art History* wrote,

> Two things emerge from the relationship between verbal and visual descriptions. The first is that the diversity of ways of illustrating textual sources means

that the text cannot be wholly reconstructed from the images of it. So although illustrations are more particular in terms of the image they present, they do not stand independent of their textual sources. In other words, we need to know the text to read the image (93).

Writing influenced by the visual arts, though, can stand independent of the image, and the image, of course, is independent. No text is needed to read visual art.

Inkblots and Psychology

The history of using imagery to influence and shape our ideas is long and complicated. According to Margaret Peot, author of *Inkblot*, the origin of the inkblot test harkens back to a game from the late 1800s called Blotto: "Using cards that showed a variety of inkblots, players would write poems based on the blots or compete in describing the blots in great detail" (14).

Physician Justinius Kerner had an accidental spillage of a bottle of ink on paper, was intrigued by the pattern, and then proceeded to produce his own inkblots to which he wrote an entire collection of poems, *Kleksographien*, published in 1857.

Influenced by the image-response techniques of his predecessors (i.e., Szyman Hens who used inkblots to study his patient's fantasies and Alfred Binet who predicted that inkblots could measure a person's creativity), psychiatrist/psychoanalyst Hermann Rorschach—son of an art teacher, with his own artist aptitude—created inkblots in 1921 for his patients as a tool to test and analyze their perceptions of the imagery. Rorschach was a product of his upbringing, his schooling, and his society. His biographer, Damion Searls, in *The Inkblots* wrote that Rorschach "grappled with the theories of Freud and Jung while also absorbing the aesthetic movements of the day, from Futurism to Dadaism. A visual artist himself, Rorschach had come to believe that who we are is less a matter of what we *say*, as Freud thought, than what we *see*" (inside cover).

While the use of inkblots as a diagnostic device has since fallen out of favor with psychologists, it is fascinating to learn how image-response was an integral part of the history of cognitive development. "What mattered was *how* people saw what they saw—how they took in visual information, and how they understood it, interpreted it, felt about it. What they could do with it. How it set them dreaming" (Searls 117–118).

Suggested Viewing: Hermann Rorschach's ten original inkblots

Artwork can stimulate all types of writing by engaging the imagination, but fear can be an obstacle. In the personal essay "This is Our World,"

Dorothy Allison wrote,

> Even those of us from the same background, same region, same general economic and social class, come to "art" uncertain, suspicious, not wanting to embarrass ourselves by revealing what the work provokes in us. Sometimes, we are not sure. If we were to reveal what we see in each painting, sculpture, installation, or little book, we would run the risk of exposing our secret selves, what we know and what we fear we do not know, and of course incidentally what it is we truly fear. Art is the Rorschach test for all of us.

Because humans have the propensity to see patterns where none were intended, image-response exercises have validity. No doubt it is apophenia (the tendency to seek patterns in randomness, to perceive connection and meaning in seemingly unrelated things) that allows artists and writers to produce art with universal appeal. In *Treatise on Painting*, Leonardo da Vinci observed, "By looking attentively at old and smeared walls, or stones and veined marble of various color, you may fancy that you see in them several compositions, landscapes, battles, figures in quick motion, strange countenances, and dresses, with an infinity of other objects. By these confused lies, the inventive genius is excited to new exertions." What do you do to stimulate the "inventive genius" within?

Is there a correlation between seeing and feeling? As viewers do we experience emotion from art because the creator created it with great feeling? Nowadays, we look to imagery to ignite the imagination, not to limit it. "Visual images, at least if they're good, produce mental states—they 'awaken an idea' in the viewer" (Searls 96).

Suggested Viewing: The drip paintings of Janet Sobel

Ekphrasis Defined

According to the Oxford Classical Dictionary, "ekphrasis" is an "extended and detailed literary description of any object, real or imagined." A common literary definition of ekphrasis is *writing which concerns itself with the arts.*

In his 1993 book *Museum of Words*, James A.W. Heffernan proposed "a definition simple in form but complex in its implications" by defining ekphrasis as "the verbal representation of visual representation" (3). He also suggested "ekphrasis" should be relegated to writing that translates not only visual images into words but also has visual art for its subject. It is Heffernan's definition of ekphrasis that will frame the scope of this book. Ekphrasis denotes an explicit connection of the writing to an artwork. Whether the text's relationship to the artwork is literal, figurative, or conceptual, is up to the writer.

The following year, W.J.T. Mitchell in his book, *Picture Theory: Essays on Verbal and Visual Representation*, called *ekphrasis* "the name of a minor and rather obscure literary genre (poems with describe works of visual art) and a more general topic (the verbal representation of visual representation)" (152).

Poet William Carlos Williams insisted, "no ideas but in things," and in this case, the artwork is that tangible thing. In the way I have structured my courses on ekphrasis, art engagement is also an opportunity to utilize the language of the art world, such as the artists' tools and techniques, art movements and trends.

In general, there are two types of ekphrases:

1. Actual ekphrases concern actual artwork.
2. Notional ekphrases concern imagined artwork.

Ek-phrassein = out + to tell, explain, point out, speak out; to call an inanimate object by name

Ecphrasis = description
Ekphrasis = verbal description of an object

An additional layer to the definition of the word concerns ekphrasis as a unique experience. Cole Swensen, in her article "To Writewithize," defines the term by its experiential dimension: "It's used to indicate the product of a writer's contemplation before a painting, sculpture, Grecian urn, Achillean shield, or other specific work of art." In other words, to bring the experience of your having attended deeply to an artwork through visual engagement to a reading audience is what is to be expected of ekphrastic writing.

For the Greeks, "ekphrasis" was a term of rhetoric (the art of persuasion). Aristotle's rhetorical situation, as illustrated by an equilateral triangle to indicate how persuasion is achieved, concerns the speaker/writer–speech/writing–audience relationship:

Writer/Ethos—convincing the audience of your authority, credibility
Writing/Logos—using facts and reason to persuade the audience
Audience/Pathos—appealing to the emotional response of the audience

Description

Successful description has the power to bring forth the intended image to the mind's eye.

Enargia = a description so effective it can vividly recreate
   something/someone in words

Description = down + to write; representation; act of depicting;
   transcribe, copy, sketch

In *The Art of Describing: Dutch Art in the Seventeenth Century,* Svetlana Alpers wrote, "To know is to name is to describe, but it is also to make" (83). So, when we know something, we can name it, and once we can name it, we can describe it, from which we can make inferences. In ekphrastic writing, for instance, the more we know about the artwork and the artist's process, the more possibilities we have to make something of that data.

As an illustration of the complicated nuances of description, as well as the magic of precise description, it would be a fun experiment to ask a writing instructor and an artist to demonstrate what the artist could produce solely based on the verbal imagery provided by the writer. In the Technology and Ekphrasis section of the book, we will look at how technology is paving the way for this type of feedback.

Descriptive precision has become so popular that it has its own reference material. *Descriptionary: A Thematic Dictionary* defines terms and is organized thematically for ease-of-use. Sections include animals and insects, architecture, environment, human body, law, magic and the occult, tools, and weapons. Specific to our work as ekphrasists, *Descriptionary* lists words under the following categories: art terms, art tools and materials, sculpture, and photography. As a lover of words, here are some that I found particularly titillating: frilling, guilloche, sfumato, pochade, scrim, lumachelle, and anaglyph.

In *How Poets See the World* author Willard Spiegelman asked fundamental questions about ekphrasis: "How does description contain or convey meaning? What do we do when we describe something? Reproduce, account for, picture, portray, trace, parcel out? How does one take the measure of the external world? How neutral or objective a form can such an effort take? Does the 'I' always interfere with, interrupt, or color the seeing 'eye'? Can language hope for a scientific rendering" (5)? What are your answers?

No matter how deft a person becomes at describing, ekphrastic doubt is a reality. To be a successful ekphrastic writer, one must be comfortable with uncertainty. After one of poet Rainer Maria Rilke's long descriptions of a Cézanne painting, he wrote:

> I'm not sure that I even managed to describe the balance of its tonal values; words seemed more inadequate than ever, indeed inappropriate; and yet it should be possible to make compelling use of them, if one could only look at such a picture

as if it were part of nature—in which case it ought to be possible to express its existence somehow..... In this case, however, the object itself is more tangible, and the words, which feel so unhappy when made to denote purely painterly facts are only too eager to return to themselves in the description of the man portrayed (C. Rilke 83–84).

In the accompanying writing guide to her book *Living with Art*, Rita Gilbert stated, "Probably the main difference between art writing and other types of writing is that art writing tends to be more descriptive. Art is, after all, a visual experience, and you cannot write meaningfully about it without describing what you see" (1). Though, as you will see with the writing curated for this book, not all writers use description when writing on art. Moreover, in this modern age of immediate access to digital images, is it necessary to describe art at all? Has description of artwork become redundant?

Of course, when we consider the visual arts, there is the tendency for our descriptions to center around vision. It is advisable though to discover other approaches to description given specific subjects. For instance, if you are an ornithologist, your descriptions will include the birds' specific sonic vocalizations. Writers new to ekphrasis will often forget auditory descriptions entirely. If you are a gardener, the descriptions for your plants include environmental conditions (both spatial and temporal), such as "deer-resistant," "drought tolerant," "vining growth," and "part sun to shade."

History of Ekphrasis

Ekphrasis began as, and in some respects still is, an exercise in rhetoric. In ancient Greece, the standard textbook was Aphthonius' *Progymnasmata* of the fourth century AD, which guided the students through exercises that would help to establish them as great orators.

Nowadays, does the average person take pride in displays of rhetoric and oration? Modes of compositional rhetoric are listed here, ordered by simplest to most complex: fable, narration, anecdote, maxim, refutation, confirmation, common topic, encomium, invective, comparison, characterization, description, argument, and proposal of law. You will notice that description (ekphrasis) is number twelve of fourteen in terms of rhetorical complexity.

Aphthonius outlined specific criteria:

Description is an expository discourse which brings the object exhibited vividly into view. One may describe persons and things, times and places, irrational creatures and in addition plants.... In describing persons one should proceed from beginning to end, that is, from head to feet; in describing things, from what precedes them, what is in them, and what tends to result from them; in describing times and places, from what surrounds them and what is contained in them. Descriptions may be simple or compound.... In description one should adopt a free, relaxed style and ornament it with different figures, and in general hit off the objects being described (15–16).

Aphthonius provided an illustration of description (of the temple in Alexandria):

A hill juts out of the ground, rising to a great height, and called an acropolis on both accounts, both because it is raised up on high and because it is placed in the high-point of the city. There are two roads to it, of dissimilar nature. One is a road, the other a way of access. The roads have different names according to their nature. Here it is possible to approach on foot, and the road is also shared with those who approach on a wagon.... The beauty is unspeakable. If anything has been omitted, it has been bracketed by amazement; what it was not possible to describe has been omitted (16).

In his epic poem the *Iliad*, circa 762 BCE, Homer was the first writer known to employ extended descriptions. It is notional ekphrasis, in that the artwork was not an actual artifact but notion born from the writer's mind. Later Virgil, in his epic poem, *The Aeneid* circa 19 BCE, also used epic ekphrasis. Other ancient literature with ekphrastic moments includes Apollonios Rhodios' epic poem, *The Argonautika* and Ovid's epic poem, *Metamorphoses*. Since then, the descriptive mode has been in vogue with virtually every notable writer turning to the visual arts and adopting description of an actual or notional ekphrasis. To name a few: William Shakespeare's play, *The Rape of Lucrece;* Miguel de Cervantes' novel, *Don Quixote;* Herman Melville's novel, *Moby Dick;* Benito Pérez Galdós' novel, *Our Friend Manso;* Henri Ibsen's plays, *The Lady from the Sea* and *When We Dead Awaken;* and Fyodor Dostoyevsky's novel, *The Idiot.*

While Homer's ekphrasis spans numerous pages, it was not until the third century AD that we find an entire book driven by ekphrasis. It is the combined work of Philostratus the Younger (otherwise known as Philostratus of Lemnos), Philostratus the Elder, and Callistratus, called *Imagines* (*Eikones*). The work includes short essays on myth portrayed in literature, myth-themed paintings, and statues. The book, originally written as lectures, is especially modern in its treatments of beauty, the human condition, and nature.

Suggested Reading: The full text of *Imagines*

In China, the mode of poets responding to artworks by emulating their themes or mood flourished in the seventh century of the Tang

Dynasty. It was during the Southern Song period that we find the first comprehensive anthology of ekphrastic poetry (c. 1187).

Ekphrastic writing is omnipresent in poetry collections, literary journals, art books, artists' biographies, museum literature, and in the forewords to works of fiction and nonfiction. In *Picture Theory*, Mitchell demystifies the mode by pointing out, "Ekphrastic poems speak to, for, or about works of visual art in the way that texts, in general, speak about anything else." Meaning, the ekphrastic mode is not extraordinary, as it is as common as using any subject to help spring forth creative ideas.

Excerpt of Ekphrastic Poetry: From Homer's *Iliad,* here is an excerpt of the epic descriptive narration of Hephaestus' making of the shield for Achilles:

> There earth, there heaven, there ocean he design'd;
> The unwearied sun, the moon completely round;
> The starry lights that heaven's high convex crown'd;
> The Pleiades, Hyads, with the northern team....

Here we have notional ekphrasis of a physical representation of power, a symbolic shield, written in a story of mythology, which will later influence metal artists to create actual shields based on what Homer had written for the notional shield. Namely, any artist who created a type of Achilles shield was finding influence from the text, thereby making text-influenced art. Traditional ekphrasis concerns the writer's dependency on the image. When the artist's image is dependent on text, which some people erroneously call "reverse ekphrasis," it is just art that happens to have words as its source.

Early verbalization of the ekphrastic tradition correlates with the boom of ekphrasis in the latter half of the twentieth century. Jean H. Hagstrum's 1958 book *The Sister Arts* used the term "pictorialism," and not "ekphrasis" to describe the tradition. Up until about the early 1980s, "ekphrasis" was used exclusively by classicists and historians. To my knowledge, the first mention of "ekphrasis" appeared in 1983 in Alpers' *The Art of Describing.* Then in the 1990s, books such as Hollander's 1995 *The Gazer's Spirit* utilized "ecphrasis"[sic], and hence the popularity of the term was born. In 1997 the poetry journal *Ekphrasis* was founded, introducing most of us writers to the previously obscure word for the movement of writing to art.

Ekphrastic writers use artifact for artistic fodder, an approach with a wide reach, yet most discussions of ekphrasis concern poetry. In truth, ekphrasis can be employed in the development of character, a transformation of setting and narrative, as well as providing a threshold through which memoirists can step. With a surge of educational programs encouraging interdisciplinary arts and inter-art scholarship, writers and teachers of all genres can benefit from a discussion on the interdependence of language and vision.

Scholarly Criticism

When dissecting scholars' criticism of ekphrasis, it is alarming to notice the diction used. Heffernan in *Museum of Words* asserts that "To represent a painting or sculpted figure in words is to evoke its power—the power to fix, excite, amaze, entrance, disturb, or intimidate the viewer— even as language strives to keep that power under control" (7). Similarly, philosopher Roland Barthes wrote, "The interaction between writing and visual art is often a 'parasitic' one in which the writing serves to diminish the effect of the art, to explain it away, to make it *say something* that is authoritative and precise" (Foster and Prevallet 148). What do you think? Do writers wish to usurp artists' power? Critic Harold Bloom also perpetuates hostility: "Poets rather ruthlessly want to write their poems, and pragmatically the gazer's spirit often reduces even the most awesome painting to so much *material poetica*."

What exactly are ekphrastic writers attempting to do? Many controversies related to ekphrasis stem from the accusation of appropriation and the assumption that ekphrastic writing inherently upstages artwork through its verbal interpretation. What's controversial about exploring the intersection of seeing and writing? What is more artistically pure than viewing art as a nexus to your own art-making? If, as John Ruskin asserted in *Modern Painters*, imagination is the highest intellectual power of humankind, then writers must ask themselves: Am I honoring the full capacity of my mind? Proponents of ekphrasis, then, would argue that ekphrastic writing is a way of charging the imagination.

Is a writer's engagement with the visual arts tantamount to poaching? Is ekphrasis a type of appropriation (that is, reworking for one's use without the creator's permission)? Ekphrasis can be born from a type of mimicry (resemblance), an imitation (used as a model), or a kind of voyeurism. Is ekphrastic writing a type of reductive art? Or is ekphrasis merely a device applied for the pleasure of the writer's muse?

Is ekphrasis controversial in the way that musical covers can be? Does the second musician have pure intentions in producing that cover? Does the musician pay homage, or does the musician believe that a better job can be done? Listeners might enjoy the cover better than the original, but what does that mean for the original version?

Grant F. Scott in *The Sculpted Word* wondered, "Why is ekphrasis more frequently seen as a transgression than a crossing or a joining? What is it about the border between the word and the image that seems so dangerous?" (xii) Why do you think there is so much scholarly criticism of ekphrasis?

Poet Paul Valéry demanded, "We should apologize that we dare to speak about painting." Do writers attempt to upstage artists? Are they assigning words to something ineffable? Are creative writers assailing the visual arts like musicians and translators assail original songs and text?

The controversies surrounding ekphrasis are arguments about supremacy. Do artists with their completed works loom over writers who stand in deference to the artists' masterpieces? In *Picture Theory* Mitchell situates the players: "The ekphrastic poet typically stands in the middle position between the object described or addressed and a listening subject who ... will be made to 'see' the object through the medium of the poet's voice" (164). Even Rilke is not immune to criticism: "Rilke is forced to grant language a stronger physical presence if his art is to compete with that of Rodin or Cézanne" (Strathausen 199).

Edward Hirsch in *Transforming Vision* writes that there is "something transgressive in writing about the visual arts.... A border is crossed, a boundary is breached as the writer enters into the spatial realm, traducing an abyss, violating the silent integrity of the pictorial." And Stephen Cheeke in *Writing for Art* summarized, "Almost all theorists of ekphrasis emphasise the paragonal aspect of the mode, or 'the struggle for dominance between image and word'" (24).

Once I heard a poetry professor warn her student, "Sometimes you speak of your work as 'art appreciation,' and—from what little I know—that phrase would be best avoided, as it suggests an unsophisticated approach to art. The reality is that editors will be looking for signs that the poems are responsive to contemporary art theory and criticism." If you're a creative writer, though, scaling the ivory towers of theory and criticism are intellectual pursuits and not a matter for art-making. It is aesthetics that ekphrastic writers are after. People wishing to engage in erudite arguments on contemporary art are perhaps flexing their muscles as burgeoning art critics, scholars, and theorists, not literary artists driven by play and curiosity, and unsettled lyrical reflections of surprise and reverie.

Are the controversies irrelevant, as ekphrastic writing cannot do anything to detract from the fact that the artwork exists? No amount of words will erase the artwork from this planet, nor can words ever unbind its beauty. Words on trees, for example, are not a stand-in for experiencing a forest. We write words to uncover what we see when we experience, but those words have no power to cover what our eyes behold.

Ultimately, should works-of-art be left to their silence? According to Mitchell, the "children should be seen and not heard" proverb "reinforces a stereotypical relation ... between the freedom to speak and see and the injunction to remain silent and available for observation" (*Picture Theory* 162). What are your thoughts about the primacy of ekphrastic writing?

Why Write Ekphrastically

Of all the ways that you could approach the blank page, why engage with visual art? Frederick Franck, in his book, *The Zen of Seeing*, wrote, "I have learned that what I have not drawn, I have never really seen, and that when I start drawing an ordinary thing, I realize how extraordinary it is, sheer miracle." Can the same be said about words? Attending verbally to a work-of-art can allow for deeper meanings, for a deeper knowing?

Rather than focusing on the description itself, your ekphrasis can be about an artful experience. Begin with your tabula rasa (blank slate) and see where art might take you, rather than where you might take it. Create with the energy of the moment, not the analysis or presupposition of the recent past, insisted artist Pablo Picasso. When you respond to the act of looking not *at* the artwork but *into* the artwork, you are positioning yourself to respond to something outside your usual experience. This, I believe, is what can render a piece of ekphrastic writing "successful."

Interpretation (an exercise of the intellectual mind for analysis) is antithetical to ekphrasis. While ekphrasis is a type of experiment, anchored in visual imagery, it is not forensics. In the medical field, x-ray images, ultrasounds, and electrocardiograms, for example, require review and analysis to aid in diagnoses. Creating ekphrastic writing involves the irrational part of the brain (that is, the unconscious mind). Ekphrasis is a method by which writers can exist outside themselves. Turning to the visual arts as creative fodder can allow writers to detach from their individual narratives.

Artist envy can be a writer's impetus for ekphrasis, though it's interesting to note examples of visual artists who have written creatively to their own artwork: Dante Gabriel Rossetti wrote sonnets on his pictures, J.M.W. Turner wrote poems to his paintings, and William Blake was both a poet and a printmaker. Besides being a master painter and sculptor, Michelangelo was also a prolific poet, in his lifetime penning hundreds of sonnets and madrigals.

Excerpt of Ekphrastic Nonfiction: Of what value is ekphrasis to writers, readers, to the general public? To the art world? To literature? In the Penguin Readers Guide to her novel *Girl in Hyacinth Blue*, Vreeland provides an answer: "To feel the grace of God in a painting of the dear, quiet commonness of a domestic interior, or in a landscape, seascape, cityscape, trains us to feel the grace of God in the thing itself in situ. Does the world need another painting of people quietly going about their lives? Does it need another story? Another poem? Yes" (7).

What compels a creative writer to the blank page? Use of images to stimulate writing? The visual arts can be seen as a mere springboard for writers, not as instrument control, but an act of gratitude. How can springboards be controversial? Do writers truly intend on upstaging an image by using that image to compel them to the page? All art is irreducible. Everything we do, though, is a type of translation. We see the image of a four-legged animal grazing in a pasture, and we say "cow." We feel a pin sticking into our forearm, and we scream "ouch." I may see a painting of a king and say, "the stars miss eating grapes right off the vines."

Some writers have been drawn to artwork as a way of avoiding the sentimental (that is, introverted writing). When writers create what Jung calls, "extroverted art," they allow themselves to become subordinate to the object, thereby abandoning conscious intent. In other words, as alluded to earlier, ekphrasis can be a mode by which to escape the self.

Stimulating the eye by rooting around visual imagery in the spirit of playful investigation can lead to "negative capability." Poet John Keats wrote about this particular state of mind that creativity requires, in which a person "is capable of being in uncertainties, mysteries, doubts; without any irritable reaching after facts and reason" (qtd. in B. Edwards).

All of this can be learned: The art of observation, of looking closely, of losing one's self in the gaze and how that close-seeing can be a kind of mediation that ushers writers closer to their compositions.

Increasing one's observational and verbal skills is a byproduct of the practice of ekphrasis. Recently, a National Public Radio journalist was interviewing a digital animation artist whose work had been television-censored. The journalist said to the artist, "Since we can't see the image, can you describe it to us?" While the man had skills in animation, he struggled with conveying that imagery through verbalization.

The argument for writing ekphrastically is the same as the argument for doing literary translations. As Rilke wrote, "With every work of art a new thing is added to the world." (Baer 140). When we translate, we produce a new version of the original by rendering it into another language. Literary translation is an intercultural celebration, which functions as a mode of pollination among countries, cultures, peoples. Think how sequestered we would be if there were no translation. For example, poets Sam Hamill and John Balaban tackled the mammoth task of translating Old Vietnamese poetry (a language which was disastrously close to extinction) into English. If a piece of literature is an irreducible experience, can anything truly be translated? The new version is "not a representation in any formal sense, but a comparable experience" (Brower).

If literary critics are so concerned with writers' treatments of the visual arts, what would be their opinion about painters who repaint masterpieces? Pablo Picasso's series of near sixty paintings, "Las Meninas," was created by performing a comprehensive analysis, reimagining in the cubist style the 1656 *Las Meninas* by Diego Velázquez. Was it admiration that prompted artist Pablo Picasso to spend many months studying and painting details and entire renderings of one of his favorite painters?

Ekphrastic Conventions

What do you make of this quote from *The Sculpted Word*, "Ekphrasis appropriates *and* liberates the image…" (Scott xii)? The author asserts that the ekphrastic writer's work is twofold. Sure, writers working in the ekphrastic mode turn to an image to stimulate the muse, but what does it mean to *liberate* the image? To free it from its framed constraints? To emancipate it from its current construct as merely a visual thing?

When ekphrasists attend to a work-of-art fully, when we look into it with rapt attention, the rest of the world falls away. To be taken captive by artwork is the ultimate goal, for it is in that spirit that our creative writing can have the most potency. It is not necessary to learn about the conventions of ekphrasis before you write ekphrastically; all that matters is that you find that spark that compels you to the page, even if it's just a single brushstroke. Yet, as with all writing, knowing the conventions can build complexity into the choices you make.

Turning back to *Picture Theory*, the author explores three moments of realization: "ekphrastic indifference," where no amount of description can amount to depiction, "ekphrastic hope," where language is used to make readers see, and "ekphrastic fear," which means "a threat to be reduced" (152–163).

Conventions of ekphrastic writing include:

1. Addressing the artwork in its entirety (*panekphrasis*)
2. Treating only a detail of the artwork (*oligoekphrasis*)
3. Narrating the artwork
4. Personifying the artwork
5. Interpreting the artwork
6. Objecting to the artwork
7. Addressing the artist
8. Giving voice to the artist

9. Describing the artist's process (*proekphrasis*)
10. Supposing the goings-on inside the studio (studio ekphrasis)
11. Imagining the life of the model (model ekphrasis)
12. Giving voice to the model
13. Remarking on the artwork's static construct (art as an artifact)
14. Recording museum ekphrasis, which is place specific (*topoekphrasis*)
15. Remarking on the individual moment of viewing
16. Exploring notional ekphrasis (imagining a nonexistent artwork and writing about it)
17. Writing the absent
18. Responding to the artwork's essence or mystique
19. Adopting the artist's artistic style
20. Describing the form or shape of the artwork (*morphekphrasis*)
21. Sound elements of the artwork are described (*phonoekphrasis*)
22. Providing or responding to historical context
23. Following personal associations
24. Addressing an artwork in which you yourself appear (*idioekphrasis*)
25. Description specifically of digitally produced art (*neoekphrasis*)
26. Visual-art-influenced writing the transcends description (*metaekphrasis*)

In 1995, Hollander wrote that as an option for ekphrastic writers, "the speaker of the poem can notionally climb into the painting and take an extended walk through the scene" (37). Of course he meant "climb into" figuratively, but there is now a museum in Paris that allows visitors the experiential pleasure of literally walking through Vincent van Gogh's paintings, which are magnified and projected on the walls, floors, and ceilings.

Metaekphrasis

Writers in their ekphrastic journey might decide to supersede the artwork's description while still communing with the artwork. Will your creative writing move beyond the actual artwork and describe something outside the frame? For instance, instead of needing to describe the art, is it the history depicted in the painting that intrigues you, or is it the memory it invokes or a mood that sparks a narrative, or is it something else beyond the image that requires description?

For writing that takes its influence from the visual arts but in which no description exists, I propose the term "metaekphrasis." During the revision process, for instance, writers might decide that the descriptive elements of their work are no longer germane to the final product, so they dispense with it. In other words, while the artwork and its description spurred them to the blank page, the writing evolved beyond ekphrasis.

Regarding layout and design, knowing whether or not your words will be printed near the image could inform your decision about the treatment of description. Alternatively, if you are like Rae Armantrout, you write the poem that comes, regardless of the image or concern about a paired display. Later we will see the image that this poet chose, but for now, here is her metaekphrastic poem:

Much
by Rae Armantrout

To know someone is to know what they think
they're doing.

"What do you think you're doing?"

is not a question to be asked
of an animal or plant.

Understanding this question
is what makes us human!

That was one idea I had.

Pretend play develops in babies
between 18 and 24 months.

They are preparing their answers.

*

I just wanted to get
an impression,

and then to make an impression
on you. Though I don't care

much for you. Don't
leave me alone

with these notions.

Topics in Ekphrasis I

Beauty

What in Fernand Lungren's painting do you notice? Perhaps it is something as simple as the reflective elements: a mirror on the back wall, the sconces, the glass decanters on each table, the shadows reflected onto the floor. The John Keats' poem "Endymion, Book I" begins, "A thing of beauty is a joy for ever...." If art is a thing of beauty, does it need to hold meaning? Can we behold beauty without intellectualizing and without assigning significance?

According to Roger Scruton in his book *Beauty,* there are four kinds of beauty: "human beauty, as an object of desire; natural beauty, as an object of contemplation; everyday beauty, as an object of practical reason; and artistic beauty, as a form of meaning and an object for taste" (124). Of course, you do not need to visit a museum to experience beauty. As an ekphrastic challenge, try seeing all four modes of beauty in every artwork included in this book.

Imagine going to a museum: you stand in front of a painting—at first, it is merely an object in a particular place. Yet, as you regard the colors, which are how the painter intended them, and regard the play among the objects in the painting, your eyes begin to lose sight of anything outside the frame. The eye gets caught at alluring moments: an arm, a pillow, the shadow in the far corner. The next thing you know, much time has passed, and you have been in a state of quiet contemplation.

Beauty enraptures. Meandering through an art gallery, it is easy to feel seduced by a particular art piece; you may attempt to pass nonchalantly by but you are halted by some irrational force: Pupils dilate and legs become stone in the presence of a beautiful thing. Writers with ekphrastic leanings might attempt to investigate their immobility by jotting down the unutterable, using words to stab at the wordlessness of that feeling. Aesthetics is the ekphrastic writer's work. Ekphrastic writers wish to stun

Fernand Lungren's 1882–84 painting, *In the Café* (courtesy the Charles H. and Mary F.S. Worcester Collection).

their eyes into getting precisely what the artists beheld, to align themselves physically with them, to lean over their shoulders close enough to smell paint. Principally, we commit ekphrasis because it is uncertain. Before an artwork, we are vulnerable and our hands are guilty. Our eyes are false and unapologetic witnesses, but we realize what we have indeed seen only after we have written it (Baugher, "Art to Art"). Words have both the power to clarify our experiences and to create them.

Though beauty is subjective, scientists will tell you that perception, symmetry, and adaptation have something to do with it. Looking can be an act of mediation, as Paul Valéry wrote, "To see is to forget the name of the thing one sees."

Excerpt from Ekphrastic Nonfiction: In the foreword to *Girl with a Pearl Earring*, author Tracy Chevalier speaks candidly about her ekphrastic process:

> I was originally attracted to it because of the glowing light on the girl's face, the beautiful blue and yellow of her headdress, and her wide liquid eyes that followed me around the room. What made an even deeper, most lasting impression over the years, however, was the ambiguous look on her face. Her expression seemed to me to be a mass of contradictions: innocent yet experienced, joyous yet fearful,

full of longing and yet full of loss. Vermeer miraculously managed to capture her caught between many emotions. I could never tell what she was thinking, and this irresolution kept me wondering about her (ix).

Writing Invitation: Begin a piece with this first line from Frank O'Hara's poem, "A Note to John Ashbery": "More beautiful even than wild ducks / paddling among drowned alley cats…"

In Oscar Wilde's novel *The Picture of Dorian Gray*, after artist Basil Hallward paints Gray's portrait, Gray becomes obsessed with the beauty portrayed in the painting and the idea that the painting of beauty is forever, while his own youth and beauty are ephemeral. In Wilde's work, we have an example of notional ekphrasis, as well as the treatment of both beauty and absence.

Suggested Reading: Wilde's preface to *The Picture of Dorian Gray*

Writing Invitation: Write about an artwork that most people might find repulsive, but which fills you with reverence.

Absence

It is your prerogative to embrace or reject the visual clues offered up by the artist (Sandbank). Let's consider the absent, invisible, and the notional. In ekphrasis, what is excluded from the artwork might seem an unlikely place on which to focus your attention. Though, that approach can lead to surprising moments for both the writer and the reader. Here is the corresponding poem to Fernand Lungren's *In the Café*. Take particular notice of the lines where the absence is considered:

The Café
(After Fernand Lungren)
by Grace Bauer

She embodies the audacity of orange,
dominating the otherwise muted palette
of the painting with a flamboyant
ensemble that requires her to perch
on the plush banquette, lean into a table
that appears to be floating on air.
    Without her, our eyes might be drawn
beyond the labyrinth of pillars and partitions,
to the other patrons who nearly fade
into the room's blacks and grays, or the somber
flower lady mid-right, whose bouquets pale in comparison.
    Without her, we might take more notice
of Lungren's mastery of translucence—

each mirror, gaslight, globe, carafe a dazzle of light
reflecting off the solid barely seen. Or seen through.
     But she commands our eyes' attention—
her slender figure taking up more space than women
tend to do. Especially in public. Especially when alone.
Especially when drinking, which she clearly is—
a hint of amber-colored liqueur shimmering
in the glass she cradles in her still-gloved hands.
     She is aware of the young man
sitting just outside the frame, scrawling intently
in his sketchbook, and likes imagining herself
a vision taking shape on the page. She pictures him
later, dabbing paint onto canvas; can almost feel
the pull of his brush in the brown of her hair. So she pauses
to allow him to capture what he can of the moment.
With her in it. Content to be both solitary and seen.

Writing Invitation: When we look at an artwork, we are looking at the sign of something that has happened, either actually or notionally. Write on artwork that the artist never produced or the artwork that the artist did produce but that you (and possibly no one else) has ever seen. Harriet Scott Chessman's *The Lost Sketchbook of Edgar Degas* (his imaginative sketchbook devoted to New Orleans) is an example of a work of fiction on notional works-of-art.

Excerpt of Ekphrastic Fiction: Alternatively, try writing actual ekphrasis by focusing on what is excluded from the artwork, as Julian Barnes did in his novel, *A History of the World in 10½ Chapters*, by creating a list of what was absent from the painting, *The Raft of Medusa* by Théodore Géricault: "Let us start with what he did not paint. He did not paint:

1) The *Medusa* striking the reef;
2) The moment when the tow-ropes were cast off and the raft abandoned;
3) The mutinies in the night;
4) The necessary cannibalism;
5) The self-protective mass murder." (126)

Writing Invitation: In general, there are two ways to draw a chair. First, draw the chair itself (positive space). Alternatively, draw everything surrounding the chair (negative space). Either way, the result should be the same: A drawing of a single, specific chair. In the same way that art teachers ask students to draw the chair by drawing what is not the chair, write an ekphrastic poem or prose piece in which you write around the subject depicted in an artwork.

Excerpt of Ekphrastic Nonfiction: Similarly, in Mary Gordon's essay, "Still Life: Bonnard and My Mother's Death," she states the absence in describing two paintings by Pierre Bonnard, *Young Women in the Garden* and *The Lesson*: "There are no flowers in the garden," the author writes of the first painting, and "We do not see her eyes," she observes in the other one.

Writing Invitation: What is included in a painting and what is not can be equally significant. Highlight the absence by creating a poem, essay, or story that's mostly "what is not." Be open to the associative possibilities; pastoral paintings, for instance, do not necessarily lead to pastoral writing.

Excerpt of Ekphrastic Nonfiction: One approach to writing the absent is to reflect on the existence of an alter ego, the other, or the shadow, as José Orduña did in his memoir, *The Weight of Shadows*, in which he engages ekphrastically with the surrealist painting, *Fenómeno* by Remedios Varo:

> When one thinks of a shadow, one typically imagines an absence—a type of nothing—but this is fundamentally wrong. In Varo's painting, the visual place where the viewer assumes a man once was, or should be, is occupied by a shadow. The black three-dimensional figure fills the rounded contours of a body, except it is made of darkness. The darkness walks, while the image of the man is relegated to the flat world of silhouette. A shadow is not the absence of light but a relationship of light with itself and with an observer (189–190).

Writing Invitation: Locate an artwork in which your alter ego exists. Create a character sketch, empathize with it, or settle on another way to engage with it.

Supposing the significance of what's invisible to the viewer is the work of the imagination. Why attempt the obvious of exploring what you see? Think about your personhood. Aren't your physical and personality traits as much about what exists as much as what doesn't?

Excerpt of Ekphrastic Fiction: *The Picture of Dorian Gray*, is an excellent example of focusing on one thing in order to reveal another. In other words, describe what the artwork is not, thereby indirectly revealing what the artwork is. The painter (Basil) says he cannot exhibit the portrait for he's "'put too much of myself into it.'" Lord Henry begins to describe the painting (notional ekphrasis). His description, though, is the opposite of what we shall see. "'Too much of yourself in it! Upon my word, Basil, I didn't know you were so vain; and I really can't see any resemblance between you, with your rugged strong face and your coal-black hair, and this young Adonis, who looks as if he was made out of ivory and rose-leaves....'" Basil reveals that it is a portrait of a man named Dorian Gray.

Most ekphrastic criticism focuses on the absence of sound and the absence of movement, but there are other opportunities in treating the absence for ekphrastic practitioners. As a writer you can shift the focus, directing your reader's attention to something outside the frame or lost within the frame, a mere notion whose context is within the frame itself but not confined to it. To the beginning writer, the frame might seem limiting, but limits provide great freedom. See John Keats' poem, "Ode on a Grecian Urn" to as an experience of the absent.

Excerpt of Ekphrastic Poetry: In the novel-in-verse *Autobiography of Red,* Anne Carson uses notional ekphrasis: "It was taking him a very long while / to set up the camera." The nine-page long list in which seven notional photographs are described ends with a curious contradiction that brings to mind the interconnectedness of product and producer. Notice also the not-knowing: "It is a photograph he never took, no one here took it."

Religion

In Albrecht Dürer's *Adam and Eve,* we are overcome by the anatomical details of the figures, as well as the fauna and foliage. Yet, it is the narrative and symbolism that lead to a question of intent. Is this a cautionary tale? Who is telling the tale and who is listening?

How to classify religious art as a topic in ekphrastic writing is puzzling. Does it address morality, cultural viewpoints, the artist's impressions, historical narratives, or is it merely mythical text-influenced visual art?

Ekphrastic Freewrite: (After Fritz Von Uhde's 1890 painting, *The Hard Pass—The Road to Bethlehem*)

Somber hues of browns and greys as two people walk past winter trees in a row (barren of fruit and leaves) on a muddy footpath. The man helps her as she leans into him. He carries wood and bags around his shoulders. She has a basket in one hand. Another hand steadies a walking stick. He cares deeply for her, her fragile state, and has whittled the staff for her. Do they have miles to go before they rest? Is their destination on the horizon? What happens in Bethlehem? The birth of the Savior, the culmination of immaculate conception, the fortitude of God upon an innocent? A woman as the vehicle for creation, perhaps the creator herself. For this is the way of artists—the hard pass to their conceptions, their artistry where the barn awaits them, an old inn-keeper agrees to shelter, and wise men abound. How do we do it? How do we walk the hard path alone with

Albrecht Dürer's 1504 engraving, *Adam and Eve* (courtesy the Clarence Buckingham Collection).

winter on our backs, mud in our boots, a basket of essentials, and a small lantern scarcely seen through the dust of our eyes?

Writing Invitation: Discover artwork that depicts religion or spirituality in which you find comfort and write from that feeling of solace.

Did the oral tradition of story-telling lead to religious art? Is the result notional or actual ekphrasis? Text-based art begetting a verbal response?

What do we learn from religious art? Does religious art, in particular, bring about more comfort or consternation to viewers as compared with other types of art? Take the images of Christ on the cross, which, more often than not, also depict mourners. What is the comment? His death wasn't an isolated catastrophe? Those left behind were his unwitting biographers?

Ekphrastic Freewrite: (After Diego Velázquez's 1632 *Christ on the Cross*)

The crucifixion alone, without mourners, without doubting Thomas, without the tears and the women, without Magdalena. Here, Christ is alone. Tens of thousands of artwork include the onlookers, Mary, the weepers—society which witnesses the death, the torture, for without society depicted, it would seem that Christ's death happened in a vacuum, without affecting others, without leaving a mark on the world. Like the proverbial tree falling in the woods—a Christ alone, hangs from a cross, his bones fall down.

Excerpt of Ekphrastic Fiction: Anita Brookner, in her novel *A Misalliance*, tackles the complication of Christ's death:

> We will not even speak of the Crucifixion, if you don't mind. And all the martyrdoms. Those poor saints throwing away their lives, the only possession they could really call their own. And the cruelty of their tortures. All so that they could be shown in painting, resurrected, in perfect form, with merely a tower or a key or a wheel as a dainty allusion to their sufferings. As if the realm of painting were taking its lead from the kingdom of heaven. I worry about that a lot (53–54).

Writing Invitation: Write a prequel to a religious narrative that's been depicted in art.

Ekphrastic Freewrite: (After Pieter Brueghel's c. 1563 painting, *The Tower of Babel*)

With baked bricks and tar for mortar, these civilians of Babylonia construct a tower to reach the heavens. See, the tower's top pierces through a slough of clouds, and down below the man who executed the construction and his disciples before him curtsy and bow to the genius who will be crowned God. This is the lift that'll take them straight to Heaven, for the only way to conquer God is to face God and to face God means to find him and to find him means to search his Kingdom. But there is a conundrum in this tower that Brueghel depicts. Although searching locally, one finds soundness in craftsmanship, fancy footwork in arch-to-arch construction. See the windows—one atop the other and see how the path slopes up gradually, winding its way closer to heaven. But assessed globally, the entire tower sits skewed slightly to the left that, given its infinite thrust upward, it will eventually fall, taking the large village below with it. So, he has depicted strength, stability, determination coupled with imbalance—that which is taken for granted, flirting with physics, greed, haste, arrogance. And the result of such a plight? God decided to strike the people, scatter them in a babble. With different tongues, we cannot unite against the will of God. God gave us "confused language" and scattered us. Instead of a united team striving toward a common goal, we fight against one another.

Suggested Viewing: John William Waterhouse's painting, *Saint Eulalia*

Here is a quatrain poem that treats Albrecht Dürer's *Adam and Eve* image beyond its iconography. Notice the sound elements, as well as how it incorporates the modern mode of imagery used in mass media:

After the Fall
(After Albrecht Dürer's *Adam and Eve*)
by Rebecca Foust

Most assume it's the moment *before* the fall:
human figures drawn in classic proportion;
the four humors (elk, rabbit, cat, and ox) all
in balance; the cat pre-pounce, and on

a high crag, an ibex poised to plunge into abyss.
But wait—Adam is looking at Eve, who looks
at the snake, its jaws brimmed with bliss
that is anything but innocent. See how Eve smirks,

and notice her hands. Both palm-up, the right
cupping an apple offered by Satan, the left twisted
behind to block Adam's view of the fruit
it holds: a second apple—I think *already* tasted—

which explains those modesty leaves, sin
slapping pasties over perfection, and a fig tree
that bears apples, not figs. And why Eden
is a dark wood, with creatures—a parrot by

an elk by an ox—that look bluescreened in.
The whole scene's an ad, and what's being pitched
is eternal desire. Look at Adam's sign,
hawking the artist, and his eyes eating Eve, transfixed

by only the next piece of fruit. After the Fall
we all hunger this way—unto death—
in its joyous chaos, its pulsing, its swollen glands
and flux and infinite forms. Until the last breath

persuaded to crave what we are forbidden
to have, and to reach with both hands.

Excerpt of Ekphrastic Nonfiction: Symbolism is especially prevalent in religious art. Symbols are powerful because they contain a message within a message that links the viewer to other ideas and experiences. Margaret Starbird, in her nonfiction book, *The Woman with the Alabaster Jar*, finds signs and symbols in Sandro Botticelli's, painting, *Mystic Crucifixion*:

> Here the desolate figure of Mary Magdalen [sic] clinging to the foot of the cross on which Jesus hangs. On the right is a figure of an angel gripping a fox, which he holds upside down by the tail. Dark storm clouds in the painting are being driven away, and from the nimbus in the upper left corner, where God the Father is pictured blessing the scene, angels are descending from the sky, each bearing a shield of white with a titled red X emblazoned on it (121).

Writing Invitation: Identify artwork that illustrates the act of worship and write a piece that uses symbolism. Alternatively, discover a type of religious ritual depicted in art and free-associate on the connections that you imagine.

Suggested Viewing: The Tibetan Buddhist ritual of creating sand mandalas

History

In Kara Walker's *Slaughter of the Innocents (They Might Be Guilty of Something)*, we're poised to wonder: Is art the most crucial voice in history? Many artists choose to respond either directly or indirectly to local, national, or global matters that they find politically significant. Art can cleave a community together.

Here's an iambic pentameter poem in classic couplets that starts with a double-entendre title in its treatment of Walker's cut-out silhouettes. Notice the tension that exists between the subject and the use of formal verse:

Cut from Darkness
[After *Slaughter of the Innocents (They Might
Be Guilty of Something)* by Kara Walker]
by Michael Spence

As if from ancient fear and wonder, my gaze
Is drawn to the central figure: see her raise

A hook above her head as she holds the leg
Of a hanging child. Someone kneeling begs

The blade to stay suspended. Is my role
To make it stay by keeping watch? A pole

With a larger hook in the hands of a man nearby
Connects him to another he's speared like a prize.

Kara Walker (American) 2016 *Slaughter of the Innocents (They Might be Guilty of Something)*. Cut paper, acrylic, and graphite on canvas. The Museum of Fine Arts, Houston, Museum purchase funded by the Caroline Wiess Law Accessions Endowment Fund, 2017.487. Artwork © Kara Walker, courtesy of Sikkema Jenkins & Co., New York. *Image courtesy of the Museum of Fine Arts, Houston.*

> The blades that he and the woman wield seem part
> Of themselves—as if their sharpness saw its start
>
> From deep within. Are victims due their fate
> Because they've fallen beneath the claws of hate?
>
> Can killing be a form of play? A demon
> Seems to make a naked woman run
>
> From his reaching hands, but a devil merely spins
> Plates on his fingertips. When innocence
>
> Appears clear, doubt lies like a hidden crack
> Painted over. All silhouettes are black.
>
> In the far corner, a woman grips a snake
> But looks away as though she hopes to break
>
> Its gaze. Does she control it now, refuse
> Its evil? Or simply fear to let it loose?

J.D. McClatchy in his introduction to *Poets on Painters: Essays on the Art of Painting* observed, "Often, writing about an old painting may prove to be the best way to write about the past." However, as evidenced by Walker's image, contemporary artists' treatment of history also provide essential framework from which ekphrasists can respond.

Excerpt of Ekphrastic Fiction: In the case of Johannes Vermeer's painting, *View of Delft,* we are reminded that artwork held great significance at the time they were created and publicized for their relevance and timeliness. In the memoir, *Travels in Vermeer* Michael White honors these elements: "The Nieuwe Kerk steeple is fully, perhaps symbolically lit—it's the brightest spot—probably because William of Orange is buried there. This great national hero, who led the Dutch revolt against the occupying Spanish, was assassinated in 1584. Vermeer's spotlighting of the Nieuwek Kerk, then, was a patriotic homage" (34–35).

Suggested Reading: Isabella Gardner's poem, "Little Rock Arkansas, 1957"

Writing Invitation: Behold an artwork of an historic scene, one that allows for entry into the past, and write about it while considering Dorothy Allison's words: "Art should provoke more questions than answers and, most of all, should make us think about what we rarely want to think about at all."

War

Are you drawn to art that illustrates aggression and violence, danger and destruction, heroism and ceremony? In the 1917 speech, Senator Hiram Johnson said, "The first casualty when war comes is truth." Are artists seen as types of historians who grasp at the truth and tug on it regardless of the consequences? Living through history and making art on historical moments with their own perspective revealed? Similarly, philosopher David Hume in *A Treatise Of Human Nature* wrote, "The victory is not gained by the men at arms, who manage the pike and the sword; but by the trumpeters, drummers, and musicians of the army."

Ekphrastic Freewrite: (After Francisco de Goya's 1814 painting, *The Third of May 1808 in Madrid: The Execution at Principe Pío*)

Goya admired the maverick monarch Napoleon, but when his army invaded Spain, Goya experienced war firsthand. In addition to conveying sympathy for the victims of war, he showed how the French soldiers were also victims, with their "just follow orders" mindset. Some soldiers cover their eyes in disbelief and choke on gun smoke and blood liberating from the luckless. The blood reaching the soil, penetrating the earth, lurching to its core, mingling with other roots and life in which God exists. The cells of the blood, the pebbles on the ground, the fine outerwear of the guards, and the night which holds each man there and can do nothing else. Cued: five prisoners, including a tonsured monk. On one side: a mound of three dead. On the other side, a group awaits the firing squad which functions as a single unit. Each of the Spaniard bearing a long shot-gun—their hat-shaded faces are staring into the eyeholes, their stance is leaning balanced on a collective bent knee. Kneeling prisoner in the center—lit by a lantern between the killers and the killed. His hands palms-up to Madrid's night sky in vain, for the group of dead beside him will rise to eight. How close we stand to death, to our rites, where brooding men loom in their top-hats and long jackets. Their full sheaths swinging beside them as they reload and take down men as easily as a tree struck by lightning. The bark flings off the tree bole, exposing the white inside. The blood of these war-captured stains the ground, disappears into a stronghold of roots destined to rot to the core, the core of the earth where men trod mindlessly over the amount of blood it takes for the work to be done. They will not reap what they sow, but the cells will descend and inhabit the soil, inhabit the land which grows the bread that these soldiers will deliver home and break for their children to eat.

Writing Invitation: Select an artwork in which violence is depicted. Write a poem, essay, or story that includes a comment about how you are not sure about what you should see and a comment about how you are uncertain about what it is precisely that you are seeing.

Here is another illustration of an artist who made art based on his experience of war: Painter/sculptor Jean Fautrier made art in response to the torture and murder of French citizens by the Nazis. His series of art, "Hostages," was created between 1943 and 1945. The Tate Museum display read, "He spent most of this period in a sanatorium on the outskirts of Paris. At night, he could hear the Gestapo torture and execute prisoners in the nearby woods. The pitted and scarred surface of *Head of a Hostage* suggests both individual features and the anonymity of bodies found in mass graves."

Writing Invitation: If Rilke was right, "all art is the result of one's having been in danger." (C. Rilke 4). Spot danger portrayed in artwork and write from the perspective of someone in danger. Perhaps it is you?

Suggested Viewing: Pablo Picasso's painting, *Guernica*

Can art elicit change? In the case of the Spanish Civil War, it was a 1937 painting that brought worldwide attention to the war. In response to the bombing of Guernica, Spain by Nazi Germany and Italian warplanes at the behest of Spanish Nationals, Pablo Picasso created an anti-war mural. As the story goes, military men under the order of General Franco stormed Picasso's studio and confronted him about the painting. "Who's responsible for this?" they demanded to know. "You are," Picasso responded unapologetically (Faigley et al 14).

Writing Invitation: Poet Richard Hugo suggested that writers never ask a question that they themselves can answer. Select an image, begin your freewrite with a question and see where that leads you.

Besides the museums destroyed and artists assassinated, artwork was seized because of uprisings, terrorism, and other acts of war. For example, under Hitler's order for the destruction of anything that he deemed "degenerate art," Nazi soldiers destroyed or seized hundreds of thousands of works-of-art, many of which have never been returned.

Suggested Reading: Miller Williams' poem, "The Curator"

Contemporary artists use photography as evidence of being at a scene, at the precise moment of horror. This adds a dimension to the art-artist connection, which can be an aspect of the resulting ekphrastic writing. In *Photographers on Photography*, famed photographer Eddie Adams insisted, "Still photographs are the most powerful weapons in the world" (Carroll 116).

While on assignment for the Associated Press during the Vietnam War, Adams witnessed the police chief General Nguyễn Ngọc Loan shooting Nguyễn Văn Lém. Two consecutive shots, first the photographer and then the General. Adams regretted taking that shot, and he wished he had been more celebrated for having taken a series of photographs of dozens of Vietnamese refugees sailing to safety in a small boat to Thailand (Haggerty).

Suggested Viewing: Eddie Adams' photograph, *Saigon Execution, 1968*

During the Iraq War, individuals in the United States Army and the CIA committed atrocities against detainees in the Abu Ghraib prison. In 2004 when photographs of these atrocities were published, it had a chilling effect. In his book *Photography* Steve Edwards explained, "The case of the 'trophy images' made by US military personnel depicting the abuse and torture of Iraqi prisoners in Abu Ghraib prison.... They are like 'tourist pictures' in that they proclaim, 'look where I went,' 'look what I did'" (115).

Writing Invitation: What feelings are evoked when you gaze at a photograph that depicts, in real time, some image of war? Given the images from the Abu Ghraib prison, we wonder what compelled the military personnel to smile for the camera. Discover artwork that stirs within you a writing of protest, polemic, lament, or rage. Start a revolution with your words.

Suggested Reading: Allen Ginsberg's poem, "America"

Death

Regard the image of the woodcut, *Man of Sorrows*. What strikes you? The subject, the pose, symbolism? Given the inevitability of death, how is it portrayed in the arts? According to sociologists, one cultural indication of how society perceives and manages death is how artists in that society treat the subject.

Ekphrastic Freewrite:
(After Christian Boltanski's 1990 photographic installation, *The Reserve of the Dead Swiss*)

Forty-two 10×10 inch black and white obituary portraits on shelves of virgin pine lined with white muslin. A small lamp hovers in the middle of each picture. What can they tell us, as we shine a light and prepare even their pictures as if for a Jewish burial? Years of dying by interrogation, by religion. As they once stood, they now ash and ash cannot be wrapped in a shroud and taken to the Jewish cemetery—where the tombstone is erected a year later when the ground has settled from the body's decomposition. Who has been kept from religious burial rites, kept from remembrance by photographs with strangers looking on, strangers in sound mourning?

Unknown artist's 1460–75 woodcut, *Man of Sorrows* (courtesy the Waller Fund; gifts of Mrs. Tiffany Blake, Thomas E. Donnelley, Emil Eitel, Carolyn Morse Ely, Alfred E. Hamill, Frank B. Hubachek, Monarch Leather, and Mrs. Potter Palmer).

The treatment of a particular subject affects our perception of it. Our perception is cultivated by our genetics, society, and the culture in which we identify. How is death portrayed in art in your culture? Given many artworks that treat death, compare and contrast the portrayal of the death of an elder versus a child, the death of a terrorist versus a victim of terrorism, death due to homicide versus suicide, or death due to illness or aging.

Suggested Viewing: Henry Wallis' 1856 painting of poet Thomas Chatterton, *Chatterton*

Are there politics to how we see? Is art a type of witness? Historians agree that David Jackson's photograph of 14-year-old Emmett Till's dead body precipitated the civil rights movement. Rather than keeping the torture and murder of her African American son a private matter, Till's mother allowed the photograph to be published. She raged, "I wanted the world to see what they did to my baby" (Griffin).

Writing Invitation: Consider these words by writer Flannery O'Connor: "Your beliefs will be the light by which you see, but they will not be what you see, and they will not be a substitute for seeing." Discover an artwork in which you consider or discount its historical context, and in which your beliefs (or the beliefs of your character) color what you see.

Can death be made beautiful? Is honoring the subjects of death and dying blasphemous? Are you familiar with cultures in which death is more or less taboo than yours? Death in nature is the subject of the photography series by Maria Ionova-Gribina. On her website she discusses her artistic vision, as well as the childhood memories that informed her art-making:

> I found these dead animals during bicycle rides to the sea in the summer. I wanted to find a way to save them for the world of art. They were so unprotected.... One or two days more and they would be eaten by worms. I remembered my childhood. When I with my brother found a dead mole, bird or bug we buried them on the border of a forest. And we decorated the grave with flowers and stones. Why we did it that way? Probably it was a children's curiosity, our first studies of mortality. In this project I work with my childhood memories and with the subject of life and death. All animals died naturally or after accidents with cars. The flowers were gathered near dead animals and in my garden.

Suggested Viewing: Maria Ionova-Gribina's series of photographs, "Natura Morta"

Writing Invitation: Find artwork that draws you into a scene in which you can imagine happening upon the death of something or someone. How would you, or one of your characters, react?

Later in this book, we will learn about the creative process, tools, and techniques of many disciplines of visual artists, including photographers. Photographer Dorothea Lange believed, "'A camera is an instrument that teaches people how to see without a camera.' She was committed to helping people in trouble. By photographing them, she hoped to awaken and inspire the more fortunate to help, too. That is why her pictures are called a documentary, a word that comes from the Latin root *docere,* meaning, 'to teach'" (Sills 19).

Suggested Viewing: Dorothea Lange's photograph, *Migrant Mother, Nipomo, CA, 1936*

Suggested Viewing: Arnold E. Hardy's photograph, *Death Leap from a Blazing Hotel*

Suggested Viewing: Reza Deghati's reportage photographs

Topics in Ekphrasis II

Nature

In Charles Sheeler's painting, *The Artist Looks at Nature,* an artist sits outside on a chair before an easel. Do you see a juxtaposition between the organic and the geometric shapes? Here is the companion poem, by a naturalist-poet whose use of rich diction elevates our poetic experience of both the image and the narrative:

The Artist Looks at Nature
by Sandra Meek

Nothing wild to this cloverless field, measures
of grass Sheeler's wall knives mid-canvas; an absent sun

severs bright lime, kelly, with a hunter-green shadow—
a blade's flat grind and barracuda tip. Walls spoke out

jaggedly, spidering limbs jointed like the *daddy longlegs*
I once plucked from leaf litter—impossible, its spindly

legs, the freckle of the high-riding body: not a true
spider at all, *Opiliones, harvestmen* for the shepherds

who'd strap on stilts to walk at once among and above
their flocks, not to lose to a failed view's wolves a single lamb they

had watch over. Bereft of venom, no silk to whisk
away on, to escape a predator the creature will self-

amputate, the abandoned leg twisting, writhing as if vivified
by electric current. If mimicry diverts, any wall, domestic

with distance, can grow monumental, foregrounded
beneath the artist's dangling foot: Sheeler's, doubly flighted,

is stepped as steep as a Mayan pyramid too sacred
to be topped: its faces' composed lines, not the wild

expansive view, what I once photographed from the rainforest
below. White-nosed coatimundi snuffled

among the leaves, ocellated turkeys ruffled feathers
iridescent as oil on seawater's sunlit skin; spider monkeys lilted

44

Charles Sheeler's 1943 painting, *The Artist Looks at Nature* **(courtesy The Art Institute of Chicago/Art Resource, NY).**

> through the canopy. Raising his arm to his drawing, the artist
> casts his shadow there. The eye cannot rest on what lies
>
> before it. What I would have held whole and alive
> and other in my hands teetered back into the field I'd
>
> released it to. In my palm, the tiny severed thing,
> still twitching.

The process of writing on nature and the writing on nature portrayed in the arts can inform one another. Much of the creative writing on nature takes the position of the speaker standing in deference to an actual land-scape or one portrayed in artwork. Engaging with nature can also lead to environmental writing (that is, the problems that arise when humans and nature collide).

Is there much of a difference between ekphrastic writing and nature writing? All good writers are astute observers in that they have the desire and ability to look very closely. Painters see shapes and hues and texture and light. Writers write concretely of the things they see, feel, and can name. Art of any type can be an extension of reflections on what you are looking at and how you are processing what you are seeing.

Suggested Viewing: Morris Graves' tempera on paper, *Summer Flowers for Denise*

John Haines is an example of an interdisciplinary artist who straddled these worlds. His career began as a visual artist and that training informed his nature writing, which in turn lead him to write ekphrastically on art-work by Edward Hopper, Albrecht Dürer, Paul Klee, Francisco Goya, and Hieronymus Bosch, to name a few. He attended art school in New York and then relocated to Alaska, where he became a celebrated naturalist writer.

Suggested Reading: John Haines' memoir, *The Stars, the Snow, the Fire*

Suggested Viewing: Emily Carr's Alaska paintings

Suggested Reading: Pattiann Roger's poem, "Alpha and Omega"

What are the common aesthetic concerns for literary writers writing on nature? Nature writing topics include resilience, beauty, hope, sense of place, growth, danger, cycles and change, order and chaos, the human spirit, and contemplation. To write well of nature, one must be in nature. Nature can be sensually experienced and described. All the senses can be exploited when one experiences nature firsthand. It takes a curious spirit and deft observational and descriptive skills. Similar to individuals who write creatively, feeling connected with nature requires we possess a level of comfort (awe, even) by what exists beyond immediate awareness.

Suggested Reading: Alison Hawthorne Deming's poem, "Genetic Sequence"

Suggested Reading: Jane Hirshfield's poem, "Mule Heart"

Psychologist Rudolf Arnheim philosophized,

Nothing is more humbling than to look with a strong magnifying glass at an insect so tiny that the naked eye sees only the barest speck and to discover that nevertheless it is sculpted and articulated and striped with the same care and imagination as a zebra. Apparently, it does not occur to nature whether or not a creature is within our range of vision, and the suspicion arises that even the zebra was not designed for our benefit.

Have you ever inspected a strawberry, really looked at one? See those oval-shaped yellow bits dotting the red contour? What are they? Well, as it turns out, they are ovaries each with a seed inside it. Celebrated painter of flowers Georgia O'Keeffe mused, "In a way, nobody sees a flower really, it is so small, we haven't time—and to see takes time, like to have a friend takes time" (Ackerman 270). Do you take time to see a flower really?

Suggested Reading: Mary Oliver's poem, "Hummingbirds"

Suggested Reading: Jorie Graham's poem, "I Watched a Snake"

Suggested Reading: Marianne Moore's poem, "The Fish"

The speaker in Sylvia Plath's poem, "Wuthering Heights" comments on the effects of the closeness one can feel for nature. Is it alluring or dangerous? Perhaps both:

> If I pay the roots of the heather
> Too close attention, they will invite me
> To whiten my bones among them.

Throughout the Fairchild Tropical Botanic Garden in Florida are sculptures, a form of public art. Here is a photo my mother snapped there of two fiberglass-reinforced plastic pumpkins by artist Yayoi Kusama.

Do you feel moved by artwork born of scientific investigation? Here is an example of how nature influenced the art of photography: In the 1800s Botanist Anna Atkins used photography to record her specimens in *British Algae: Cyanotype Impressions*. Published in 1843, it is the world's first book of photography.

Suggested Viewing: Vija Celmins' photo-based drawings and paintings of nature

Suggested Reading: Pablo Neruda's poem, "Oda a la Alcachofa"

Writing Invitation: Consider this quote: "Once the artist is able to enter this 'uninterrupted realm' of pure being, he becomes one with a nature that looks back at him" (Strathausen 27). Locate an artwork in which flora or fauna is central, or consider carefully something in nature and begin a long description predicated upon deep-looking.

One method of writing a response to nature is through the mode of anthropomorphism, which in literature is referred to as "pathetic fallacy." If you have never given voice to a plant, animal, or insect, it can be quite fun and revelatory. Here is an example of that mode in this ekphrastic flash-fiction piece influenced by Louise Bourgeois' 2003 sculpture, *Spider Couple* (see Kristina J. Baugher's drawing of a similar subject, *The Argument*).

Yayoi Kusama at Fairchild Tropical Botanic Garden, Miami, Florida. *Pumpkin: Big*, 2009 and *Pumpkin: Medium*, 2009.

The Harder Choice
by Peter Grandbois

After we made love, she begged me not to impale myself on her fangs. I thought I'd make it easy for her. You know. Avoid the mess, not to mention a scene. But she wouldn't hear of it. She wanted me to take up running again, said she loved the way I sprinted across the bathroom floor at the first sign of trouble. When I thought of running, I thought of disappearing. I didn't tell her that. Better to be daggered and mourned. I threw myself at her. But she knocked me away with her pedipalps and called me a coward. I crept to the other side of the web. Counted flies until I could sleep. When morning came, I wasn't any better off. She was still there, if anything, bigger than before as if she'd found her purpose and sucked the life out of it to nourish her own. She'd always had that kind of clarity. And I, well, let's just say, yesterday marked the first real decision of my life. It should have been my last. Slowly, careful not to make the slightest vibration, I tight-roped off the web and down to the floor, away from her. If she wouldn't kill me, I'd do it myself. But just as I stepped toward the white whirlpool where I'd seen so many leave this world, the two-legged giant who terrorizes our home opened the door, showering our web with light. I froze. My eight eyes panning from the whirlpool to her and back again. The linear path of death or the tangled odyssey of love. The shimmer of gold refracted off the labyrinthine web, and for a fleeting moment, I saw my path outlined like a poem.

Suggested Reading: Brigit Pegeen Kelly's poem, "Iskandariya"

Suggested Reading: Kobayashi Issa's many haiku

Writing Invitation: Examine artwork in which an animal or insect is featured and write a piece in which that species is honored in some way.

Besides fine art that is relegated to galleries, museums, and in the homes of private collectors, there is also site sculpture and other types of public art. In both these cases, art exists in nature, and at times, the artwork is natural or nature itself.

Suggested Viewing: Robert Smithson's earthwork sculpture, *Spiral Jetty*

Suggested Viewing: James Turrell's large-scale artwork, *Roden Crater*

Suggested Viewing: The image from the documentary, *Planet Earth*, "Nature Takes Over at Chernobyl Ghost Town"

Writing Invitation: Consider this quote from plant scientist, Anthony Trewavas: "Metaphors help stimulate the investigative imagination of good scientists," and find the artistic possibilities in nature, such as Poland's Crooked Forest in which there are 100-year-old pine trees that grew at ninety degree angles before reaching up to the sky.

Suggested Viewing: The three waterfalls of Niagara Falls

Suggested Viewing: Frank Lloyd Wright's house, Fallingwater

Suggested Reading: Patrick Syme's nonfiction book, *Werner's Nomenclature of Colours: Adapted to Zoology, Botany, Chemistry, Mineralogy, Anatomy, and the Arts*

Writing Invitation: Locate photography that captures the exquisite hues (lilac, navy blue, baby blue, brown, mauve) found on the bird, the lilac-breasted roller. Rilke wrote, "Most people do not know at all how beautiful the world is and how much magnificence is revealed in the tiniest things, in some flowers, in a stone, in tree bark, or in a birch leaf" (Baer 85). So, what can that one bird teach you?

Suggested Reading: Rachel Carson's nonfiction book, *Silent Spring*

Suggested Reading: Jane Goodall's nonfiction book, *In the Shadow of Man*

Suggested Reading: Sylvia Earle's nonfiction book, *The World Is Blue*

Writing Invitation: Whether consciously or unconsciously, many artists find within nature their own self-portrait. Artist Frida Kahlo, for instance, painted self-portraits which she titled, *Wounded Deer, Self-Portrait with Thorn Necklace*, and *Hummingbird*. Uncover a work-of-art that depicts nature and in which your own self-portrait exists.

Especially before anatomy books were published, how did representational artists create art with precision? George Stubbs, best known for his paintings of horses, took matters into his own hands. In the service of his art, he spent a year dissecting horses. Whether he slaughtered the animals for his pleasure or not is something I do wish to know. Consequent to his being intimate with the equine physique to support his artistry, he decided to share his knowledge (verbal and pictorial) and produce a book. Although it was published in 1754, Stubbs' *The Anatomy of the Horse* is still hailed today as an essential instructional guide for those in the field.

Ekphrastic Freewrite: (After George Stubbs' 1763 painting, *Mares and Foals in a Landscape*)

Three mares and two nursing foals under a linden tree next to a lake. The mares, I imagine, seem to be speaking to each other, with the children being incidental. This field and horses are fabricated? The musculature is precise: the wistfulness of their manes and tails—shimmering, translucent. They whisper about the dissecting painter, no doubt. Only from the vantage of a corpse could he study the muscle and sinew. He would pull the horse apart, ripping muscle from bone, sectioning it off from circulatory and nervous systems. How strained his hands must have been, but this method led to the accuracy of his portraits. The horses would prefer to be ill-represented, with a little guesswork. Is it better to be scientific in your creation or imaginative?

Writing Invitation: What animal from your childhood holds significance? Examine photographs of that creature or artwork that reminds you of it and write autobiographically.

Landscape

Consider landscape portrayed in the visual arts. According to D.W. Meinig in his article, "The Beholding Eye: Ten Versions of the Same Scene," there are numerous ways in which landscape can be viewed: We can choose to see landscape as

1. nature,
2. habitat (nature and humans blending),
3. artifact (humans exist everywhere),
4. system (intricate system within a system),
5. problem (corrections are needed),
6. wealth (monetary value),
7. ideology (representative of values, philosophies of a culture),
8. history (record of nature and humans blending), and
9. aesthetics and place (unique coordinates).

Suggested Viewing: Edgar Degas' landscape painting, *Beach at Low Tide*

Suggested Viewing: Joan Mitchell's cityscape painting, *City Landscape*

Writing Invitation: Given Meinig's manners of seeing landscape, which ones resonate with you? Identify artwork that ignites the various ways in which you view landscape. As a challenge, attempt each of these ten versions in a single poem, essay, or story.

Again, in *Beauty,* Scuton explores the difference between landscapes and objects d'art:

> Hence it is easy to describe the natural objects that we can hold in our hands, or move into view, as we would describe works of art: and this conditions the kind of pleasure we take in them. They are *objects trouvés*, jewels, treasures, whose perfection seems to radiate from themselves, as from an inner light. Landscapes by contrast are very far from works of art—they owe appeal not to symmetry, unity and form, but to an openness, grandeur and world-like expansiveness, in which it is we and not they that are contained (51).

Is enjoying a work-of-art limiting as compared with physically experiencing a landscape? What are your thoughts on "it is *we* and not *they* that are contained"? Consider this idea of containment in your next freewrite.

Suggested Viewing: Anna Ostroumova-Lebedeva's cityscape, *Chain Bridge in St. Petersburg*

Suggested Viewing: Loïs Mailou Jones' painting, *Jardin du Luxembourg*

Writing Invitation: Do you see landscape as being devoid of something, or do you see it as full? For instance, what does an urban or rural landscape say about its inhabitants?

What do landscapes (exterior scenes) have that interior scenes do not? Said another way, what can an artwork of an interior accomplish that artwork of an exterior cannot? Consider these words from John Muir, "Into the forest I go, to lose my mind and find my soul."

Suggested Reading: Robert Wrigley's poem, "Anything the River Gives"

Suggested Reading: Patricia Goedicke's poem, "The Sea"

Suggested Reading: Theodore Roethke's poem, "Meditation at Oyster River"

Writing Invitation: Locate an artwork on nature that uplifts your spirit and write about it. Alternatively, write a topographical or loco-descriptive poem (one that describes and praises a place).

Given the experience of an actual landscape, gestaltism comes to mind: While the details of place—colors, textures, shapes, depth, sounds, smells—are evident and can be experienced individually or together, the entire scene (the whole) transcends its parts and becomes a reality unto itself, one in which we can see context—relationships among concepts, categories of things, connotations, and the like. What is the appeal of artwork that represents nature and landscape? A token of a place that's available to us, if only through our imagination? As a relic of a place we have been and which we hold as nostalgic?

Suggested Viewing: Alexis Rockman's futuristic landscape paintings

Suggested Viewing: May Vale's landscape paintings

Writing Invitation: Consider the words "escape" and "landscape." Either find an artwork that depicts a pastoral scene (such as, mountains, oceans, meadows) that you would like to escape to or one that you would never want to visit, and write an epistle poem, essay, or story from that setting.

Suggested Viewing: Thomas Eakin's painting *The Champion Single Sculls*

Suggested Viewing: Aleksandra Ekster's cityscape painting, *View of Paris*

Writing Invitation: Consider this quote from Henry David Thoreau: "No method nor discipline can supersede the necessity of being forever on the alert. What is a course of history, or philosophy, or poetry, or the most admirable routine of life, compared with the discipline of looking always at what is to be seen?" Find artwork that relates to the writings of Thoreau and study the form of linked haiku (renga). As is customary of the form, use nature as your subject and keep the language literal.

Suggested Reading: Honoré Willsie Morrow's historical novel, *Seven Alone*

Writing Invitation: Identify artwork that has some relationship to an adventuresome person, such as Meriwether Lewis, William Clark, or Sacagawea, or artwork that depicts the benefits or challenges of travel, or that evoke in you yearning for adventure. Alternatively, find artwork that treats the subject of travel, such as old maps, or art with locomotives, luggage, or stamped envelopes.

Writing Invitation: Perhaps you are composing a story that lacks tension or in which your character requires conflict? Locate artwork whose subject matter is a natural disaster or the weather (such as lightning storms, hurricanes, snow) and let that imagery inform your story.

Writing Invitation: Explore an object in nature (or an artwork that features a natural object), read Wisława Szymborska's poem, "Conversation with a Stone," and embark on your own conversation.

For Spanish architect Antoni Gaudí, nature was his muse, and there is no better illustration of that than his Barcelona cathedral, Sagrada Família. His biomimetic architecture boasts spiral stairways, honeycomb gates, grand arches, metal vine work, conical shapes on the roof, gargoyles in the shape of animals, and impressions of leaves. In his architecture, he strove to emulate the perfection he admired in nature (Peach).

Suggested Viewing: Georgia O'Keeffe's landscape paintings

Suggested Viewing: Edward Burtynsky's industrial landscape photography

In his novel's preface Oscar Wilde wrote, "All art is at once surface and symbol. Those who go beneath the surface do so at their peril.... It is the spectator and not life that art mirrors." What symbolism exists for you in nature? In the time of William Shakespeare, for example, the symbolism associated with flowers was highly accepted. To illustrate, in "Hamlet," Ophelia doles out actual flowers, as well as their figurative symbols: "There's rosemary, that's for remembering"; "And there are pansies, they're for thoughts"; "Here are fennel and columbines for you—they symbolize adultery"; and "I'd give you some violets, flowers of faithfulness, but they all dried up when my father died." The flowers hold multiple connotations for Shakespeare's characters, as well as his audience. If it serves your writing, find symbolism in what you see and decide if your characters need symbolism in their lives as well.

Given the image of Mondrian's painting, what do you first notice? Why do you think your eyes were drawn to where they were drawn? Does it remind you of a place you have visited? Because this image is in a book, you can hold in your hand, turn it, and view the image upside down. What do you notice? View the image on its sides. Does your experience of what you see change?

Ekphrastic Freewrite: (After Allison Collins' 2002 painting, *Steptoe Butte*)

The squares of yellows and oranges like a library—all angles in their places until an unsuspecting hand ... a melding, a greeting of hand to angle, of that which is fresh and sinewy and pale to the stacks, a landscape of yellow boxes and orange boxes amid a landscape of green expanse and lavender above. Who lingers here and who drives through. Who knows how to mix the rhythm of green—that undulation of grass not yet harvestable for straw, but plumbing in nutrients, hay perhaps, grain or crops, those that someone nods to on his way to the city where cement stacks

Piet Mondrian's c. 1916 painting, *Farm near Duivendrecht* **(gift of Dolly J. van der Hoop Schoenberg).**

ride on brick and the sky turns a pink some nights because of the smog, and it makes him recall the purity of a lavender sky astride the velvety green of field, makes him recall the symmetry of these shapes like books on the shelf of his own body.

Writing Invitation: Consider a place depicted in an artwork or a place depicted in one of your own photographs. What is the importance of that place? Is it from your past? Is it notional? Write a place-influenced piece that also speaks to inner reflection, or write about a devotional or meditative act.

Science

Physicist and philosopher of science Albert Einstein declared, "The most beautiful thing we can experience is the mysterious. It is the source of all true art and science." What do you think? Coming from a man of science, does it surprise you that he would celebrate what is unknown, the mysterious?

Try naming the group of practitioners that I describe in this list: persistent investigators; explorers of the mysterious, who strive for certainty and precision; users of language in creative ways to convey the ineffable, and creators of terminology; those with stellar observational skills who live in a state of wonderment. These qualities describe creative writers, visual arts, and scientists. Given the similarities among the disciplines, it is not difficult to imagine a surplus of ways that all of these practitioners can cross-pollinate.

Suggested Research: Notable scientists include Rosalind Franklin, Marie Curie, Irene Joliot Curie, Ada Lovelace, Lise Meitner, Gertrude Elion, Maria Goeppert-Mayer, Barbara McClintock, Dorothy Hodgkin, Jocelyn Bell Burnell, Miriam Daniel Mann, Kathryn Peddrew, Christine Darden, Annie Easley, and Mary Jackson.

In the introduction to his anthology *Verse & Universe: Poems about Science and Mathematics*, Kurt Brown remarked on the relationship between art and science:

> Perhaps the kind of imagination it takes to conceive of a radical and complicated new scientific theory, and prove it, is not so different from what is required to envision, compose and successfully execute a great poem. The human mind may not be as compartmentalized or fractured as we tend to believe. If science and art have anything in common, it exists in the resources of the human brain and our ability to create something unforeseen and revolutionary out of our dreaming.

Writing Invitation: Consider Brown's passage above, and identify artwork in which you can appreciate either a cross-disciplinary approach (viewing one discipline from the perspective of a different discipline) or an interdisciplinary approach (wherein the artist has knowledge of two disciplines and portrays them both in the artwork).

Isn't it fascinating how when we shift our perspective just a minuscule amount, we can see more than we ever imagined? Take, for example, scale. What is our fascination with miniatures? Similarly, what is our fascination with an enlarged view of the microscopic? Do we feel like explorers? Is the feeling voyeuristic? Henry Carroll in his book *Read This If You Want to Take Great Photographs*, introduced the term "macro photography" as "the art of photographing extreme close-ups" which "has the ability to transform everyday objects into alien forms and totally change our perception of the world around us" (99).

In *Poetics* Aristotle discussed beauty and perception this way: "[B]eauty depends on magnitude and order. Hence a very small animal organism cannot be beautiful; for the view of it is confused, the object being seen in an almost imperceptible moment of time. Nor, again, can one of vast size be beautiful; for as the eye cannot take it all in at once, the unity and sense of the whole is lost for the spectator." Do you concur with Aristotle's assessment? As a writer, when do you experience the feeling of vastness or the feeling of evanescence?

Recent strides in technology have allowed for new forms of art. Photomicrography is an art form that unites digital time-lapse stills of specimens seen through light microscopes. The microscopic, usually relegated to the lens, has been liberated through this process, thereby allowing for inquiry from those viewers who would not otherwise have access to the images. Additionally, the art that results from this process is kinetic, which begs the question: what visual arts discipline would it be categorized under? Video art? Performance art?

Suggested Viewing: Persian miniatures (small paintings on paper)

Suggested Reading: Ernst Haeckel's book, *Art Forms in Nature: The Prints of Ernst Haeckel*

With the recent interest in S.T.E.M. education (science, technology, engineering, mathematics), it is not difficult to find art that corresponds to each of these fields of study. While illustrations of the natural sciences have already been tackled, here are some ideas for technology, engineering, and mathematics:

Suggested Viewing: Sam Taylor-Wood's film art, *Still Life, 2001*. Compare this display of time-lapse rotting fruit with the iconic 1615 still-life, *Flowers in a Basket and a Vase* by Jan Brueghel.

Suggested Viewing: Kinetic sculpture of Alexander Calder, inventor of mobiles. Compare Calder's art with the ancient art of origami

Suggested Viewing: Hamid Naderi Yeganeh's mathematical formulas drawings of birds in flight. He calls himself a mathematical artist and explains that he first defines birds by trigonometric functions: "In order to create such shapes, it is very useful to know the properties of the trigonometric functions. I believe these images show us an important fact: We can draw with mathematical formulas."

Suggested Viewing: The mathematical origami artwork by Erik Demaine

Humans

Portraying the complexities of the human figure in the arts is an ancient conundrum. Although the human body is the commonality we share, the history of the depiction of the human form in the arts is long and controversial. However, the relatability of the human form in the arts can indeed be a celebration of the self. Do we have the ability to see ourselves in other people? Do we have the capacity for an empathetic gaze? Is the human form in the arts a circus of differences or a parade our commonalities?

Ekphrastic Freewrite: (After Francis Bacon's 1952–53 painting, *Study of a Nude*)

There is a small man full-bodied with his back to us, mid-canvas. He's balanced on a merely drawn line, a beam, the edge of a pool, or a bed's metal frame—I can't make it out. His hands are up over his head, and the cranium is tilted downwards. Are his hands bound? Is there a rope from the structure that's overhead? The pool or bed below is a grey-purple blue, and one can make out a semblance of his shadow. Is he there by will, or is it a languished crime and punishment? How strange that "Study of Nude's" subject would have his back turned toward us, as if in modesty. Has modesty left him hanging in effigy, or is he preparing to dive into it? The breaching of nudity and wake, how sober the unclothed. There are faint light grey rays emanating from under where the figure stands. But the dark background is strewn in thick lines running vertically. The yin and yang of things—circularity of naked and confinement of modesty— our fine lines that we are must be praised by that which we set ourselves against. His feet are splayed out, but his legs are tight together; he is firm on that thin, unstable ground.

Suggested Viewing: Lucian Freud's portrait paintings

Suggested Viewing: Alice Neel's portrait paintings

Writing Invitation: Locate artwork in which a body part is depicted. Free-associate on what you know about the body for a couple of minutes and then free-associate for a few minutes on what you do not know about the body. Which was easier to produce, the known or the mystery? Weave these notions together in couplets.

Excerpt of Ekphrastic Fiction: In the story "Medusa's Ankles" from the collection of stories *The Matisse Stories* by A.S. Byatt, we have a surprising verbal description of a visual representation of a character: "The rosy nude was pure flat colour, but suggested mass. She had huge haunches and a monumental knee, lazily propped high. She had round breasts, contemplations of the circle, reflections of flesh and its fall" (3).

Research on babies shows that they respond to the representation of human faces within a few weeks after birth. And, compared with other species, they favor their own. Facial expressions are widespread—anger on a face, for example, is recognizable worldwide. And our brains are wired to dislike distortions. Though, it is called adaptation when we get used to such anomalies. So, skilled artists are fortunate if they can portray a wide array of facial expressions, for the recognition of faces is a type of universal language.

Suggested Viewing: Jenny Saville's portrait paintings

Suggested Viewing: Alberto Giacometti's paintings

Writing Invitation: Discover a face in an artwork that gives off the air of malaise or frailty. What future does that face behold?

As humans, we value growth and connection. We wish to feel significant and offer contribution. We thrive in certainty but also appreciate uncertainty. Ultimately, our needs are quite simple. One theory about the importance of art in our lives is this: "Our favourite works of art seem to guide us to the truth of the human condition and, by presenting completed instances of human actions and passions, freed from the contingencies of everyday life, to show the worthwhileness of being human" (Scruton, 108). Do you hold the opinion that art enriches your life because it is a reminder that your very existence has value?

Suggested Viewing: René Magritte's painting, *The Human Condition*

Writing Invitiation: Uncover artwork in which you see the truth and humor of the human condition revealed and write a senryu. Alternatively, write on the pain you perceive in an artwork. How does this relate to the pain that you have experienced?

Earlier, we saw the image, *Man of Sorrow* by an unknown artist. Here is the corresponding poem, one that does not take the apparent route of responding to a religious artwork by becoming a poem on religion. To whom does the speaker relate?

Sundays
by Erin Belieu

after church, she shucked the grip of shoes, of service, of talcumed hands
and White Shoulders, the peace beings of neighbors, the puce-faced elders
and pilly hangings, and that soft, sad man with his sorrows,
no business of hers.

Looking up where he drooped, where there's smoke, there's fire, she thought,
choosing one adult fib that seemed, for once, more possible than not; she felt
him contagious, a man with his torso gouged like that, of no-thank-you
troubles, and terrible holes.

She was sorry for him, though decided his story likely a lie, unlikely stories
abounding, aplenty, for little girls to buy. But she wanted no truck nonetheless,
nuh uh—and what had she done?—how bad could she be?—and whose son
was this, this sad, soft man another would hurt like that?

So Sundays, she shucked, and ran and climbed, the birch in her yard
no scourge. Who'd put, she thought, a gift worth having at the end of a whip?
Such adult

nonsense; if she needed beseeching, better the leaves now candling their verdigris,
   in spring,
where a girl could be, redeemed, redeeming, sewing herself
into what anyone who looked could see was something true.

Reckless, she went, farther, higher, climbing clean into the birch's crown,
the limbs growing greener and thinner, the girl now certain it was only a father
who'd do that to a kid, and call it a lesson. How lovely that spirit, and her at the top
knowing no one could reach her.

Ekphrastic Freewrite: (After René Magritte's 1928 painting, *The Lovers*)

A portrait of a couple posed side by side. The painting cropped at the chest, the landscape behind them a meadow, bushy trees, the sky is a solemn blue with clouds. She in a dress and he in a suit and tie. Their heads tilt toward each other. White cloth is draped over their heads and necks. Just the hint of features under the cloths—point of a nose, a chin, the cloth is close to the face. They have only their bodies to give each other in their senseless love. Two lovers without a harsh word for one another. Words that stench and stink and sting cannot fester in the mouth (a cauldron of venom) nor the ears (a rancid pit). Without eyes to criticize, to close when they should be open, remain open when they should be otherwise. They press their heads together and grin for the artist.

Writing Invitation: Identify illustrations of loneliness in numerous works-of-art and weave notes on each into a single poem, essay, or story.

Ekphrastic Freewrite: (After Peter Paul Reubens' 1630–40 painting, *Cimon and Pero*)

His hands are bound and his eyes open. She holds the breast out for him, and the prisoner drinks from it, onlookers at the window. Devoted daughter this is the ultimate feeding, your buffet for the man who bore you. See how long his hair and beard have gotten? White wisps. Her buxom banquet buoys another day of living for him. How she is captive by his needs. Selfless and gentile, honorable and ghostly. Why expose the expanse of her chest rather than merely the spigot? Patriarchic Pero. Refreshing the thirsty, feeding the hungry, visiting the sick, comforting the captive: four acts of charity (out of seven) in one. Oh, to be able to give what I have, and to give it freely.

Writing Invitation: Identify artwork that illustrates caring for another human or animal, or some other act of charity. Create a poem, essay, or story in which giving or receiving reveals a relationship.

Have you ever talked to a friend who reported she was feeling feverish and nauseous, and as soon as the call ends, you begin to feel those same symptoms? Some people are more susceptible to suggestive illness and pain than others. It is the mirror neurons in our brains that allow for our reactions to notional pain in a similar manner to reactions of actual pain. How can you apply this principle to art-viewing? This is all to say that the ways in which we respond to art can be as fiercely felt as if we were literally experiencing what was being depicted. This art-engagement can lead to not just empathetic ekphrasis, but sympathetic ekphrasis.

Suggested Reading: poems contained in issues of *The Journal of the American Medical Association*

Lilly Martin Spencer's 1854 painting, *Young Husband: First Marketing* **(gift of Max N. Berry, 2015).**

Suggested Reading: *Articulations: The Body and Illness in Poetry* edited by Jon Mukand

Here we have Spencer's painting, *Young Husband: First Marketing*. The title of this painting provides us with information—not just any information, but a narrative—beyond the frame. Do you find this contextualizing title distancing or welcoming? What alternative titles might you have given the painting?

How we depict the human body is dependent on our time and culture. Historically, as homo sapiens making art, we first made the human figure distorted, then we made the human figure anatomically accurate, then we move to exaggerated musculature. In other words, as a species, we enjoy embellishing reality.

Writing Invitation: Consider how artists represent the people in their artwork. Idealistically? Stereotypically? Sympathetically? Discover art in which you feel that humans were represented in one of these manners and write a poem, essay, or story.

Ekphrastic Freewrite: (After Gustav Klimt's c. 1907 painting, *Water Serpents I*)

Here: the world of water serpent and river nymph, forest and flower. Two lovers walk. A ground of whale head, of seaweed—brown-blubber, green, spiral tails, of divided hues—burnt sienna and umber. There they fall into each other: opening. The one is holding the other, holding her to the valley of bloodshed, elemental grief and the pliancy of sea-grass. Their two heads melded into one. Hair flowing as delicate as seaweed, as strong as the sun. Their torsos, opaque, sullen-mouthed. The new flesh of brine—serpenting in curves, undeniably two shes, two of them there on man's canvas. Not two female humans, two water serpents. See, they have no middles, no discernible legs. The subjection of body and movement—see the beach, its onerous sunset? Taste the grey sand and see these two collapse into each other, mending the times we are alone despite the sea, lonely despite the lover. Who to search for minerals between our shells, search for the one antiquated body? The one who is all beach, sand, sun.

Consider the ancient practice of body art (tattooing). Do you believe this is an art form? Indelible ink on a human's dermis. Live canvas. Is the human skin an ephemeral or an eternal canvas? Do all artists make art to last? In some cultures tattooing is forbidden; in other cultures it is ceremony. What was your ancestors' relationship with tattoos? Not all live canvases gave their consent.

Suggested Reading: Reginald Shepherd's poem, "Black is the Color of my True Love's Hair"

Writing Invitation: Discover artwork that concerns human dermis as a type of canvas. What do that picture and your skin have in common? Where are they divergent?

Art-viewing can lead to a deeper understanding of the human body. Consider human figures depicted in the fine arts, as well as in anatomical and scientific illustrations. In a world in which we can often feel divided, most any depiction of the human figure can be viewed as a commemoration of our commonalities.

Suggested Viewing: Here are some examples of the terms to use when researching anatomical and scientific illustrations—Female/male figure, anterior and posterior views; muscular system, anterior and posterior; hand and wrist; foot and ankle; hip and knee; skeletal system, anterior and posterior; vertebral column; respiratory system; the heart, external and internal views; vascular system; digestive system; urinary system; nervous system; female/male reproductive systems; eye, horizontal section; the ear canal; and the brain, base view.

Similar to the Körperwelten Exhibition, which is a traveling display of dissected human bodies donated to science and preserved by a technique called "plastination," the Anatomical and Obstetrics Collection at the Museo di Palazzo Poggi in Bologna, Italy is an extraordinary collection of anatomical waxworks from the 18th century. Sculptor Ercole Lelli used human skeletons on which he layered wax, thereby emulating musculature.

Suggested Viewing: The Körperwelten (Body Worlds) Exhibition of plastinated human corpses

Suggested Viewing: Victor Brauner's figure painting, *Force de Concentration de Monsieur K*

Suggested Reading: Denise Duhamel's poem, "Facing my Amygdala"

Suggested Reading: Alice Jones' poem, "The Larynx"

Writing Invitation: Search works-of-art in order to discover the inner workings of your anatomy, and write a series of flash-nonfiction.

Is there a preponderance of stereotyping in art? For instance, while a majority of museum art has been created by males, it is the female gender that is depicted most often—which makes us wonder, through whose gaze are we seeing art? Additional matters of stereotyping include the caste system, racial prejudice, and cultural appropriation.

Suggested Viewing: Hans Bellmer's artwork of dolls

Writing Invitation: Identify art that illustrates an ideology that matter to you and begin your freewrite. For example, how are members of your gender, race, culture, religion portrayed in a given artwork?

The biblical story of adultery, "Susanna and the elders," has influenced innumerable works-of-art. What is so intriguing about the narrative of Susanna bathing in her garden, securing the door to ensure her safety, but bathing modestly nonetheless, when all the while, the voyeurs kept her in their gaze? Compare and contrast the portrayal of this scene in the paintings all entitled *Susanna and the Elders* by Rembrandt, Artemisia Gentileschi, and Paolo Veronese. Find contemporary art that treats this same scene and decide how Susanna and her story have changed over the years.

Writing Invitation: Voyeurism and the politics of seeing: what do you make of any unwelcome gaze? Take a political position and respond to an artwork of your choice.

Excerpt of Ekphrastic Fiction: Susan Vreeland's story "Cradle Song" from her story collection, *Life Studies* concerns Édouard Manet's painting, *Berthe Morisot Resting*. What do you notice about this description? Regard the mixture of concrete with abstraction, the rhetorical questions, and the introduction of a supposition of an alternative viewpoint: "In the painting Madame's eyes are large and dark and full of feeling. She is looking out with an open look. At whom? The person painting her? She is wearing a black bow around her neck, and her black dress has a low, lacy neckline. Men would like it. She is beautiful" (65).

Family

In Richard Billingham's photograph, we have an interior scene with a seated man looking away and a standing woman looking toward the man. With her parted lips, she is seemingly speaking. One hand is making a fist. She bears flower tattoos on her biceps and forearm and a white dress with a pattern of intersecting lines. In the background, a cabinet with a display of figurines. The man's shoulders are hunched over, and his eyes are downcast. The woman's neck is protruding toward him, and her torso inclines, too. There is a flowery pattern on the wallpaper. It feels like a still shot in a film about a family that no one wants to watch because it is too real. The photographer himself on his gallery's webpage expressed, "The pictures shown here are of my father Raymond (born 1931): my mother Elisabeth (born 1950). Ray is a chronic alcoholic and has drunk for as long as I can remember. He has not worked since he was made redundant from his job as a machinist around 1980. Liz very rarely drinks but she does smoke a lot of cigarettes." This was the artwork that poet Rae Armantrout selected, which resulted in her poem, "Much."

Do you believe that the relationship we have with our family mem-

Richard Billingham's 1994 (80 × 120 cm) Fuji long-life color print on aluminum, *Untitled (RAL 25)*, © Richard Billingham, 1994.

bers has less to do with reality and more to do with our perceptions of reality? Family politics include the members and their roles, power, loyalty, belonging, abandonment, companionship, and love. Is it true that, "Persons appear to us according to the light we throw upon them from our own minds" (Laura Ingalls Wilder)? The portrayal of family is a potent subject for art. When we see artwork that depicts family, what emotions are stirred? Disillusionment, devotion, discontentment, delight?

Excerpt of Ekphrastic Nonfiction: Despite the fact that our collection of familial associations can be astronomical, our ekphrastic descriptions do not have to echo that. Obvious observations and banal descriptions can also lead to enhanced knowing. In his essay, "Symmetrical Universe," scientist Alan Lightman wrote:

> I find myself looking at an old photograph taken in 1949. I am a baby, held in my mother's lap. Standing directly behind her is her mother, and further behind, on her right and left are her two grandmothers, my great-grandmothers.... One of my great-grandmothers, called Oma, has a mouth that droops slightly on the left side, breaking the symmetry of her face. I associate that droop with the sadness of losing her husband only a few years into her marriage. If I look even more closely at the photograph, I can see a blemish on her right cheek, possibly an age spot.

Suggested Viewing: Joaquín Sorolla y Bastida's painting, *Pepilla the Gypsy and Her Daughter*

Suggested Viewing: Ammi Phillips' painting, *Mrs. Mayer and Daughter*

Suggested Viewing: Florine Stettheimer's painting, *Family Portrait, II*

We consider things relationally. We regard stimuli and wonder what that has to do with us. At some point in our development, we realize that we are also an object to be seen. For some people, this is a source of discomfort. For others it is delight.

Ekphrastic Freewrite: (After Rineke Dijkstra's photographs, *Julia 1994*, *Tecla 1994*, and *Saskia* 1994)

Three women, each holding their rubbery pink newborns after having just given birth. The first is naked but for gauze briefs that hold in place a blue sanitary napkin. Her legs are a comfortable distance apart. The second one—her legs two inches apart—has trickles of bloodletting down which runs the length of her left leg, onto the floor. The third has a new slice of the abdomen, and her legs are together in a dancer's first-position. Each woman braces her newborn with two hands against the chest. The middle babe suckles. The faces are pressed to the mothers, and only the side profile of the last is seen by the viewers.

Suggested Viewing: John Butler Yeats' portrait of his son, *William Butler Yeats*

Suggested Viewing: Vanessa Bell's portrait of her sister, *Portrait of Virginia Woolf*

Suggested Viewing: Clara Rilke-Westhoff's sculptures of her husband, Rainer Maria Rilke

Writing Invitation: Unearth artwork in which a family or family members are depicted. How are individuals similar or dissimilar to people in your family? Alternatively, what are the politics associated with painting family members? For example, both Pierre Bonnard and Paul Cézanne painted dozens of portraits of their wives.

What is your relationship to being photographed or filmed by a family member? Let's say you confront your father with your fantasy of gathering up all the hundreds of tapes he filmed of the family and incinerating every last one of them shortly after he has taken his final breath? And what if, in response, he got quiet, a sour look erupted on his face, and he warned, "I really wish you wouldn't"? This would beg the question, then, whose property are those private home moments?

What personal associations do you have with being photographed? Marianne Hirsch's *The Familial Gaze* offers a context and rationale for family photographing:

Since the introduction of the "Kodak" in 1888, the family photograph has become the family's primary instrument of self-knowledge and representation—the means by which family memory is continued and perpetuated. Such pictures tend to follow rigid conventions which seem to consolidate and perpetuate dominant familial myths and ideologies, supporting a self-representation of the family as stable and happy (backcover).

Writing Invitation: Consent for shared experiences? Who has the power? Who has the agency? How does the recording of family shape our memories and our myths of the family?

Suggested Viewing: Carrie Mae Weems' *Untitled (Woman and Daughter with Make-Up)* from *Untitled ("Kitchen Table Series")*, 1990

Suggested Viewing: Fillide Giorgi Levasti's painting, *Vita Quotidiana*

Suggested Viewing: Emily Carr's painting, *Breton Church*

Suggested Reading: Eavan Boland's poem, "The Room in which my First Child Slept"

Writing Invitation: Find artwork that, for you, represents a certain abstraction associated with family (happiness, conflict, security, loneliness, deprivation, fear, shame) and write concretely of that abstraction. Alternatively, locate a work-of-art that marries dichotomous notions, such as beauty and pain. Attempt to write associatively and personally, even if nonfiction isn't your usual genre.

Here is a list of some more family-related topics for your ekphrastic writing: scenes that mirror everyday family life; grandparents and distant relatives; caring for loved ones (humans, pets); family values; domesticity (marriage, child rearing); and notions of home—also, interior landscapes, urban-living, being part of a society and the values thereof.

Excerpt of Ekphrastic Nonfiction: Again, from Allison's essay, "This Is Our World":

For those of us who grew up hiding what our home life was like, the fear is omnipresent—particularly when that home life was scarred by physical and emotional violence. We know if we say anything about what we see in a work of art we will reveal more about ourselves than the artist. What do you see in this painting, in that one? I see a little girl terrified.... I see a mother, bruised.... I see a man with his fists raised.

Suggested Reading: Sharon Old's poems, "Blue Dress" and "The Elder Sister"

Writing Invitation: Find and explore artwork that compels you to write about a sibling you never had.

Excerpt of Ekphrastic Nonfiction: Consider José Orduña's memoir, *The Weight of Shadows.* What do details or descriptions say about the photographed, the photographer, and the occasion? In the excerpt below, you will see an example of how a picture can turn from the action of the photographer, to what the viewer can see, to what the subject is subverting, and then what the subject is revealing. With the present tense of that first verb below, the position is of Orduña, in the past, getting his picture taken. In the next sentence, despite the consistent use of the present tense, the writer is commenting on the product, which indicates that we have been transported into the future:

> Chelsea snaps a photo of me standing in front of glass doors etched with the presidential seal. The backlight turns me into a black, featureless silhouette in the center of a ring of stars. My body covers the eagle and the olive branch it clasps in its left talon, but the thirteen arrowheads peek from behind my right elbow and a halo of rays emanates from around my head (119).

Writing Invitation: Locate a work-of-art that sparks your interest in switching back and forth from one perspective to another.

Excerpt of Ekphrastic Nonfiction: Here is another example of a writer who weaves personal photography with the imagination. "Six Glimpses of the Past: Photography and Memory" by Janet Malcolm is not merely a piece of writing that includes some moments of ekphrasis, but it is an entire ekphrastic personal essay. Malcolm's nonfiction, which includes seven photographic images, unites the known with the unknown and utilizes ekphrasis to structure her six-part piece. Each part boasts at least one picture from which Malcolm discusses her memories, stories, or personal philosophies. Because it is rare to find an entire ekphrastic prose piece, let us dive deeply into this essay (you'll read my commentary) so as to appreciate the intricacies of Malcolm's ekphrasis: "I am looking at two pictures..." in which an 1832 Ingres portrait is considered, as well as "a black-and-white snapshot of a two- or three-year-old girl." A few paragraphs later, she admits, "The child in the snapshot is me. I know nothing about where or when the picture was taken." As you can see, she easily maneuvers to the not-knowing. The second part begins, "A black-and-white photograph, three and a half by two and three-quarters inches, shows a man and a woman and a little girl looking out of the window of a train." Here she begins prosaically and even describes the handwritten words on the back of the photograph. For, literary description does not have to be lofty or abstruse. Additionally, one could argue that the essay's ekphrastic elements are altogether redundant, for, while we are reading the verbal descriptions, we can cast our gaze upon the images printed alongside. How does such a presentation of words and images function? The third section deviates a bit in how it begins: "I never knew my maternal grandmother...." She starts relationally, rather than ekphrastically. In the penultimate section, instead of describing the woman in the photograph in the present tense, as in *we see a rotund woman*, the writer instead describes the woman as when she was alive. She "was an obese woman with short, straight hair and course, swarthy skin...." In the last section, the corresponding image is of a smiling man, but in contrast, the opening of this section references "an ugly expression" that would appear on the subject's face, "when something displeased ... [him]." In this case, the picture sets us up for one mode of thinking—how a man's smile corresponds to a sense of joy, happiness, sentimentality—yet the opposite is described verbally.

Suggested Viewing: Horace Pippin's painting, *Sunday Morning Breakfast*

Writing Invitation: Compose a personal essay that entirely revolves around artwork. Similar to the modes described above, play with perspective, tense, and audience expectation.

The Visual Arts
History, Perception, Illusion

Overview

Just because all the work selected for the book, as well as the artwork listed as "suggested viewing," is categorized as *fine art* does not hold that you should limit your ekphrastic writing to work that falls into this category. Any object can be treated as if it were an objet d'art. The best ekphrastic writing comes from first feeling enchanted by an object that you select. It is up to you to see the value in any given object.

What constitutes art? Painter Charles Emerson defined art in this way: "Art is changing reality in order to make a greater reality." Who makes art? How do artists view the world? What is their motivation? For instance, N.C. Wyeth received commissions to make illustrations for books, Diego Velázquez was court-appointed, and Henry Darger made art solely for aestheticism. What is the purpose of art? For recognition, storytelling, reportage, entertainment, escape?

How do we look at art? What are we supposed to see? What interpretations are valid? Before we can determine what the artwork signifies to us, we need to look closely to see. Most importantly, viewing art is symbiotic: You must give as much as you aim to receive.

Though relatively late in the history of our species on Earth, humans began making art ~30,000 years ago. If it suits your writing, take a class on art history or do an independent study. Of course, knowledge about art history or art movements, many of which are similar to movements in literature, is not a moral imperative. However, here is an overview:

History

Stone Age (~30,000–2500 BCE)
Mesopotamian (~3500–540 BCE)
Egyptian (~3000–1000 BCE)
Greek, Hellenistic (~700 BCE–1 AD)
Roman (~500 BCE–500 AD)
Indian, Chinese, Japanese
  (~650 BCE–1900)
Byzantine, Islamic (~300–1300 AD)
Medieval European (~500–
  1400 AD)
Renaissance (~1400–1550)
Mannerism (~1530–1580)
Baroque (~1600–1700)
Rococo (~1700–1800)

Neo-Classical (~1750–1850)
Romanticism (~ 1800–1850)
Realism (~1850–1900)
Impressionism (~1850–1900)
Fauvism, Expressionism (~1900–
  1935)
Cubism, Futurism (~1900–1920)
Dadaism, Surrealism (~1915–
  1950)
Abstract Expressionism (~1940–
  1950)
Pop Art (~1960s)
Contemporary (1970–present)

Movements

Abstract Art
Art Deco
Art Noveau
Assemblage
Avant-garde
Bauhaus
Baroque
Black Arts
Confessional Art
Conceptual Art
Constructivism
Cubism
Dadaism
Deconstructivism
Digital Art
Ecological Art
Environmental Art
Expressionism

Fauvism
Fluxus
Folk Art
Futurism
Gothic Art
Graffiti Art
Harlem Renaissance
  Art
Hyperrealism
Impressionism
Installation Art
Interactive Art
Magic Realism
Minimalism
Modernism
Naturalism
Neo-Classicism
Optical Art

Performance Art
Photorealism
Plein Air
Pointillism
Pop Art
Post-Impressionism
Pre-Raphaelitism
Process Art
Realism
Rococo
Romanticism
Spatualism
Street Art
Surrealism
Symbolism
Video Art

    In the book's previous sections, we traced the mode of ekphrasis, including its conventions and topics. This current section offers a broad overview of the visual arts. Some ekphrastic writers tend to latch onto an artist's working method rather than an ekphrases of the artwork itself.

Each poem, essay, and story that you compose will determine how much or little research is needed to get you where you are going. So, I have provided just enough information for a springboard to additional research as it suits your curiosity.

Before writing to art, it is advisable to see more deeply what you are looking at. A suggested first phase of engaging with art is to read both its visual and design elements: *composition*—how objects relate to each other; *line*—the visual journey created by a moving point, defines features; *quality of lines*—to suggest depth, movement, object; *space*—the empty part of a page or other surface, which tends to draw attention to the objects; *shapes*—organic and geometric; *color*—hues; *texture*—the quality of surfaces; *focal point*—where a viewer's attention is directed; *perspective*—the angle of viewing; *scale*—the size of something in relation to standard size; *proportion*—the relationship of sizes; *rhythm*—systematic visual repetition; *balance*—actual weight, illusion of weight; and spatial organization.

Here are some ideas for freewriting and free-associating:

1. What does the artwork depict?
2. How is that subject represented?
3. Describe the lines, shapes, use of space, colors, textures.
4. Describe elements of balance, proportion, and scale.
5. How do the subject and the artist's tools or techniques relate?
6. Will research about the artwork vitalize your experience?
7. What is the historical context?
8. What memories does this artwork evoke?

Employing the journalist's six questions as an approach to your blank page can also be productive. Some answers will be factual, and some answers will beg your creativity:

1. What—What is being depicted?
2. How—How is the scene being depicted?
3. Who—Who is being depicted?
4. When—Is the setting time-specific?
5. Where—Is the setting place-specific?
6. Why—Why was this particular scene created?

Once you learn to identify the visual and design elements, you can start to guide your gaze around the canvas. Examine the artwork side-to-side and top-to-bottom; discover what exists in the background and foreground; consider the balance of light and dark; inspect the relatability of lines and shapes; behold the visual clues around the focal points; identify the different textures; hunt for visual patterns; investigate the details; and contemplate how all these components are working together.

Excerpt of Ekphrastic Fiction: In the short story, "Death by Landscape" (from the collection of stories, *Wilderness Tips*), Margaret Atwood's character considers perspective:

> And these paintings are not landscape paintings. Because there aren't any landscapes up there, not in the old, tidy European sense, with a gentle hill, a curving river, a cottage, a mountain in the background, a golden evening sky. Instead there's a tangle, a receding maze, in which you can become lost almost as soon as you step off the path. There are no backgrounds in any of these paintings, no vistas; only a great deal of foreground that goes back and back, endlessly (145).

Furthermore, your ekphrastic writing does not have to involve the entire work-of-art. Perhaps you admire a single detail, which becomes your focus. In the article "Notes on Ekphrasis," Alfred Corn declared, "A more realistic goal is to give a partial account of the work." What is most vital is that you find artwork to which you have an emotional resonance. There are no rules in terms of how much of the artwork you have to reference. You might locate your poem, essay, or story in one part of the canvas, a single detail, a single hue, or merely the artwork's title.

If you have the chance to visit the Detroit Institute of Art in Michigan, you can behold the series of frescos by Diego Rivera, "Detroit Industry Murals", informed by his months-long study of factories and factory workers. The murals adorn all four walls in a single grand gallery. Contained in the mural on the east wall is an image of an infant curled in a fetal position. As the husband of painter Frida Kahlo, viewers can wonder if their childless life together had any bearing on this particular detail. This is all to say that while murals of industry, for example, might not tempt you to the page, the onus is on you to find in any work-of-art something that intrigues you. David Foster Wallace encouraged us to, "Be conscious and aware enough to choose what you pay attention to and choose how you construct meaning from experience."

Writing Invitation: Latch onto a single, surprising aspect of an artwork, dispense with the rest of the piece, and begin your ekphrastic writing there.

Countless variables affect how a person responds to art: from an innocent experience (a naïve reception, possibly superficial) to a sophisticated experience (wherein a comprehensive analysis of the potential complications of the art-making are taken into consideration). How open and willing are you to dive into the multitudes of art? Are you curious? Are you an explorer, a seeker? Moreover, are you open to seeing the poetic possibilities of all things and making inferences based on the details you notice? Yes? You, then, are primed for the pleasures of ekphrastic writing.

Additional questions for art-engagement include:

1. Is the artwork based on fact or imagination?
2. Are the renderings realistic or distorted?
3. Do you accept the artist's portrayal?
4. Is there lyricism or reverie?
5. Is there skepticism or truth?
6. Is there knowledge or mystery?
7. How do you feel being the spectator?
8. What purpose does art hold in your life?
9. Is art for understanding?

As students, we are instructed to be *active readers*, yet how often are we instructed to be *active observers*? Especially in this modern day of advertisers inundating us with their imagery, have we become desensitized to the purely aesthetic lure of images?

Learning to look in order to see more fully is an aesthetic exercise. How observant are you? Not investing in visual imagery is passive seeing. Conversely, taking time in active seeing—deep-looking—allows you to uncover the creative possibilities that exist inside an object. It is in the verbs: if not *glance, peek, glimpse*, then what? To *look* is to direct your eyes; to *see* is to notice; and *to watch* is to look at something over a period of time. Ekphrastic writers *admire, study, search, hunt, seek, recognize, consider, speculate, discern, identify, detect, stare, gaze, notice, observe, scrutinize, scout out, attend to, focus on*, and *hope*. The muse, though, might require a more charged type of seeing: *penetrate, pierce, ogle, leer*, and *witness*.

You can lead viewers to art, but you cannot make them see. Thomas Henry Huxley observed, "There are some people who see a great deal and some who see very little in the same things." How can you make meaning out of what you see? Arnold in *Art History* maintains that "it is the interaction between viewer and object that gives art its meaning and decides the way in which the visual is read" (104). Do you agree?

Art-viewing is a unique experience, so it is incumbent upon you to discover your way to the art that you love. In "What the Brain Can Tell Us about Art," Eric R. Kandel reminds us of the permission to see and write of the seeing with confidence, for its uniqueness: "[A]rt is inherently ambiguous and therefore ... each person who sees it has a different interpretation. In essence, the beholder recapitulates in his or her own brain the artist's creative steps."

The eye travels around, picking up what it needs. As in life, we take what we can, each moment, and convert it into what we need. The relationship between object and admirer of said objects is a dual relationship. The pen leads a writer to know that the eye has seen; otherwise, the moment is ephemeral. Our eyes are slow and partial witnesses—imagining, imagine, image.

Writing ekphrastically holds the same premise found in the lines in William Blake's poem, "Auguries of Innocence":

> To see a World in a Grain of Sand
> And a Heaven in a Wild Flower,
> Hold Infinity in the palm of your hand
> And Eternity in an hour

Since most of the body's sense receptors cluster in the eyes, it is no doubt that vision is our most coveted sense. However, seeing happens in the brain, and each brain has its own agency. Through neurological pathways, the brain organizes and synthesizes all visual input (Baugher, "Art to Art").

The eye itself? Its job is to capture light, for seeing actually happens in the brain. Margaret Livingstone in *Vision and Art* describes the intricate process: "Light passes through the pupil; the lens focuses an image on the retina at the back of the eye, and the retina performs the first calculations on the image before transmitting its signals to the brain" (24). The iris of the eye changes the size of the pupil, through which the light enters the eyeball. "When light falls on an object, some is absorbed. The light that isn't absorbed is reflected off the object's surface; this is the light we see" (17).

Just as writing comes before rewriting, seeing and experiencing visual data comes before your ability to process verbally what you are seeing. Also, anticipation is a factor, as explored in Berger and Mohr's *Another Way of Telling*: "In every act of looking there is an expectation of meaning. This expectation should be distinguished from a desire for an explanation. The one who looks may explain *afterwards*; but, prior to any explanation, there is the expectation of what appearances themselves may be about to reveal" (117).

When artist Alberto Giacometti wrote, "To truly see is to forget the name of the thing seen," he was remarking on the meditative qualities of deep-looking. You're transformed while transfixed on an artwork. Something shifts within you, before you, in spite of yourself, and, as Rilke wrote, suddenly you have "the right eyes" (C. Rilke 43). Is art-viewing a transcendental experience for you?

Perception

Our perceptions are made up of complex systems in which we have stimulation responses to visual data (for example), our treatment of which is contingent upon our anatomy (genetics), our receptiveness (choices), and our previous experiences.

As evidenced by the fact that we can continue to enjoy the same books, songs, and works-of-art over a lifetime, often in new ways, it is our perception that is changing, while those words, notes, and images remain the same. In Plato's *Phaedrus*, Socrates addresses Phaedrus on the matter of the limitation of attending to art:

> You know, Phaedrus, that's the strange thing about writing, which makes it truly analogous to painting. The painting's products stand before us as though they were alive, but if you question them, they maintain a most majestic silence. It is the same with written words; they seem to talk to you as if they were intelligent, but if you ask them anything about what they say, from a desire to be instructed, they go on telling you just the same thing forever.

By "same thing forever," it's the same words, notes, brushstrokes, but the way in which we receive that input is capricious. First, we perceive sensations, and then our brains process those sensations, wherein we can explain and make meaning through interpretation—predicated on memories and associations.

According to Arnheim in *Art and Visual Perception*, there are many forces in visual perception. Let's focus on three: balance, shape, and form—the visual balance is seen as "two forces of equal strength that pull at each other in opposite sides" (19). Visual data and shape-relations are contingent on past experiences in that "What we've seen before informs what we're currently seeing" (48), and lastly, form "is the visual shape of content" (96).

While these perceptions might seem individual, our brains are conditioned to perceive structure amid chaos, patterns within disorder, and organization amid discord. The Gestalt laws of grouping (based on Gestalt theory that the sum is greater than its parts) are divided thusly:

1. proximity (Are objects in a close relationship connected?)
2. similarity (Are objects that look alike related?)
3. continuity (Is an object that appears to continue another object related?)
4. closure (Are objects that complete each other connected?)
5. connectedness (Are objects that are bound together related?)

Though, as ekphrasists, we are not restricted to using the entirety of the artwork; fixating on any one detail can invariably be a portal through which we can comment on a universe beyond it.

Besides considering how we perceive, primarily when it deals with illusion, it is essential to remember that an artist created the data that we perceive. How do artists achieve specific effects? Regarding depth, as Arnheim writes, it can be accomplished in several ways:

1. "How do objects partake in the third dimension? By tilting away from the frontal plane and by acquiring volume or roundness" (258).
2. "Depth by overlapping. When one component cuts off the other, we perceive that the one cutting off is the figure, the one cut off is the ground" (248).
3. "Buildings close to us look larger than the smaller ones which appear further away. A visual paradox ... look[s] different and alike at the same time. This is the perception of depth" (289).

Likewise, the illusion of luminance can be appreciated in many works-of-art. If you regard a painting, drawing, or photograph in their colorless states, you can more easily discern shapes, texture, and line. It is luminance that allows us to make out these definitions. Said another way, contrast in a black-and-white artwork can enhance the viewing experience. If there is relatively no contrast, the piece looks cloudy, without the discernment of lights and darks. Knowing that it was possible that the images for this book were going to be rendered in black-and-white, I had to determine which art had enough contrast to render the elements of the artwork readable. If you also view digital renderings of these masterpieces, it is worthwhile to study black-and-white versions in order to evaluate its luminance.

Color Perception

Wearing a pink dress, Albertie-Marguerite Carré sits before painter Morisot. Does this portrait have compositional elements that you admire? Does it feel as though the artist is capturing a narrative? Besides the woman and her dress, what else can you describe? Do you perceive movement or stillness? Look closely, for example, at her delicate hands.

We do not all see precisely the same colors, for colors do not occur in the world, as stated before, they exist in the mind. The color we see is always the one being reflected. We see the rejected color, and say "an apple is red." However, in truth, the object is every other color *but* red. Your own color connotations are something worth exploring.

The color wheel consists of primary colors (colors that can't be created by mixing other colors: red, yellow, and blue), secondary colors (colors made by mixing primary colors: orange, green, and purple), and tertiary colors (the mixture of primary and secondary colors). Black represents all colors of light being absorbed, and white represents the absence

Berthe Morisot's c. 1870 painting, *The Pink Dress* **(courtesy The Walter H. and Leonore Annenberg Collection, bequest of Walter H. Annenberg, 2002).**

of color. Some color composition options include: using opposite colors on the color wheel, such as red–green; using analogous colors; or using a color that is all the same value, like shades of grey.

Suggested Research: Any image of the color wheel

How does our brain process different hues? In *Psychology in Everyday Life*, authors Myers and Dewall explain the Young-Helmholtz trichromatic theory as, "the theory that the retina contains three different types of color receptors—one most sensitive to red, one to green, one to blue. When stimulated in combination, these receptors can produce the perception of any color" (145).

Suggested Viewing: Elizabeth Murray's bold-colored paintings

Suggested Reading: Federico García Lorca's poem, "Romance Sonambulo"

Suggested Reading: Johann Wolfgang von Goethe's book, *Theories of Colour*

When determining the importance of color for your ekphrastic writing, one suggestion is to structure the engagement with another version of the journalist's questions:

1. What was applied (specific hues)?
2. How was it applied (application tool and technique)?
3. Who applied it (was their style common of the time or innovative)?
4. When was it applied (the historical context)?
5. Where was it applied (which hues in which areas of the artwork)?
6. Why was it applied (what effects might have been sought)?

Here is another ekphrastic poem in which deep-looking is evident. Notice that it is the hue that the poet spotlights, followed by a sense of yearning:

The Pink Dress
(After the painting by Berthe Morisot)
by Lucille Lang Day

The dress looks delicious
as pink icing, sweet and frilly
as a garden of carnations,
but the girl with blue eyes
will learn that a clown with
a round red nose, checked pants
and floppy shoes might wear
a grin over sorrow or anger.

Even now she might be less
innocent and delicate than
her ruffled dress. How can
we know whether a girl
in a pink dress is thinking
of planting tulips and peonies
or wondering whether God
or the Devil is in the details?

Does she know that chocolates
with cherry filling delivered
to her doorstep might not
be from a suitor but from
someone with a cruel intent?
Her eyes say yes, she sees
the dagger in the roses; she
isn't lost in cotton candy mist.

She knows that death might
be quick as a hummingbird
darting from fuchsia to
lupine or might linger
like the slow movement of

a violin concerto in G major
and sweep her softly over
the edge of a pink abyss.

Color is a type of illusion-making. Is it transparent, translucent, opaque? In other words, what is its visual density? Does it appear solid or amorphous? The use of colors that are the same warm colors is an example of tonal painting. Painter Emerson lamented, "Color is a major problem." For instance, yellow (a translucent color) is difficult to make look solid. Master painter Hans Hofmann, after decades of work, solved this problem for himself by troweling about a quarter inch thick of yellow paint to render it solid. So, not only is what was applied to the canvas relevant but how it was applied. Painter Josef Albers, whom some believe was the most acclaimed colorist who ever lived, astutely articulated, "Color is only color according to amount and placement."

Suggested Viewing: Clarice Beckett's tonal paintings

Suggested Viewing: Hans Hofmann's abstract paintings

Suggested Viewing: Josef Albers' series of paintings, "Homage to the Square"

Writing Invitation: Behold artwork with colors that thrill you. Focus on the artist's palette and write with the mood that the colors stir within you.

Excerpt of Ekphrastic Nonfiction: *Letters on Cézanne* is a collection of Rilke's musings (mostly) on the artwork of Paul Cézanne. Here is an entry that, surprisingly, treats synesthesia—"joined perception"—which is where stimulating one sense (such as a color) results in the response of another sense (such as with sound): Cézanne's colors,

which are never insistent or obtrusive, produce this calm, almost velvetlike air.... Although one of his idiosyncrasies is to use pure chrome yellow and burning lacquer red in his lemons and apples, he knows how to contain their loudness within the picture: cast into a listening blue, as if into an ear, it receives a silent response from within, so that no one outside needs to think himself addressed or accosted (87).

Writing Invitation: If it suits your writing, incorporate in one of your ekphrastic works-in-progress the mode of synesthesia.

Excerpt of Ekphrastic Nonfiction: *Letters on Cézanne* also includes Rilke's observations on other artists. Because of Rilke's own artistry, he was on a quest to learn from great artists, to let their creative processes, as well as their products, shape his work. Regarding Vincent van Gogh's painting, *Night Café*: "The night café I already wrote about; but a lot more could be said about its artificial wakefulness in wine red, lamp yellow, deep and utterly shallow green, with three mirrors, each of which contains a different emptiness" (61).

Rilke arrived at a surplus of ways to describe the hues of the blue applied by Cézanne. The poet used these imaginative terms (keep in mind, though, that this list has been translated from the French): "an ancient Egyptian shadow-blue," "self-contained blue," "bourgeois cotton blue," "light cloudy bluishness," "densely quilted blue," "wet dark blue," "juicy blue," and "full of revolt, Blue, Blue, Blue" (C. Rilke xx).

Suggested Research: Hoffman California-International Fabrics—Style 1895 Watercolors. Hundreds of fabric colors are assigned with imaginative names: celestial, new grape, hollyhock.

Suggested Reading: Muriel Rukeyser's poem, "Ballad of Orange and Grape"

As a young ekphrastic practitioner, I assembled a list for myself of common words that could also denote specific colors: tawny, lovat, fawn, rouge, sienna, alabaster, sable, khaki, opal, ash, claret, fox-red, mustard, spruce, putty, umber, citrine, cloud, adobe, sapphire, loden, mercury, graphite, bark, russet, putty, sap, blush, cobblestone, honey, peridot, bay leaf, glacier, molasses, brandy, cardinal, iris, Bordeaux, steel-blue, slate, pewter, acorn, ebony, lilac, mist, canary, pearl, olive, umber, lagoon, lead, coral, sepia, cinnamon, egg yolk, creosote, heather, mauve, and peach. For the love of wordplay, assemble your own list of colors.

Excerpt of Ekphrastic Fiction: Let's look again at Byatt's story collection, specifically "Art Work" in which there is this vivid description of an artwork by Henri Matisse: "It is a dark little image on the page, charcoal-grey, slate-grey, soft pale pencil-grey, subdued, demure. We may imagine it flaming, in carmine or vermilion, or swaying in indigo darkness, or perhaps—out-doors—gold and green" (32).

Suggested Viewing: Herbert Aach's DayGlo paintings

Suggested Reading: Robert Haas' poem, "The Problem of Describing Color"

Writing Invitation: While much of this section of the book concerns specific facts of art-making, it is worth emphasizing that at every turn, your imagination should not be neglected. After having looked at many colorful artworks, try free-associating. Find imaginative ways to describe what you see. Allow connotations to direct your word choices.

Illusion

Given the image of Carmen Herrera's painting, what do you notice? Cut the piece in half lengthwise and regard the pattern. Now cut the piece

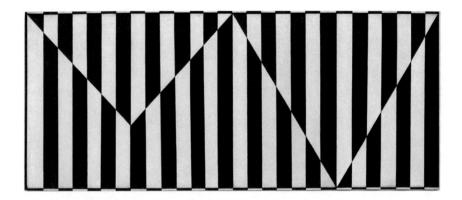

Carmen Herrera's painting, *Untitled, 1952* (permission granted by the artist, © Carmen Herrera).

in half widthwise and express how the various ways of dividing the visual field affect your perception of the entire image. What is the significance of her using only black and white? What is the significance of the number of columns? In the Drawing section of this book, you will see this painting's companion poem.

An illusion is a type of misperception based on our brain's best guess of what it is seeing, and as Diane Ackerman reminds us in *The Natural History of the Senses*, "We think of our eyes as wise seers, but all the eye does is gather light" (232). Painter Georg Baselitz created inverted paintings as a way of really seeing the objects rather than allowing his brain to "think up" the object. In other words, in the service of subverting his "best guess" mode of functioning artistically, Baselitz's inversions allowed him to cultivate his own form of deep-looking.

Now that we've gleaned some knowledge about the eye-brain-perception relationship, you'll perhaps concur with this summary: "In particular there is the idea of art as illusion—what we are really looking at is brushstrokes on canvas; the rest is made up of our cognitive and intellectual processes that give the picture its meaning—in terms of recognizing it as a portrait and the ways in which it plays with our senses of perception" (Arnold 21).

Suggested Viewing: Bridget Riley's optical art

"It is not what you look at, but what you see," Thoreau warned. Through unintentional acts of deception, both sight and words fail. Each looking event is a fusion of mis-seeing (*trompe l'oeil,* French for "fool the eye") with seeing. That is, the viewer's own proclivity for a skewed seeing is fed by cerebral and anatomical uniqueness. For example, artists born with abnormal depth perception (stereopsis) such as Rembrandt and Picasso compensated for their compromised vision by excelling in shading and other techniques, which ultimately rendered them masterful at creating perspective. The creative writer's work involves making creative use of both inadvertent and essential errors (Aristotle). In other words, "[A]rt is an illusion—paint on canvas, carved marble, or chalk on paper—it is what the viewer brings to it that makes it 'represent'" (Arnold 91). When an ekphrastic writer gazes at an object, both real and imagined visions are at play.

Suggested Reading: Edward Hirsch's poem, "The Horizontal Line" (After Agnes Martin)

Artist Alberto Giacometti, remarked on the critics' assessment of his elongated figures, "All the critics spoke about the metaphysical content or the poetic message of my work. But for me it is nothing of the sort. It is purely optical exercises. I try to represent a head as I see it" (Ackerman 268).

How is our art affected when we are afflicted with abnormal vision such as dyslexia or color blindness? Specific pathologies contribute to an imagined or creative vision. Let the eye be tricked for the delight of the muse. The art of deception, as in tricking the eye, is one way in which a writer can make creative use of artwork. Allow your unique neurological pathways to lead you to your own authentic ekphrases.

How do artists achieve desired effects, such as illusions of space, motion, and depth? Seeing things three-dimensionally can be accomplished by artists in numerous ways. "Part of our ability to see three-dimensionally is known as *stereopsis* or binocular depth perception, and it exists because our eyes register the world from two slightly different perspectives" (Livingstone and Conway 35).

1. As a matter of course, thick lines we perceive as coming forward and thin lines we perceive as going back.
2. Impasto technique administered by artists, such as Giorgia Morandi, Nicolas de Staël, and Rembrandt: "Using a thick application of paint can also produce an illusory sense of depth by taking advantage of the fact that our stereopsis is more sensitive to abrupt depth discontinuities than to gradual depth changes" (Livingstone 143).
3. The way we physically interact with works-of-art affects how we see the intended illusions: "As we move around within a space, for instance, we are processing images of many different views of the same object to enable us to register a fully three-dimensional image within its three-dimensional setting" (Smith 351).

4. "Normally your brain computes motion based partly on its assumption that shrinking objects are moving away (not getting smaller) and enlarging objects are approaching" (Myers and Dewall 150).

The complexity of our brain is made more so when we consider our brain's parallel processing centers: Research indicates that our brains assign "different teams of nerve cells the separate tasks of simultaneously processing a scene's movement, form, depth, and color" (Myers and Dewall 146).

Excerpt of Ekphrastic Fiction: In *Girl in Hyacinth Blue*, the novelist Vreeland has her character react to a painting's illusions. The description is reverent, as well as affecting physiologically: "I walked toward the painting, took off my glasses to see that close, and it was as he had said. If I moved my head to the right or left, brush strokes subtly changed their tint. How difficult it was to achieve that. In other places the surface was so smooth the color must have floated onto the canvas. I suddenly found myself breathing fast" (8).

Writing Invitation: Artist René Magritte contended "Everything we see hides another thing, we always want to see what is hidden by what we see." Locate artwork in which you're compelled to consider what's in sight and what's out of sight.

In brief, it is two brains that contribute to our ekphrastic creations: theirs and ours. The creation of illusion is based on their anatomy and artist technique, as much as it is based on our perception and receptivity to illusion.

Perception and Empathy

Given the title of Auguste Rodin's sculpture, we have much information. First, "Hanako," which we can easily research, denotes "little flower." Then, we have her nationality and her occupation. However, art-viewing is only partially a lesson in fact-finding. The associations we bring to each work-of-art becomes the foundation for the art that we, in turn, produce. Is it true that "language translates what the sculptor transmutes" (Rilke, *Auguste Rodin* 15)? Here is the poem influenced by Rodin's mask. Consider the relationship between fact and association, as well as how brevity aligns with the sculpture's form:

Mask of Hanako 4
by Marilyn Chin

I recognize the scar
On her flat nose

Moth eyebrows
Plucked by a ghost

Double lids cast downward
Hint of a topknot
Ancient furrows

Lips parting   just   so
Master
Let me go

Art can transport you, triggering a range of emotions. The portrayal of real human emotions (first accomplished by the Greeks poets) means that those depicted in art are relatable to us, the receivers. Whether we are making art or engaging with art "our immediate context, and the motivation and emotion we bring to a situation, also affect our interpretations" (Myers and Dewall 139).

Our brains strive to make sense of the world around us via two distinct processes: sensation ("bottom-up") and perception ("top-down"). Simply, in the first type, our "sensory receptors and nervous system receive and represent stimuli." In the second type, our brain "creates meaning by organizing and interpreting what your senses detect." In other words, top-down processing "creates meaning from the sensory input by drawing on your experiences and expectations" (Myers and Dewall 134). What is the significance of this? As ekphrastic writers, it is essential to know the layers of our engagement with the arts. We do not merely take in stimuli, but we process stimuli uniquely. Ask 1,000 people to absorb themselves in the same work-of-art, and you will get 1,000 different responses, for those responses united both the bottom-up and top-down processes.

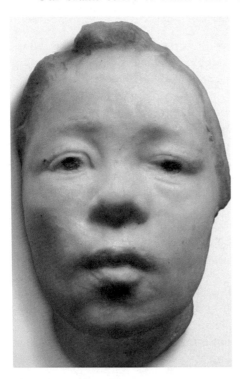

Auguste Rodin's 1911 sculpture, *Mask of Hanako, the Japanese Actress* (courtesy the Philadelphia Museum of Art, bequest of Jules E. Mastbaum, 1929, F1929–7-43b).

What experiences have you had in terms of feeling moved by art? Author Leo Tolstoy, in *What is Art*, explained, "The activity of art is based on the fact that a man, receiving through his sense of hearing or sight another man's expression of feeling, is capable of experiencing the emotion which moved the man who expressed it.... And it is upon this capacity of man to receive another man's expression of feeling and experience those feelings himself, that the activity of art is based."

In her 2008 Harvard Commencement Speech, author J.K. Rowling made a startling connection between the brain and the heart: "Imagination ... is the power that enables us to empathise with humans whose experiences we have never shared." Reiterating her point, she posited, "[H]umans can learn and understand, without having experienced. They can think themselves into other people's places." Have you met someone who seemed to have no heart for other people's plights? What I have found is that these are the same people who are often distanced from their imagination. Could the adage be wiser than we knew?—To imagine walking in another person's shoes, to feel what they felt, is an act of *imagination*?

Some people are either more susceptible than others to suggestions of emotions (an automatic process), or they are better at acting the stoic (voluntary process). Authors Myers and Dewall maintain: "Hearing sad music can tilt the mind toward hearing a spoken word as *mourning* rather than *morning*" (140). So it is verbal imagery that has the most potency in our writing, for "When you write smells, or images, or sensations, you are actually gaining access to the emotional area of the brain" (Bushnell 4). The conduit for both verbal imagery and visual imagery is feeling.

Though, there are undeniable similarities between the literary and visual arts, as well as differences. John Updike, in his essay, "Writers and Artist" explained the matter rather crudely:

> Whereas the writer only has to say "table" to put it there, on the page. Everything in the way of adjectival adjustment does not so much add as carve away at the vague shape the word, all by itself, has conjured up. To make the table convincing, a specified color, wood, or number of legs might be helpful; or it might be too much, an overparticularized clot in the flow of prose. The reader, encountering the word "table" has, hastily and hazily, supplied one from his experience, and particularization risks diminishing, rather than adding to, the reality of the table in his mind. Further, the table takes meaning and mass from its context of human adventure (196–197).

Surrealist René Magritte's painting *The Treachery of Images* is merely a realistic painting of a pipe with the scripted words, "Ceci n'est pas une pipe." ("This is not a pipe.") Viewed together, the word-image pair creates a paradox. Or does it? When we see a *painting* of a pipe, do we see a pipe? When we read the words, "this is not a pipe," isn't it true that the words indeed aren't a pipe? Though, when you say or read "pipe," do you imagine a pipe? Moreover, have we grown so accustomed to seeing an image and believing the reality of the image that, although we know we are looking at a representation, we speak of it (think of it, even), as the thing itself and not merely an image of the thing?

Essayist Jericho Parms in *Lost Wax* writes about an experience similar to the scope of Magritte's series of word-images paintings: "The installation on view at New York's Museum of Modern Art asks viewers to consider how these three representations communicate the common fact of the object. We see a chair. We see the visual image of a chair. We see the etymological definition of a chair. How do they differ? Which representation constitutes the true nature of the form? Which has more chairness?" (53) What is your answer?

So, if art is only representation and not reality, then what is real? What is reality's relationship to our perception? When a writer writes "oak tree," I see it. In that respect, the writer and I together create the image. Given this assessment by critic Sigurd Burckhardt: "[W]hether [a painter] paints trees or triangles, they are corporeally there for us to respond to.... The painter's tree is an image; but if the poet writes "tree," he does not create an image (Krieger 266). Do you agree that you're no image-maker, writer?

On the whole, responding creatively to imagery allows us to halt intellectual inquiry for our muse's enjoyment. Painter Charles Emerson offers us some levity with: "In the end, it's just paint. It's not water, sky, cloud. Once you get past that, you can just enjoy it for what it is, a painting."

Art Forms

Art-making is merely decision-making. An artist has a vision that translates as a composition. What kind of composition? Which tools to accomplish that task? On which material? By what techniques?

Again, in *Read This If You Want to Take Great Photographs* Carroll wrote, "Composition is all about how you choose to order the visual elements in your picture" (9). Additionally, emphasizing light and shadow are important compositional decisions for artists. He continues, "Great compositions take you on a journey. Your eyes are guided around the image on a specific path" (10). Specifically, the orientation matters: horizontal begs a side-to-side eye movement, while a vertical orientation elicits an up-and-down eye response (12). Furthermore, those well-versed in the visual arts discipline can evaluate the compositional elements of a work. Here are those ingredients: "A well-composed painting has carefully arranged forms, shapes, and edges; a balance of color and tonal values; and foreground, middle ground, and background that merge harmoniously" (Horowitz 71). Imagine discussing a literary composition on these levels: "carefully arranged," "balanced," and "merging harmoniously"?

There are many decisions for an artist to make before actually making art. Typically, writers do not give much thought to the material on which they are composing. A screen or a notebook? Ruled paper or not? White paper or not? Serif or sans? Virginia Woolf had purple pens, James Joyce, confounded by ink and stylus, opted for pencils. Knowing how and why artists choose specific tools, materials, and methods can lead to important ekphrastic moments.

Drawing

The 2019 drawing *The Argument*, takes its influence from the 2003 sculpture *Spider Couple* by Louise Bourgeois. Earlier, you read the corresponding ekphrastic flash-fiction piece.

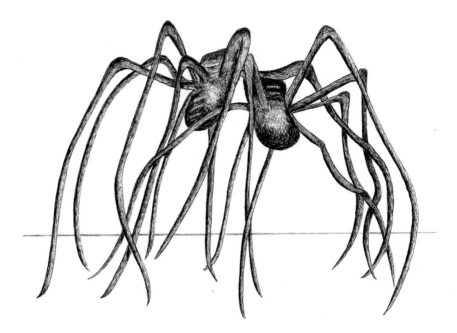

Kristina J. Baugher's 2019 ballpoint pen drawing, *The Argument* (permission granted by the artist, © Kristina J. Baugher).

Artist's Comments

I read Peter Grandbois' "Hard Choice" to get a clue if the writer had described any of the actual details of the spiders' anatomy. Instead, the flash fiction piece was based on the emotional involvement of the pair themselves. I then decided to soften the pair, to move away from the sculptured look, and focus on their entanglement—their "argument" that I imagined was taking place. As I was drawing the right spider's legs, I did accidentally entangle a pair of legs and was going to correct it, but I stopped. Actually, that entanglement was exactly what the drawing needed, even though in the Bourgeois sculpture, the legs were not entangled (Kristina J. Baugher).

Drawing: it is one of the genres of the visual arts in which a person uses a drawing instrument on a two-dimensional medium. For some artists, drawing is the prelude to a painting, sculpture, or even a photograph. For some artists, the drawing is the thing.

Rudy De Reyna in her book *How to Draw What You See* breaks it down for us: "Every object that you see has a structure or form based on either the cube, the cylinder, the cone, or the sphere. Any object may be based on one or a combination of these four geometric solids. A solid, for our graphic purposes, means an object that has three dimensions: height, width, and depth" (11).

"What is it?" we typically ask children who share their pictures with us. What is the validity of that question? Does the creative brain concern itself with *what is it*? Adults and children tend to have wildly different thoughts on art, as illustrated in opening pages of Antoine de Saint-Exupéry's book, *The Little Prince*:

> I showed my masterpiece to the grown-ups and asked them if my drawing frightened them.
>
> They answered: "Why should anyone be frightened by a hat?" My drawing did not represent a hat. It was supposed to be a boa constrictor digesting an elephant. So I made another drawing of the inside of boa constrictor to enable the grown-ups to understand.
>
> The grown-ups then advised me to give up my drawings of boa constrictors, whether from the inside or the outside, and to devote myself instead to geography, history, arithmetic and grammar. Thus it was that I gave up a magnificent career as a painter at the age of six (10–11).

As the adage goes: art is process, not product. As viewers, we behold the finished products, but insight as to the artists' processes can also stimulate our creative writing.

In *Drawing on the Right Side of the Brain*, Betty Edwards explained, "The object of drawing is not only to show what you are trying to portray but also to show *you*. Paradoxically, the more clearly you can perceive and draw what you see in the external world, the more clearly the viewer can see you, and the more you can know about yourself. Thus ... drawing becomes a metaphor for the artist" (23). What do you make of her connection between the art and the artist?

Given the title of Edwards' book, it's no surprise that she has some insight about the brain's capacity for creativity and the artist's ability to apprehend that place in which the muse resides: "Recent research on human brain-hemisphere functions and on the information-processing aspects of vision indicates that ability to draw," and, Edwards asserted, "may depend on whether you have access to the capabilities of the 'minor,' or subdominant, right hemisphere" (32). I myself believe that every human has the capacity to be creative.

It is fascinating to learn that the struggles that some writers have feeling free to create are shared with artists of other disciplines. For creative types who struggle with the critical voice within, there are ways to combat this problem. Working quickly—a technique used by both writers and artists—is one method by which you fool the brain into forgoing its tendency to criticize. Writing or drawing more quickly than you would normally short-circuits the logical brain that strives to keep up with its rigid processing. More on the function of the brain and creativity in the next section of the book.

All artists must start simply. By learning the basics, you will create a foundation on which your art-making can thrive. The first exercise for artists who wish to draw is to draw a straight line.

Here is the poem that treats the Herrera image. What do you see as the relationship between the painting and the poem? What is the significance of the poem's epigraph? De Reyna specifies, "You must arrange your basic forms … so that they *relate to each other*" (37). Is this also true of creative writing? Discuss how all parts of this poem relate to each other. What poetic associations are most surprising?

Untitled 1952: 14 Lines Inspired by Carmen Herrera
("There is nothing I love more than to
make a straight line." Carmen Herrera)
by Major Jackson

(1) A calm objectivity engulfs my ribs.
(2) On this day, the Brooklyn Bridge calls out over avenues and parks
     to the George Washington, its cables guiltless and loud.
(3) Ladies and gentlemen, I keep Cal's noise within earsight:
     The painter's vision is not a lens, / it trembles to caress the light.
(4) Backgammon alone has a calculable end.
(5) Let's plant a white calf in blackest earth, you said.
(6) If out of nowhere, a man should turn a corner with a fist of calla lilies
     and spontaneously thrust them toward you, by all means,
     land like a crow in snow.
(7) If a man should peel back two envelope flaps sent by the artist who
     airmailed them sixty-seven calendar years ago, a burst of moon light
     will suffuse his eyelashes.
(8) Who stands to gain like calabash embezzling rain?
(9) Watching me sleep, women have explained things to me with their
     calligraphic eyes.
(10) Soon, I heard even California under her fingers.
(11) Should you cross your eyes nature will reveal itself like calypso.
(12) The Ballad of the Three-Fingered Woman: *What calisthenics should I
     demonstrate today?*
(13) The almost survivors peering behind calamitous bars: sunken cheeks,
     soon evanescent.
(14) A dark subjectivity calks my ribs.

[Note: (3) includes two lines from Robert Lowell's poem, "Epilogue" from Day by Day *(Farrar, Straus and Giroux)]*

Writing Invitation: Identify artwork in which various objects are arranged. Focus on the relationship among the objects and write a multi-part poem, essay, or story.

Writing Invitation: Use the notion of learning to draw a straight line as an analogy about your philosophy on what constitutes a happy life.

De Reyna describes two other perspective terms: "Eye level refers to the *height at which your eyes observe an object*" (15). Specifically, objects will always appear in one of three ways: precisely at, below, or above eye level. Next, "The *horizon plane* is simply the surface that extends from the horizon, as you look straight ahead, to your feet, as you lower your eyes" (39).

Excerpt of Ekphrastic Nonfiction: In her novel *Blue Arabesque* Patricia Hampl offers an extended description of the subject in the Henri Matisse painting, *Woman Before a Fish Bowl*:

> The woman's head is about the size of the fishbowl and is on its level. Her eyes, though dark, are also fish, a sly parallelism Matisse has imposed. Her steady eyes are the same fish shape, fish size, as the orange strokes she regards from beneath the serene line of her plucked brows. The woman looks at the fish with fixed concentration or somnolent fascination or—what *is* the nature of her fishy gaze that holds in exquisite balance the paradox of passion and detachment, of intimacy and distance? (4–5)

Here's a list of some of the tools and techniques of artists who draw: basic utensils (pencil, piece of metal, brush and ink, charcoal, graphite, pen and ink, chalk), color utensils (pens, pencils, pastels, crayons, ink), paper options (color, weight, texture, size, orientation), ways of creating texture (use of scratching, use of rubbing-in technique with your finger, as seen with charcoal and pastels), use of dry brushes, and drawing with an eraser.

If the paper is showing through or left alone in places, it emphasizes the flatness of the drawing or painting. There are reasons to leave part of the paper exposed: to reveal the artwork's flatness or to make use of the color of the paper itself.

Writing Invitation: Find art in which you can discern the paper or canvas beneath the marks made by the artist. Next, consider how you exploit white space in formatting your own literary work. What philosophical comparisons can you make?

Suggested Viewing: Aboriginal Dreamtime art (ancient Australia)

Writing Invitation: Given this headline, "73,000-Year-Old Doodle May Be World's Oldest Drawing discovered in Blombos Cave in South Africa," write a story about the person responsible for the drawing and how that story relates to the person who discovered the drawing and recognized it as art.

Recall the earlier discussion of absence as a topic in ekphrasis and that how to create the chair, the artist will draw what is not the chair—in other words, focusing on negative shapes so as to uncover positive shapes in a drawing. When artists draw entirely around an object, they are providing the illusion of the object. Instead of focusing on the positive shape of the object, the desire is to reveal the negative space around it. Through drawing space surrounding an object, an artist creates a type of "negative" image (Sibley).

Art students are asked to invert objects (for example, human figures) on their canvases, so they are *looking* and not merely guessing at the details. Echoing Georg Baselitz and his upside-down paintings, try viewing a world map upside-down, thereby obscuring the typical ways of thinking you know what you are seeing. The brain's 'guess' is not always correct.

Painting

Let us begin this section with the companion poem to Mary Cassatt's painting, *The Bath*: Recall the topics in ekphrasis already discussed (beauty, absence history, nature, family), as well as ekphrastic conventions. Which topics and conventions can you appreciate in this poem? Also, pay particular notice to how the speaker is physically positioned:

The Bath
by Peter Cooley

We're in the air, our wings invisible
somewhere, a hundred years above the scene.

Heaven gives angels this view or the dead
come back to judge, hungry to be alive.

But here we have only to assume calm.

The mother, her gown striped with gray and brown,
immerses the daughter's feet in the huge bowl.

The rug in the foreground, the wallpaper and chest
along the background, the mother's gown: clash.

Nothing is pretty but our assumption
this is a sweet scene. Nothing is beautiful.

As we leave, let's maintain our aerial view,
our hummingbird invisibility.

Fly above your next moment. Suspend your gaze.

In this section, we tackle the artistic genre of painting. How much artistic painting have you done in your life? Here are just a few of the multitude of decisions the painter must make: paints (oil or acrylic paints, watercolor, pigments—historically, painters would make their own from minerals, precious stones, and plants—gouache, tempera, encaustic); method of application (paintbrush, sponge, paint knife, roller, airbrush); and support (canvas, watercolor paper, wood, stone, clay, glass, a wall).

Suggested Viewing: David Hockney's painting, *A Bigger Splash*

Types of painting include narrative, landscape, portraiture, figurative, still-life, allegorical, symbolic, political, and abstract, to name a few. Painter Charles Emerson insists, "A good painting is always logical, consistent, and convincing. But it doesn't have to be logical in a customary way; it can invent its own logic. It is up to the viewer to respond to it, to see it. For example, many Cézannes are solving a problem, rather than just being a picture of something; if you cannot recognize the problem, you'll never understand how the logic is sound." Do you concur that making art is a type of problem-solving?

Painters of fine art are well-versed on color relationships, illustrated by the color wheel, and categorized, as mentioned before, by primary colors, secondary colors, tertiary colors, and so on. Consider the art, the science, and the chance elements at play when an artist mixes colors. Recall, though, that color is not a reality, it is perception—which we interpret and imbue with associations.

From each of these decisions, though, more decisions emerge. If you choose to use a paintbrush, then what type, soft hair or hard hair? Once you decide on the type of brush, then at every moment in the application of that material, you determine which brushstroke to use to obtain the desired effects. If you choose to use colors, will they be transparent, opaque, or iridescent? Purchased paints or hand-made? Will you use direct painting, or will you mix colors? If so, how? By physically mixing them before application, color-mixing by overlaying washes (scumbling), or placing certain hues next to other hues—thereby blending adjacent colors? Will you use primary colors, secondary colors, or tertiary colors? If you choose to use paper, what type (dry or wet paper, purchased or handmade paper, white or toned)? If you choose to use fabric, what type (purchased or hand-stretched canvas, white or toned)?

Suggested Viewing: Yves Klein painting with "live paint brushes," *Anthropométrie: ANT I 30*

Sumi-e, the Japanese word for *black ink painting*, is a technique of applying ink to a surface (paper, a scroll) in which the emphasis is on the beauty of each brushstroke. One striking aspect of this technique is the process of allowing the ink to run entirely off the paintbrush—leaving jagged, disappearing lines, as well as the raw paper itself. Can the image of something vanishing work as a metaphor for your life?

Writing Invitation: Locate artwork of the Sumi-e tradition. Next, consider calligraphy as a type of text-influenced art, as well as the fact that Chinese artists use the terms "writing a painting" in addition to "painting a poem."

Oil paints (produced from pigment being mixed with oil), which give an opaque effect, have some unique names: Venetian red, isoindolinone yellow, transparent gold ocher, indanthrone blue, dioxazine violet, viridian, cobalt green, terre verte, lamp black, and cremnitz white. Names of acrylic paints include cadmium red, azo yellow, raw sienna, burnt umber, phthalocyanine blue, chromium oxide green, titanium white, and ivory black, to name a few. Do you find the name of artists' tools and techniques particularly intriguing?

The reductive mode of art-making is employed by certain artists. The scratchboard technique, for example, involves the thick application of paint that the artist scratches through. With the use of a scraper, the painter can create layers of paint hues like sedimentary rock. Here is a freewrite in response to that technique:

Ekphrastic Freewrite: (After Frank Auerbach's 1977 abstract painting, *To the Studios*)

How deep is abstraction, the sands of abutment? That which exists in the heart can never live in a home. What is this poem about? There is control in a room of simplicity and the way the oil gets caught in your nose. Oh, how you dreamt of that smell. Laborious years at your canvas, paint atop paint so that someday you will actually see that thing you are aiming to see; your model or a glance, shackles on your hands and feet, following the path on which you are confident of the nothing of scratching down to the surface. A polarized silence until blood and flesh, the capillaries wail, and the years you learned to mix paint and which finger was best. How you sleep in oil, travel on brush hairs and nothing vacant or trivial is really such, for all is color and grand and just another way of seeing.

Absent oil paints, an artist might select acrylic paints, which use a plastic base, resulting in their "plastic" effect. The paint can be "extruded (squeezed) through a nozzle into plastic strands of dried paint that can be pulled off the canvas and knotted, braided, or otherwise manipulated in very unconventional ways" (Smith 221). Some artists make creative use of the sculptural-like quality of acrylics:

Ekphrastic Freewrite: (After Bernard Réquichot's 1957–58 *Le Reliquaire de la Forêt*)

Theater boxes of mounds of paint. The use of red, blue, white to depict derangement and how life is cruel. This looks like the white matter and grey matter of brain has unraveled into spools of filaments, thick as a ponytail or paint from tubes. But why a requiem for the forest? He connected glob to glob by string, the tubes, or the tube-caps themselves. How to convey chaos, the cacophony in one's head if one is a visual artist? What is the pictorial opposite of order? How long before the mountains of paint dried? Did they moisten-up when the artist suicided?

Watercolor

In this anonymous watercolor, *Radha, the Beloved of Krishna*, we see a side-profile of a woman. We can describe what we see: the mane of black hair down her back; hoop earrings and wisps of hair about her face in pliant curls; the definitive arc of her eyebrows and eyeliner; pointy nose and evanescent lips; necklaces and bangles, but nothing in the background. For some writers, description is the first step. However, you will later see that the companion flash-fiction piece dispenses with description in a metaekphrastic approach.

Watercolors use water as a medium, the effects of which are transparent (that is, the paint does not entirely obscure the paper beneath). Deciding how much water and how much paint determines the artistic effects.

Here are some of the tools and techniques of the watercolorist: Select your watercolor paper (archival, which texture, what weight); select your

Unknown artist's 1750s ink and opaque watercolor on paper, *Radha, the Beloved of Krishna* (courtesy of Cynthia Hazen Polsky and Leon B. Polsky Fund, 2005).

brush (natural or synthetic, level of stiffness, shape); and decide on your technique (drybrush, flat wash, graded wash).

Suggested Viewing: J.M.W. Turner's watercolors

Suggested Viewing: Andrew Wyeth's watercolors

Suggested Viewing: Alice Schille's watercolor, *Bow Spirit*

Suggested Viewing: Jane Peterson's watercolor, *The Pier, Edgartown*

Suggested Viewing: Frances Macdonald MacNair's watercolor, *Spring*

Writing Invitation: Given that "Transparency is the most unique quality of watercolor, as it allows the white of the paper to shine through" (Horowitz 41), what do you believe is the value of transparency in creative writing? Examine artwork that feels atmospheric to you and write not "about feelings" as our teachers have cautioned us against, but "with feeling."

Printmaking

Prints are created by an ink-transfer from a type of matrix onto paper or other material, with basic techniques that include relief, intaglio, planography, and stencil. Common matrices include metal plates, polymer plates, stone, wood, and linoleum. Historically, pictures in illustrated children's books were prints, for one of the unique features of printmaking is the opportunity to create multiple impressions from a single matrix. Have you seen this designation before—1/100? With printmaking, it means that you are seeing the first print in an edition of one hundred total prints of that same image.

In general, artists prepare their chosen matrix (based on material, size, orientation), draw on that matrix (for example, the artist can draw with a black marker on a piece of linoleum), use a gouge to carve out the linoleum, apply ink, and then the image is imprinted on paper.

Printmakers introduce ink onto their rollers, and they roll the ink onto a matrix (woodblock, linoleum cut). A sheet of paper is placed over the inked matrix, and if a hand-cranked printing press is used, they send the matrix-paper complex through the press. Finally, the paper is peeled away to reveal the image.

In relief printing, "The ink is applied to the raised surface and an impression is taken of the block or plate. Areas cut away by the artist, or which do not stand out in relief, will remain blank on the printed paper" (Smith 230). The print studio can sometimes feel like a chemistry laboratory: "In etching, the lines are scratched through an acid-resist ground, then bitten into the surface of the plate by acid" (Smith 24).

There are many variables to control in printmaking. For instance, what to do if you over-cut your woodblock or linoleum? What if you leave your plate in the acid for too long? What if the lithograph stone hasn't ground down evenly? Hence, for all artists, there are moments of risk, surprise, mystery, and significant leaps of faith.

Given Katsushika Hokusia's woodblock print and reading from its title that it is part of a series, it's impossible not to be curious about the other nine prints. If you're piqued, then find the other prints in the series and see how viewing all the prints together changes your feeling about seeing just a single print from that collective. See the clouds, full moon, trees, water, rocks, grass? The composition is such that there is no telling where the bridge is leading the figure. It is possible that this print was text-influenced, for scholars believe it mimics these lines from a 1303 poem (translated by Matthi Forrer):

> When I was cutting horsetails
> The autumn moon appeared
> Shining through the trees
> On Mount Sonahara.

Writing Invitation: Examine artwork that spans the techniques of printmaking and evaluate the surface methods, as well as comparing the quality of the line work in each. Discover the poetic possibilities of print-makers' creative processes.

Writing Invitation: The reversal of the image is one dimension of printmaking: "the print is always the mirror image of the plate" (Peterdi 15). Contemplate your mirror image, and what others see of your face as compared with what you see, what you perceive. Are those versions at odds?

Suggested Viewing: Andy Warhol's silkscreen prints, *The Electric Chair*

Writing Invitation: What might be Warhol's comment in utilizing the delicate fabric of silk on which to project images of an electric chair. Silkworms and individuals sentenced to death have a commonality, perhaps?

Soon you will see the response to Hokusai's woodblock. If you were familiar with printmaking studios, you might recognize that the size and shape of this poem echoes that of the average linoleum cut used by student printmakers. What point-of-view is employed, and how is that perspective functioning in the poem? Does the poem hover in that ancient time in which the woodblock was produced, or does the poem place itself into the twenty-first century?

Katsushika Hokusai's 1835–39 color woodblock print, *A Peasant Crossing a Bridge,* from the series *A True Mirror of Chinese and Japanese Poems* (gift of Mr. and Mrs. Samuel M. Nickerson).

A Peasant Crossing a Bridge
(After the painting by Katsushika Hokusai)
by Gerard Wozek

It's as if at any moment, the bridge might fail,
imploding into the white capped torrents below.
Instead it holds firmly, as the peasant balances
two bundles of spiny horsetails, his tip toe ballet
in tattered slippers and rags, watched solemnly
by the autumn moon. Perhaps those gathered
sticks will become a storm shelter. A second roof
to cradle the forthcoming snows. Come December,
the echo of soft flute music will fill the concave
slopes of Mount Sonahara. His smiling lips
pressed softly to reed pipes cut carefully from
the rushes. Quiet notes touching mountain peaks.

Suggested Fieldwork: Visit a printmaking studio for demonstrations on how the various techniques are executed.

Writing Invitation: Research how one particular print was made and incorporate the surprising aspects of the technique into your creative writing, thereby uniting research and imagination.

Sculpture

What is sculpture? In *Living with Art*, Gilbert wrote, "The study of sculpture confronts us with the third dimension, with the concept of depth" (265), the materials of which can be virtually anything—clay, stone, marble, metal, wood, plastic, and found objects to name a few. *Additive* sculpture media includes clay (ceramics), in which you add material by way of modeling, and *reductive* sculpture media includes stone, metal, rock, in which you remove material by way of carving. In sculpture in which there is a physical building, an artist can also choose to make multiple pieces and stack them for larger or more intricate works.

Suggested Viewing: The Terracotta Army (depicting the armies of the first Emperor of China)

Writing Invitation: Poet William Carlos Williams observed, "A poem is a small or large machine made of words." Write a poem, essay, or story in which the speaker constructs or destructs something.

Here are some tools and techniques specific to sculptures made of clay:

1. Tools include dowels to roll out clay, serrated ribs for scratching, forks for scoring, small loop tools, rubber-tipped tools, artists'

fingernails, and stain to create false shadows and a sense of depth.

2. Texture can be represented through pattern and details, where the overall positioning of texture can create the illusion of forms (a garment, for instance). To create the same patterns over and over, in an original sculpture as well as over the lifetime of an artist, plastic molds can be used.

3. Actions include pinching, paddling, coiling, scoring, modeling, aerating, carving, depressing, smoothing, painting, firing, and cooling.

4. Malleable clay dries, loses water, becomes brittle, and shrinks. The drying process takes days or weeks, depending on your environment and the thickness of the clay. Invariably there are no guarantees and artists must be flexible enough to make creative uses of mishaps.

Suggested Viewing: The sculptures of Barbara Hepworth

Writing Invitation: Write a dialogue in which two or more sculptures speak to each other while you (the writer) eavesdrop.

Given George Rodriguez's pair of sculptures, *Tia Catrina & Uncle Sam*, do the poses convey stasis or action? What textures exist? What stories do the sculptures have to tell? What techniques, do you suppose, have been adopted (for example, coil and pinch, slab and casting, casting and use of molds)?

Suggested Viewing: Nancy Graves' sculptures

Writing Invitation: According to artist Adrian Arleo in *The Figure in Clay*, working with clay, artists can construct facial features this way: "Features such as eye sockets are pushed in, and the cheeks and chin are pushed out. The nose and lips are made from small coils added to the scored surface, then defined with tools" (Tourtillott 31). The eyes, they say, are the windows to the soul. Examine an artwork in which the eyes give you pause. Write from that feeling of being arrested, from the impulse to know more.

In *The Figure in Clay*, a book in which numerous sculptors discuss their creative process, artist Doug Jeck explained,

> Establishing a face and an implied persona can involve weeks of work. I often cut off the head after several days of working and begin again.... As is true for the body, making the face and head involves pushing and stretching from the inside and the outside. I'm forming features, scratching lines, brushing, carving, pressing, squeezing, and looking for a complex personality to arrive (Tourtillott 97).

Do you resonate with Jeck's explanation? Is your approach to writing similar?

George Rodriguez's 2017 *Tia Catrina & Uncle Sam* **(image courtesy of Foster/White Gallery with permission from the artist. © George Rodriguez).**

Suggested Viewing: Camille Claudel's sculptures

Writing Invitation: There is fragility to clay in that it is reactive to touch. Interestingly, wet clay captures the fingerprints of the maker. Settle on a sculpture that prompts you to use this image of the artist's fingerprints.

Ekphrastic Freewrite: (After Alberto Giacometti's sculptures)

Start with a metal skeleton of what serves your pleasure: a house, a mug, a human figure. Then, take clay and obliterate the metal with it, rendering it inexhaustible of air and mind and any wayward form that disagrees with this surface. You may add mounds of clay or as little as possible. In this manner, you will sculpt Everyman, and how you depict him here people will remark on: Did you make him portly, disheveled, mute? Is he capable of doing anything? Have you captured motion, devolution, mutation? This figure remains lean. Scarcely clay beset the metal, the bones of which poke out of him—he with his elongated, attenuated, atrophied limbs. His head looks straight on, his features are cast in bronze, yet I cannot tell his eyes from nose. Does he feign movement of thought and promise—a solitude that starves ourselves? Merely alone, we are left in the skeleton of our daily skin, the way the bronze catches the light and absorbs it into itself—that color, that light that spreads around a room only hibernates there inside Giacometti's thin figure. I imagine him falling off the edge.

Suggested Viewing: Judy Pfaff's sculptures

Writing Invitation: Fired ceramics are hollow, vessels; they have an interior space. The artist must reach inside, thereby shaping it from the inside-out. Ponder this quote by philosopher Alan Watts: "You can never have the use of the inside of a cup without the outside. The inside and outside go together. They're one." Behold an artwork that reminds you of your relationship with yourself or your art-making process. Consider two sides of a thing, the inside, and the outside and the relational dimensions.

Suggested Viewing: Augusta Savage's sculptures

Writing Invitation: Sculptor Louise Bourgeois said, "A work-of-art doesn't have to be explained. If I have not touched you, then I have failed." Write a piece in which you explain or refuse to explain what you are doing in something you have written.

Photography

Consider this image by Sandy Skoglund, *Babies at Paradise Pond*. Does it surprise you know that this isn't a painting? There are many types of photography: photojournalism, photorealism, photo-surrealism, photography and abstraction, and postmodernism photography, to name a few. Furthermore, some photographs are purely conceptual, existing only to capture light. How would you classify this piece? Is there a narrative that can be extracted from the photograph? If so, who would be the narrator? Later, we will see not one, but two companion ekphrastic poems influenced by this photograph.

In general, cameras work in this way: a camera records an image; light passes through the lens; the shutter keeps out light out until it's released; too much or too little light renders the image over- or underexposed; a flash is utilized when there's insufficient light; and the lens is focused further from the object or closer to it (Sills 73).

Writing Invitation: Given the directionality of light, "side lighting, back lighting, overhead lighting, and diffused lighting" (Horowitz

Sandy Skoglund's 1996 photograph, *Babies at Paradise Pond* **(permission granted by the artist, © 1996 Sandy Skoglund).**

59), explore how reflected light in a specific photograph says something about you.

"While a photographer does use a mechanical tool, the camera, to capture an image, it is *how* and *why* it is done that can make a photograph art" (Sills 4). The photographer's decisions determine the nature of art. These decisions include what film to use and how to develop it; whether to use color or no color; whether to improvise or be spontaneous; how to construct a composition; the selection of a light source, including location and intensity; which details to focus in on; where the photographer is positioned; the position of the subjects; how, why, what to crop; and the size and orientation of the photograph.

Here is another connection made between art and the inkblot, this time by photographer Jason Fulford:

> [A] photograph is similar to a psychologist's inkblot because, right after we inter-pret the literal aspects of the image ... we enter into a second, much more per-sonal reading. The second reading is informed by elements such as our memories, personal experiences, tastes, and cultural background. In other words, the first reading is based on what the photograph imposes on us and the second is based on what we impose on the photograph. As we are all different, this second reading

is unpredictable and entirely outside the photographer's control (Carroll, *Photographers* 56).

What do you make of these connections? What have your experiences been with viewing artful photography?

Writing Invitation: If you were to ask, an expert photographer would tell you, "A photographer must learn how to see before she can shoot" (Carroll, *Read This* 7). Does the photograph reduce the person, place, or event that's otherwise irreducible?

Similar to the hostile language use by scholarly critics on the topic of ekphrasis, the terminology used by photographers is charged, as photographer Ishiuchi Miyako explains: "'Shoot' a picture, 'fire' the shutter, 'capture' the subject, 'load' the film. Peel back photography's innocuous mask and underneath you will find an art form pulsating with aggression." Consider the politics of photographing children, strangers, and family members who may or may not have given consent. Miyako continues, "This violence goes beyond mere terminology. The concentrated act of looking that photography demands is, in itself, aggressive. We all know what it is like to be on the receiving end of someone's prolonged gaze—we become the prey. Conversely, we all know what it feels like to spy on someone from afar—we become the hunter" (Carroll, *Photographers* 106). How is writing similar or dissimilar to photography in these ways?

Here is a single-stanza sonnet influenced by an iconic photograph by Sally Mann. Notice the use of concrete language, coupled with philosophical musings.

Sally Mann
(Emmett, Jessie and Virginia, 1989)
by Jonathan Johnson

Remember when our skin held everything—
or what then seemed everything—river sand
and blood, snot, strawberry ice cream,
mud dried to dirt cracking the creases of your hands?
It's not that the world was ours. We were
the world's. Paint, sun, leaves, others' warm skin,
smear and silk of grass found us at the blurred
edge of ourselves. Kiss, scab, fist on the chin.
Remember touch without time or knowing
our perfection or naming it our soul
or knowing we would end, apart, in clothes?
We'd have never thought to call ourselves whole.
Our bodies weren't bodies. They were summer and feral.
We'd not yet begun to abandon the world.

Writing Invitation: What is vital enough to photograph? Who gets to decide? Has anyone in your family destroyed a family photo? Consider image ownership and who mandates which moments get recorded. What photographs do you display in your home? Why?

Writing Invitation: Susan Sontag in *On Photography* observes, "the camera makes exotic things near, intimate; and familiar things small, abstract, strange, much further away. It offers, in one easy, habit-forming activity, both participation and alienation in our own lives and those of others" (167). Find photography of interiors and photography of exteriors. Which pleases you? Given all the pictures we take of ourselves (close-ups), are we losing perspective? Write a poem, essay, or story in which you unite the near and distanced elements in a photograph.

Ekphrastic Freewrite: (After Christian Marclay's 1994 installation, *White Noise*)

Found photographs pinned to the museum wall 12 feet by 20 feet each by a single stick pin. Their images are facing the wall. The handwriting on the backs of the photos in cursive, the curlicues in swift ups and downs in English and German. The mosaic of gradations of white photographic paper: shades of pale, beige, white, yellowed, the color of age. Are you curious about what is underneath, don't you want to flip them over? Gaze into the eyes of strangers to know them, yet one can never know—regardless if they are flipped or not. Pins perpendicular to the photographs pressed shyly to the wall. There is safety there—in a neat row—blinding the viewers' eyes of the images' truths.

Writing Invitation: In *Another Way of Telling* Berger and Mohr caution us, "A photograph is a meeting place where the interests of the photographer, the photographed, the viewer and those who are using the photographs are often contradictory" (7). Given a specific family photograph from your album, explore this "contradictory" notion.

You cannot take a picture of religion or happiness or depression, only symbols therein. In other words, it is the specifics, not abstractions that are the objects for photography, though abstraction might indeed be the artwork's subject matter.

Suggested Viewing: Nick Ut's photograph, *Trang Bang (Napalm Girl)*

Writing Invitation: Berger and Mohr also remind us, "There are many reasons for not taking a picture" (78). Settle on a photograph and instead describe the picture that the photographer did not take (notional ekphrasis).

Abstract Art

What do you notice about the image by Lo Ch'ing? Do you see the elements of realism and abstraction? What do you make of the composition? Do you see shadow, outline, symbols?

Abstract art is abstracted from reality, in which designs or forms may be definite and geometric or fluid and amorphous; in abstract art, you will

Lo Ch'ing's 2016 ink-color painting on rice paper, *Post-Industrial Society Has Arrived* (permission granted by the artist, © Lo Ch'ing).

typically discover action, movement, and the mechanical. Abstraction in the visual arts, though, exists on a spectrum: in realistic art, you will find details of abstraction, and in abstract art, you will find artwork that's only partially abstract. Abstraction can exist in the subject matter presented or in the manner in which it is presented, and, as with ekphrasis, abstract art can be based on something notional. Consider this: can a human figure be made abstract?

Suggested Viewing: Joan Mitchell's abstract painting, *Girolata*

Suggested Viewing: Lee Krasner's abstract paintings

Ekphrastic Freewrite: (After Carlos Mérida's 1960 *Variations on an Old Theme*)

Colors in lieu of notes, but what's ironic is this painting's lack of color—only maroon, black, blue, and brown remedies. And those figures look like notes themselves: half, quarter, whole. An expression of angularity and the need for color, like the need for song when none will soar, when the colors can't reach him like ears refusing notes. Sound's inability to transcend time, space, and color. The sound it takes to cure color and curve. All that's here is darkness and line, for in that emptiness, the hope for a musical score, when fused form man's expression, form the shape of this artist's inner workings. But see, he's a failure. He can paint the notes, yet he's not privy to their song. Perhaps he's made it colorful, but all the viewers know is darkness, is the void—that which died in him, that dead crescendo aria, of the fabric of tone and pulse and pitch, repetition of vibration from instruments to player. So, that which is kept from him he keeps from us—to warn us of our own fate—how when something so intrinsic leaves us, all we can do is paint the void, those maroons and browns that wrap their notes around our hearts, expunging all sound and fury, all reason to be and to create, all reason to keep beating, to keep the beat, the beat, the beat.

Suggested Viewing: Agnes Martin's abstract paintings

Suggested Viewing: Helen Frankenthaler's abstract paintings

Ekphrastic Freewrite: (After Marcel Duchamp's 1912 *Nu Descendant un Escalier No.2*)

She's everywhere and nowhere at once, on all planes (past, present, future). Her hips steadying the torso, the legs bend at the knees, a collection of blurred parts, a static recollection of spinning in a woman's body, and the way that five degrees one way or the other can kill her. The joints must be fluid, and the head tilts to check for each step; she's mindful not to trip, not to suspend this movement he captures in taupe, red, black. The entire canvas (shaped rectangular to frame the woman) is held up by the figure bending to lower herself onto a lower plane while I stand smug in a Pennsylvania museum.

Writing Invitation: Spiegelman declared that "If representational art encourages description of both its technique and its subject matter, nonrepresentational art forces a different kind of descriptive and emotional response" (135). So, instead of attempting to describe an abstract work-of-art, try instead to emulate the style of the artist's in your own writing. For example, make typographical decisions that echo those of the artist's, the result of which may be a concrete poem or prose piece.

Conceptual Art

Conceptual art is born of concepts or ideas. Rather than aesthetic concerns, the conceptual artist has an idea that's driving the creative process. Additionally, the tradition tools and techniques that might ignite or flummox the artist can be irrelevant to the conceptual artist. For this discipline, it is no-things-but-ideas. One way to enter this type of art is to focus on the juxtaposition of materials.

Suggested Viewing: John Baldessari's painting, *What is Painting*

Ekphrastic Freewrite: (After *Concept of Space, 1958*, a "slash picture" by Lucio Fontana)

Canvas painted black. Blending the line between painting and sculpture. Perhaps the canvas fell onto a table corner, ripping it open like flesh. In one instance: a planer field morphs to three-dimension. There was no going back. He began another piece. Initially, the cuts were hesitant, like someone new to murdering. Then the cuts became more efficient. But, the fabric didn't rip kindly, see how it's jagged, imperfect—as if a dull knife where used. Through thirty-three slices, one can peer to the backside of the canvas, the cavity in which the artist's secrets lie. Black on black like a night in which you hear a sound coming from the woods, knowing it's an animal you cannot name, but then the sound grows more obscene, high-pitched, and then wrestling sounds and then the screeching so that now you hope it's no animal you know being attacked perhaps, so you alter the scene—the sound emanating now from a formless thing, or just sounds themselves without origin, without fur, blood, without eyes like Saturn.

Ekphrastic Freewrite: (After Giuseppe Penone's 1980–82 *Trees of 12 Metres*)

He made this work using a chainsaw and chisel to cut back the layers of growth from a single timber beam. He worked carefully around the knots to reveal the internal structure of narrow core and developing branches. The form of a young tree is exposed, while part of the beam is left untouched to signify its status as a human-made object. By returning the tree to an earlier stage of its growth, Penone reverses the effects of time. Or does he?

Writing Invitation: With two to three character sketches in mind, view conceptual art firsthand or virtually and consider how your characters might relate to what you're seeing. What concepts are they particularly drawn to? How does their alignment with specific artwork speak to their personhoods?

Assemblage Art

Assemblage artists take materials and build or assemble them in some way. Usually, there is a three-dimensional element to it with objects that are added to the structure. Collage art is considered the two-dimension version of assemblage art.

Ekphrastic Freewrite: Traveling is like creating collages, wherein the whole is built of disparate parts. Part sculpture, part collage, Joseph Cornell's shoe-box-sized assemblages are fronted with a glass pane in which he arranged items (photographs, flotsam, bric-à-brac). In each encasement are his precious mementos coupled with found objects. Presenting the two groups together in a shared space—what is familiar and what is foreign—creates a juxtaposition in which each viewer must conclude meaning. A simultaneous near and far, we are privy to, yet held from, with each unusual item. We carry assemblages each of us. Some days the contents spill out, and some days the contents are battened-down.

Suggested Viewing: John Latham's assemblages of deconstructed books

Suggested Viewing: Joseph Cornell's assemblage, *Untitled (Bebe Marie)*

Suggested Viewing: Romare Bearden's assemblages

Ekphrastic Freewrite: (After Henri Matisse's 1954 gouache cut-outs, *L'Escargot*)

When a painter is dying, he's not necessarily incapable of creating. Long before Matisse's snail, Picasso and others were using found materials such as newspapers and cigarette packages and incorporating these things into their painting. Real objects adorning an imaginary space. Like artists are wont to do, Matisse studied the minute, snails in this case, in their ability to spiral or to grow linear at will. While he was on his deathbed, he considered the oft-dubious relationship we have with the external world, and how it can be a great comfort to shell up. So, he asked for paper and scissors, and he began the snail's composition. Onto a white mat, he framed the area in asymmetrical strips of orange paper, then he cut out eleven shapes of sundry colors and arranged them. How not unlike we are to Matisse's elder self, a snail. Constantly configuring ourselves in our arrangement to our environment, until one day we find the fit, that instance when we can be as content as block of light-lilac, purple, forest green, lemon-orange, navy blue, olive green, rust orange, and black—in each color where we can be who we are, content in that imprecise relationship to ourselves, our bodies.

Mixed Media Art

Mixed media artists use a mixture of disparate materials to create a single artwork. Imagine that. Here are some examples of combinations: tradition painting with found objects, marble sculpture and fabric, and photography adorned with human hair.

According to McQuade and McQuade in their book *Seeing & Writing 2*, one way to engage with an artwork that's mixed media is to ask these questions: What type of materials were used? Were any of the materials considered "found" objects? Is the piece two-dimensional or three-dimensional? What textures? What shapes? How do the materials speak to one another to form a unified whole? Has the visual artist introduced text into the piece? As a viewer, how are the text elements functioning as compared with the non-text elements (675–677)?

Suggested Viewing: Howardena Pindell's mixed media art

Suggested Viewing: Tracey Emin's mixed media art

Ekphrastic Freewrite: (After Arman's c. 1967 mixed media sculpture, *Venus with Red Nails*)

Inclusion of mannequin hands inside a female torso made from polyester. Some brown mannequin hands, but mostly Caucasian. The fingernails have been painted red. Some have chipped off, and some have been met with polish remover. Hands inside a woman's torso, feeling their way around. But it's female hands, so it's not caustic or reproachable, right? We all have experienced this phenomenon—things that scratch our innermost core. Why should we ourselves comfort our depths? Because no one else can reach them.

Performance Art

Performance art, a type of process-based art, is ephemeral. This form of art usually has these four elements in common: time, space, audience-performer interaction (overt or covert), and the performer (either the artist or a medium that represents the central character). There is no right way to experience performance art, not even seeing it live. How performance art is documented is another form of artistry. Merely a single still image from Yoko Ono's *Cut Piece* can be more significant, not secondary, to experiencing her performance directly. Ono's performance art involved the artist inviting her audience to cut off her clothes while she sat passively on stage, which challenged the relationship between art and art viewer (Concannon). Have you seen performance art? Were you at ease or uncomfortable with the experience? Could you imagine conceiving of your own performance piece for an audience?

Historically, dance and music have been embraced based on their abstractions; therefore audience members don't typically evaluate those art forms on the level of meaning and comprehension in the same way some readers do with creative writing. To truly experience an art form, whether it is based on imagery, performance, sound, or words, is to focus on its experiential qualities, as a thrill for the senses rather than an assignment for the intellect.

Writing Invitation: Either in person or digitally, find a way to experience performance art. Describe what you see and pluck out your favorite details, which may or may not lead to a coherent whole.

Writing Invitation: Identify one artwork that's based on destruction and another artwork that's based on construction and write a single poem, essay, or story that merges the two.

Installation Art

On the next page is a photograph of one aspect of the installation art project by Etsuko Ichikawa. Of course, this image is no substitute for the bodily experience of Ichikawa's installation. However, if you are unable to visit the museum in which this installation was a temporary exhibit, you can still research this art online to see other pictures, read the artist's statement, and perhaps even hear from those visitors who enjoyed the experience themselves. Earlier in this book, we read the ekphrastic poem by Alice Jones.

The museum experience for installation art is integral to the work itself. How the art is displayed, especially with conceptual art (the category

Etsuko Ichikawa's 2015 installation art, *HAKONIWA Project—To Touch & To Be Touched* (art reproduced courtesy the artist, © Etsuko Ichikawa. Photograph credit: Peter Kuhnlein).

under which installation art exists), is something to ponder. Installation, which is three-dimensional by nature, is not medium-specific, but it is site-specific and is concerned with space. In other words, an installation has no permanent home.

Ruskin writing about nature and space and the observer echoes the relationship between installation and viewers: "A garden is not an open space like a landscape, but a surrounding space. And that which grows and stands in it, grows and stands *around* the observer" (67). Given your experience with art installations, did it feel as though you were surrounded by art, by the artist's vision? Did it feel as though it were participatory—as if your presence there were necessary? How might you correlate these notions of spatial associations to your writing?

Ekphrastic Freewrite: (After Cornelia Parker's 1991 installation, *Cold Dark Matter: An Exploded View*)

How do you illustrate the moment of explosion? Retrieving the destructed pieces, threading them with fishing line and tethering them together in a colossal mobile. In a small garden shed, she placed found objects inside—hand-push lawnmower, hair curlers, a bicycle, cans, and tools—and she solicited the British Army to detonate it to smithereens. She then collected the remnants, strung-up the smaller objects, and the larger pieces (the shed's wood planks). In the gallery space, we see this isolated, inertial momentum—projected deconstruction and shadows off the gallery wall like the tentacles of our confused lives. Our debris is never wholly self-contained.

Ekphrastic Freewrite: (After Rebecca Horn's 1986 installation, *Ballet of the Woodpeckers*)

Imagine a room with four white walls and two colossal mirrors on each. How lost would you feel in that infinite reflecting? What name would you answer to? And what if there were mechanized birds which intermittently tapped the glass in an orchestration of tinny pecks? Do they want inside your reflection? Are they attempting to accost their own? She spent months institutionalized because her art sickened her, and this room of self-scrutiny and isolation and duplicity is her response.

Writing Invitation: Research where installation art is on display and visit that place. Was it an experience for your body as well as your mind? Ponder the artist's and museum curator's display decisions.

Artist's Studio

Have you ever seen an artist at work? If not, you can surmise what happens in artists' studios, which includes artists' tools, techniques, methods, and subjects. Artists' studios can be an interior space separate from their homes, in their homes, or out in nature. Perhaps "the consciousness of the studio itself alludes to the consciousness of the painter" (Kolosov 126). What does your writing studio say about you as a writer?

Some artists choose to work with sentient beings, and some choose to paint still-lifes. Compare and contrast three artists' treatments of similar still-lifes:

Suggested Viewing: Anne Vallayer-Coster's painting, *Vase of Flowers and Conch Shell*

Suggested Viewing: Clara Peeters' painting, *Still Life with Crab, Shrimps and Lobster*

Suggested Viewing: Fede Galizia's painting, *Still Life*

In addition to responding to what you see, you can imagine or research where artists produce, with whom, for whom, and in what manner:

Artists (general)—consider all the possible relationships between the artists, their purpose (including their subjects), and their audience; (internal)—personal motivations, thoughts and emotions during the making; (external)—professional motivations, the time in which it was made (historical context), narrative and action depicted, compositional decisions, overall tone, and whether it's a depiction of the whole or part.

Was the artist destitute? Was commerce a consideration? Did the artwork require the artist to compromise artistic integrity?

Models

Models (general)—imagine all the possible relationships between the models, their purpose, their audience (including both the artist and the

114

viewers); (internal)—explore personal motivations, thoughts, and emotions during the posing as well as their physical comfort; (external)—consider professional motivations and what exists outside the frame. As an aside, some portraits aren't the result from the artist having settled on one actual person's likeness, some are composite sketches, and some are entirely fabricated.

Suggested Viewing: Théodore Géricault's painting, *Study of a Model*

Is modeling for an artist a type of collaboration? An eleemosynary contribution? For example, Gertrude Stein sat for Paul Cézanne and Pablo Picasso numerous times, and Pierre Bonnard's wife submitted to being his model for years. Why do it? Employment, obligation, pleasure, or altruism?

Writing Invitations: Imagine you are the artist. Imagine you are the commissioner. Imagine you are the model. Imagine you are a voyeur inside the studio.

Ekphrastic Freewrite: (After Caravaggio's 1606 painting, *David with the Head of Goliath*)

The politics behind the model-artist relationship and the mode by which the artist portrays the model. The darken decapitated head of Goliath: the artist's self-portrait. Pure brown hues, darkening gradations of sienna, umber, ochre without gory details. Not the brilliant hues, for this is maelstrom, blasphemy: David was modeled by a mere commoner—a merchant, servant, drunk, beggar. But why did Caravaggio do it? These indigents were available and posed cheaply. Here he is immortalized. Those people in the township who spat at him were forced to regard his demigod likeness. Goliath, ruler once, defeated finally—the head is held out by indifferent David. Held in the foreground, so it's twice standard size: his downward eyes, his mouth agape. The corrugators are furrowed, the brows are quizzical as if he were caught by surprise as if he didn't have a prayer. David's unsure of his catch, melancholic, seemingly humbled. Look, the two faces stand in opposition to each other: relaxed but closed-mouth David versus Goliath's dropped-jaw. David's eyes are upward gazed yet seem to be fixated on nothing, just somewhere from off from the palette and brushes of a man in his studio doing his work—immobilizing a nomad, and depicting himself as the slain. At the museum, a backlash from the townspeople: using the town drunk to depict the pious, biblical figure! Are these times over, knowing the model and artist, and having a say regarding who deserves to slay the beast?

Suggested Viewing: Andrea Solario's painting, *Salome with the Head of Saint John the Baptist*

Writing Invitation: Volunteer to model for an artist or an art class and see what writing comes from that experience.

Artist Jean Dubuffet's approach to portraitures was infuriating to some: He would invite individuals to sit for him, then he would never set the date. Instead, months later, he would display these portraits (which had no resemblance to the actual people), and even name the individuals, without them ever having sat for him. Suffice it to say, his absentee "models" had unfavorable opinions about the portrayals of their likenesses.

Writing Invitation: Change the narrative by imagining that another model sat in the place of the original.

Besides relational concerns, imaging that physical studio space can be a fecund creative exercise. What sights, smells, and sounds did those studio walls witness? What objects? Was the place pristine and orderly or filthy and chaotic? How does the interior of the studio symbolize the artist's process?

Suggested Viewing: Johannes Vermeer's painting, *The Art of Painting*

Excerpt of Ekphrastic Nonfiction: In the foreword to her novel, *Girl with a Pearl Earring* author Tracy Chevalier speaks about her creative process and how imagining Vermeer's making of his painting (as well as his model's thought process) lead Chevalier to a revelation about her own story-making: "On that November morning, however, for the first time I had a new thought: All of those feelings of hers were directed at the painter. What did Vermeer do to her, I thought, to make her look at him like that? Suddenly the painting became a portrait not of a girl but of a relationship" (ix).

Excerpt of Ekphrastic Fiction: Similarly, author Harriet Scott Chessman in *The Lost Sketchbook of Edgar Degas* allows Degas' fictional model to speak on her behalf: "He painted my eyes like dark caves, my skin pasty as dough, my lips a cadaver's pale slash" (11).

Writing Invitation: Imagine the model staring at you. Alternatively, imagine the sitter is looking at something you cannot see. Follow the sitter's gaze and imagine what exists outside the confines of the frame, to which you can write a notional ekphrastic poem, essay, or story.

Excerpt of Ekphrastic Fiction: Not only does the model have a voice in Chessman's novel, but the model has a life and has friends who hold opinions about her job: "It's art, though, René. It isn't trying to show any truth about you as an actual person. You're just a cheap model for Edgar!" (123).

The relationship between the model and the painter can be symbiotic, antagonistic, charitable, strained, familial, compulsory, a tribute, or a business arrangement. Which begs the question, are all portrayals true?

Excerpt of Ekphrastic Fiction: In another Harriet Scott Chessman novel, *Lydia Cassatt Reading the Morning Paper*, the model speaks and makes an illuminating connection: "To model for someone is always a surprise; you never know what they'll make of you" (60).

Is the surprise the model refers to similar to the surprise of writing to artwork and not knowing what the words you will make based on vision and how your brain processes stimuli?

Writing Invitation: Imagine what happens in the studio before, during, and after the making of the artwork. Visit an artist's studio and see what writing comes from that experience.

Excerpt of Ekphrastic Fiction: Again, in *Lydia Cassatt Reading the Morning Paper*, we see the surprising moment that the model is regarding the artist's (May) portrait of her. At first, the model speaks in a detached way about the painting in which she's portrayed, and then the subjective comes into view: "I look. May has created a calm scene: a woman in a garden, with a white lace bonnet and a blue dress, edged with colorful embroidery, and a dusky red row of plants behind her, leading up the allé, to the dark windows of the villa. She's crocheting something blue. And what is that double band of red on her lap? Ah, the sash of my dress. It startles me" (99).

Excerpt of Ekphrastic Nonfiction: In another ekphrastic treatment of the artist's model, Patricia Hampl, in her memoir, *Blue Arabesque* imagines this: "The model rises. She discards the alluring costume, the bright yellow beads, the masquerade that was so necessary to beguile her truth to canvas. She leaves it all, she walks behind the cloister screen, into her own life, where she cannot be seen but only imagined" (208).

Creative Process

I selected Vilhelm Hammershøi's image to punctuate this section on the visual artist's creative process because I felt that the emptiness of this space, along with the pregnant canvas on its easel, was a haunting nod to artists at work—infinite possibilities before us, the quietude, and a space divested of people. What about being an artist appeals to your personhood? What do you wish were different?

Here is Hammershøi's companion ekphrastic poem, which makes use of repetition and slant rhyme, as well as couplets that build toward an unanswerable question. What ekphrastic approaches are at play? What

Vilhelm Hammershøi's 1912 painting, *Interior with an Easel, Bredgade 25* (courtesy the Open Content Program at J. Paul Getty Museum).

topics are being treated? If you have not already been enjoying the curated writing on this level, here is a reminder to read these pieces aloud for the full bodily experience.

Copenhagen, Bredgade 25
by Cole Swensen

Light walks quietly through an empty room.
Light empties the room quietly within

the dove whose grey was here made warm,
the dove whose room slants carefully home

to the careful squares stretched by sun.
Hammershøi's doors are always open

either wholly or slightly making way.
To love a room is to love space for its own sake.

The doorway belovèd and how we loved the window
taking light out of itself like out of a pocket

and out of the easel, itself another window
at which another dove hovers, entirely a color

treading air and feathered out among angles,
each angle also a window, which means that each bird

is a fleck of light—or is it precisely not that? Does, in fact,
a flinch of light become avian automatically

repainting a room whose flight silently anchors
a window of sight diagonally across a wall

or does the diagonal itself create a kind of light
that annihilates the very concept of a wall.

Jung asserted, "The creative process ... consists in the unconscious activation of an archetypal image.... By giving it shape, the artist translates it into the language of the present, and so makes it possible for us to find our way back to the deepest springs of life.... The artist seizes on this image, and in raising it from deepest unconsciousness he brings it into relation with conscious values, thereby transforming it until it can be accepted by the minds of his contemporaries according to their powers" (Campbell 319). What do you make of Jung's transcription of how the creative process works?

Suggested Viewing: Marie Bashkirtseff's painting, *In the Studio*

Regarding their flow processes, would it surprise you to know that artists of all disciplines make similar pronouncements of their creative processes, practices, and elements of chance? Reverie, risk, repeat. Artists must love their tools enough for patience, play, and missteps. When I asked a classroom of young writers, what is the writer's beloved tools, no one answered "words."

> "When you don't know what you're doing, you just fill in the spaces."—Hartmut Austen

> "The painting has a life of its own. I try to let it come through."—Jackson Pollock

> "I'm painting and painting until the right thing happens."—Elizabeth Murray

> "Only when he no longer knows what he is doing does the painter do good things."—Edgar Degas

> "Paintings come out of painting."—Charles Emerson

Ekphrastic Freewrite: (After Pierre Bonnard's 1897 painting, *Rooftops*)

He threw his studio window open in order to get the landscape. Warm harmonies of brown and grey enlivened by the yellow dot of the birdcage. A blocked view by the steep pitch of the roofs. Flat surface pattern of walls, window, roofs showing the interplay of geometric shapes. There's a figure in the one open window. It's a woman, of course, see her red figure. What's brilliant white that sits between the cage and her? Gradations of brown, that flat expanse which carries the eyes up and up to an uncertain sky.

Writing Invitation: Imagine one of your favorite artists working. What was happening on the street directly outside the studio at the time the artist was at work?

Painter Claude Monet traveled to Rouen, France, rented an artist studio across the street from the Rouen Cathedral, and he sat at the window for months, creating thirty paintings of that cathedral in different conditions such as sunlight, cloud cover, rain. The results of that activity are atmospheric, ruminative paintings that remind us of the importance of changing light, perspective, and chance.

Suggested Viewing: Claude Monet's series of paintings, "La Cathédrale de Rouen." Examples of his paintings include, *Rouen Cathedral, West Façade, Sunlight*; *The Portal of Rouen Cathedral in Morning Light*; *Rouen Cathedral, Façade and the Tour d' Albane. Grey Weather*; and *Rouen Cathedral, Façade (Sunset), Harmonie in Gold and Blue.*

Writing Invitation: Which version of Monet's "Rouen Cathedral" is your favorite? Why? Think about a story you're composing; which Monet version would make for a plot-driving motif?

Suggested Viewing: Claude Monet's series of paintings, "Haystacks"

Writing Invitation: In what ways is this statement true of the themes your treat in your writing: "The angle of light you choose affects your subject matter" (De Reyna, 51)?

Ekphrastic Freewrite: (After Edward Hopper's 1963 painting, *Sun in an Empty Room*)

Does a room harbor sun when no one's there to receive it? How to shine a light on a void? What appeals to us of a womanless room angling in sunlight? Yes, the room can get on without her. The yellow walls and floor, even the naked window can shimmer in light and heat despite the emptiness. Do the two shafts of light represent two absent people, yet the room still vibrates from them having been there? Do humans emit vibrations? The vibrations of a common thing, like a bowl, when moved close to a microphone, emits sounds. Music of a common thing. The music of an empty, sun-filled room. The lyricism of the diurnal. "I am very much interested in light, particularly sunlight, trying to paint sunlight without eliminating the form under it, if I can," Hopper once said.

Writing Invitation: Author Carlo Dossi argued, "All ideas are already in the brain just as all statues are in the marble." Describe the artist's creative process itself, thereby imagining how the artwork arrived at its final state. Alternatively, create an ars poetica ("the art of poetry").

Suggested Reading: John Ashbery's poem, "The Painter"

Ekphrastic Freewrite: (After Michelangelo's 1525 sculptures, *Prisoners: Bearded Slave, Awakening Slave, Young Slave, Atlas Slave*)

Imagine Michelangelo in his studio chipping away at the marble. In the end, were his pieces actually "non-finito" (not finished) or were they exactly in their proper state for exposure to the world? He had something to break open, something to coax out. The shy, the imprisoned, the victims. They whisper, but all are immune to it except for artists capable of goading goodness out of the intractable. He knew which tools were required to reach inside. He spent years releasing the trapped, setting free the slaves and their unmuted cries.

Ekphrastic Freewrite: At times the visual artist will choose to work en plein air: A man today sidewalk sitting on a small stool and leaning over a canvas as he painted the building before him. The scene was quite savory, the grey-stoned, white column mansion. The strangling ivy clinging to all sides. The shades of the elm and maple trees that lined the street, in perfect alignment. I get this process—how even though it is loud out here, the wind, passers-by, the traffic, the mind finds its stillness. Have you strutted past this place many times and finally decided on a day to paint it? Are you new to town? Perhaps a loved one is in hospice somewhere, and you were in the neighborhood. Perhaps the ill one is you—and although the doctors cannot be convinced of it, this is the only panacea that will soothe your edges, buff your shine, temper your spires.

Excerpt of Ekphrastic Fiction: Irving Stone, in his biographical novel, *The Agony and the Ecstasy* explores Michelangelo's exhaustive creative process during the completion of the commissioned fresco, the ceiling of the Sistine Chapel:

> He painted sitting down, his thighs drawn up tight against his belly for balance, his eyes a few inches from the ceiling, until the unpadded bones of his buttocks became so bruised and sore he could no longer endure the agony. Then he lay flat on his back, his knees in the air, doubled over as tightly as possible against his chest to steady his painting arm. Since he no longer bothered to shave, his beard became an excellent catchall for the constant drip of paint and water (531).

How often have you wondered about the artist's process of making?

Excerpt of Ekphrastic Nonfiction: In the memoir, *Old Many Goya,* author Julia Blackburn writes ekphrastically of Francisco Goya's creative process. Consider whether research or simply her imagination might have led to her composing these lines: "He uses Rembrandt's technique of painting acid directly on to the plate with a brush to achieve the effect of drawing with diluted Chinese ink. He uses dry point to enlarge the traces not made sufficiently clear by the acid and a tool called a burin to make wider, rougher lines" (76–77).

Suggested Viewing: The series of contemporary artist interviews in their studios, "Art21"

Self-Portraits

In the image of Elaine de Kooning's painting, we have a smocked woman sitting on a cushioned chair. Open book in her lap, legs crossed, coffee mug and ashtray on the floor underneath her. What else do you notice? Does this image stir within you a story?

In Jackson's poem below, the speaker asks a series of questions, and ultimately, the notion of absence is considered. Given the ekphrastic conventions listed earlier (for instance, addressing the artwork, dictating what the artwork says, writing an interpretation of the artwork, or meditating on the moment of viewing), which one or ones are evident in this poem?

Considering Elaine de Kooning's Self-Portrait #3
("Everything was a matter of tension..." Elaine de Kooning)
by Didi Jackson

Is she the small thunder
on either side of my house
on a smock-blue day
as neighbors roll
trash bins to the curb,
rid themselves of all
they don't want or need?
Or the half-drawn valentine
on the back of the chair
where she sits
in this painting?
Or even the reflection
of a chickadee—a tiny tornado
at the glass window
of my front room?
As I move towards her and away
I am afraid she is

the echo of Willem,
a cigarette normally snug between
her fore and middle finger
like a coiled seraph: not there.
An early self-portrait.
The coffee cup and ashtray
clean and as empty as her
sketch book. So many hard
angles: the tapestry, the photos,
the sharp cut of her hair,
the ghostly pages she reveals.
What is put in a portrait
is as important
as what is left out.

Elaine de Kooning's 1946 oil on masonite, *Self-Portrait #3* (courtesy the Elaine de Kooning Trust, National Portrait Gallery, Smithsonian Institution).

Not always is the self-portrait a portrait of the self. A miasma can be a self-portrait. A discarded infant pacifier found on a New Jersey beach in December can be a self-portrait. In Cheeke's *Writing for Art* we are cautioned, "This demand that art should work in some ways like a mirror and reflect things as they are, but at the same time that it should somehow make things better than they are, is a deeply persistent one in our culture" (124). What expectations of art have you had in the past?

Excerpt of Ekphrastic Nonfiction: Returning to Blackburn's *Old Man Goya*, here is another extended ekphrasis, but this time it is on the creative process of making, specifically, a self-portrait, as well as a description of the painting itself:

> In 1815 he made a portrait of himself. He must have sat at the easel and leant out sideways so that he could stare at the reflected image that confronted him in a mirror. He is sixty-nine years old. His curly hair is grey around the temples, but it becomes black within the swirling darkness that surrounds him. His white shirt is open to reveal the vulnerability and unexpected softness of his aging skin, the weight of the flesh around the jaw, the thickening of the neck. The expression of the face is tired and serious but curiously detached; it is as if the man who is being painted is preoccupied with his own thoughts and quite unaware of the fact of being observed so closely (125).

Suggested Viewing: Frida Kahlo's self-portraits

Suggested Viewing: Paula Modersohn-Becker's self-portraits

Suggested Viewing: Joan Brown's self-portraits

Suggested Viewing: Rose-Adélaïde Ducreux's painting, *Self-Portrait with a Harp*

Suggested Viewing: Louise Elisabeth Vigée–Le Brun's painting, *Self-Portrait*

Suggested Viewing: Adélaïde Labille-Guiard's painting, *Self-Portrait with Two Pupils*

While it serves you to study the work of other ekphrastic practitioners if you aim to join the ranks, do not be discouraged by the work of other writers. For example, I wonder how many people have deigned to publish an ekphrastic poem on Parmigianino's 1523 painting, *Self-Portrait in a Convex Mirror*, given the fact that John Ashbery has already done so. Adopt the attitude of, "Well, his poem is just one version, and my poem can be just as good."

Ekphrastic Freewrite: (After Parmigianino's 1523 painting, *Self-Portrait in a Convex Mirror*)

Twenty-year-old in his parlor immortalized some 500 years later. Was the mirror his canvas? Why not paint directly onto that which reflects? Why not color-in your likeness? Revealing yourself to your-self happens slowing and imprecisely. The realistic hues: the browns, black and white, the peach color for face and hand. A little orange for the pinky-ring. The other hand is missing. Who knows your hand? See how the mirror captures you, holds you captive. Abandon the canvas and paint directly on a convex mirror and hang it in Vienna. Must you have been at ease fixating at your own likeness? Who could guess a con-vex mirror could hold such honor—a boy unabashed, un-boy-like in his proud gaze from reflection to rendition, from glass that gives its infinite reflection 500 years after his flesh has rotted. His nose and all orifices turned inward, all his convexes into concaves, when all the while his likeness fossilized, preserved and refracting the gallery lights on you and me as we stroll by, all of us in reflection.

Ekphrastic Freewrite: (After Albrecht Dürer's 1500 painting, *Self-Portrait at Twenty-Eight*)

He once said that his art was his hand. Artistry, a combination of seeing and doing. Fur-trimmed coat, clothes of a scholar. He begins with himself, for how can artists paint others if they haven't painted the self? Know what's close first to be able to move outwardly. Bits of yellow and white streaks show the gleaming blonde in his hair as wavy as a woman's.

Ekphrastic Freewrite: (After Vincent van Gogh's 1889 painting, *Self Portrait with a Bandaged Ear*)

After a heated altercation with friend and fellow artist Paul Gauguin, this evidence of self-mutilation. Not for any trivial reason, such as unre-quited love. The face is pasted between an almost blank canvas to the left and a Japanese print to the right—self-reflection at the moment of realiza-tion that his artist colony will never happen. An artist's dream to colonize the masses, to sponsor a haven for the wayward, the orphan artists of the world. See the long white strokes of bandage leveled against the swifter, tinier strokes of paint for the face, raging against the clipped, black strokes for the hat's brim?

Suggested Reading: Diane Wakoski's poem, "I Have Had to Learn to Live with My Face."

Writing Invitation: Settle on one self-portrait and address it di-rectly. For example, to van Gogh's bandaged ear painting, you might ask him about why he chose to document a painful moment in his life. Wasn't the narrative lousy with shame and embarrassment? Are these feelings a matter of art?

Ekphrastic Freewrite: I once observed a painter making a self-portrait. He wasn't afraid to look at himself. He needs to look, to see in order to translate his image onto the canvas. How does the nose's bridge intersect the face? How tall are the ears? How many hairs extend beyond the confines of eyebrows? What does an inverted hand look like—for the right hand must be drawn at the same time as it is drawing? The small mirror, balanced on the painter's desk to get what's seen of a face, or to get what the inverted looks like in the little mirror which usually lives inside the artist's art bin with watercolors, blades, brushes, pens, pencils, and erasers.

Writing Invitation: What is a work of art? Are you a work of art? In that spirit, find inspiration from your flesh and study of the hand. Look superficially and then initiate deep-looking. Consider the palm lines, the scars, the fingerprints, the tough bones underneath the skin, the musculature, the stories the hand can tell, and the metaphors that exist.

Writing Invitation: Mirror gazing. Spend ten minutes looking at your face. Say nothing negative to or about yourself. What do you notice as you looked deeply at your reflection? What do you know of your face that no one else knows? See yourself and beyond. What is transparent? What is a mystery? Who or what is being reflected in the mirror? How much of your vision is real, and how much is imaginary? Are you an apparition before your very eyes?

Excerpt of Ekphrastic Fiction: Revisiting *The Picture of Dorian Gray*, let us consider the correlation between the portrait of a person and the self-portrait:

> "Harry," said Basil Hallward, looking him straight in the face, "every portrait that is painted with feeling is a portrait of the artist, not of the sitter. The sitter is merely the accident, the occasion. It is not he who is revealed by the painter, it is rather the painter who, on the coloured canvas, reveals himself. The reason I will not exhibit this picture is that I am afraid that I have shown in it the secret of my own soul" (9).

Writing Invitation: Regarding contemporary artist Cindy Sherman's early start, it has been said that "a photography professor helped Cindy understand how she could be an artist. She gave her a problem: to photograph something that made her feel uncomfortable. Cindy chose to photograph herself naked" (Sills 64). Are you shocked by the assignment or by the artist's response to the assignment? What would you have done? Discover one artist who has created numerous self-portraits. Use elements of those artworks to write your self-portrait.

Museums

A woman is seated in a chair, the back of which you can scarcely see, in a painting called, *Girl with Cherries*. Even though the style of this artwork is realism, much abstraction can be gleaned from it. Look deeply—what do you see? While having access to digital images is marvelous, there is no substitute for standing before an actual masterpiece. Are you inclined to mark the moment of viewing art with words? Does curiosity about what you see compel you to the tabula rasa? The museum experience for poet Wozek (which you'll see later) was a vital component to his creative process.

A museum is an organization that conserves a collection of artifacts of artistic, cultural, historical, or scientific significance. There are an estimated 55,000 museums worldwide, with the first public museum being the Ashmolean Museum in 1677. The Louvre Museum in Paris opened in 1793. The Tate Modern Museum in London opened in 2000, and in 2006 the world's first underwater sculpture park opened off the coast of Grenada. As eluded to earlier, in 2018 the Atelier des Lumieres opened, Paris' first museum of digital art wherein visitors experience walking through the featured artwork.

Writing Invitation: Imagine climbing inside a painting of your choice and taking a stroll through that scene. Aside from walking about, what else would you do? What interactions with objects or people would you have? What would you say to them about your presence?

Besides art museums, numerous other types of museums exist, such as agricultural and biographical museums, history and natural history museums, sex museums, and maritime and science museums. Zoos and botanic gardens are also types of museums. And art can be found virtually anywhere. A museum is any rich environment teaming with creative fodder, which can take the form of a school campus, a forest, a library, an urban setting.

Writing Invitation: Make a pilgrimage to a museum or gallery for the express purpose of welcoming any experience as it comes. I recommend you travel there alone so that you may minister to your own thoughts. Be receptive to the intimacies of that experience, and begin composing lines in your journal while you're there.

How to look in order to truly see? Giving your full attention to the artwork is a type of meditative practice. Art enters into a symbiotic relationship with its audience. The artwork gives, and the respondent must receive and give. It is synergistic. Kandel in his book *The Age of Insight*, in expressing the work of art historian Alois Riegl declared that,

Eva Gonzalès' c. 1870 painting, *Girl with Cherries* (courtesy the Mr. and Mrs. Lewis Larned Coburn Memorial Collection).

Art is incomplete without the perceptual and emotional involvement of the viewer. Not only does the viewer collaborate with the artist in transforming a two-dimensional likeness on a canvas into a three-dimensional depiction of the world, the viewer interprets what he or she sees on the canvas in personal terms, thereby adding meaning to the picture. Riegl called this phenomenon the "beholder's involvement" (189).

In quietude and stasis lies the possibility of something revelatory. Visual artist Marcel Duchamp explained, "Art is not about itself but the attention we bring to it." Unfortunately there are people in galleries all over the world walking up to paintings and two seconds later walking away, saying dismissively, "I don't get it."

Museum ekphrasis includes expanding the narrative, speculating about the creative process, or supposing about the fellow viewers. Arrive at an approach that's productive for you. Starting your freewriting in the museum and completing the piece elsewhere is the process for many ekphrastic writers. What is divulged on the page to the writer in the moment of the deep-looking—the dictation of the present moment—can not be replicated.

To be in the presence of something powerful and monumental is, for some art viewers, similar to a religious experience. In that moment of viewing, the object can be more tangible than words, though it has been a matter for modern, lyrical poems: "the presence of a gazer, reporting what he or she sees, variously describing what is there to be seen, is framing a moment of experience" (Hollander 32).

As promised, here is Wozek's ekphrastic poem. Notice the use of quatrains loosely in iambic pentameter but sometimes with extra feet. What is the point-of-view? What is the tone? Notice the use of literal description and associations?

Girl with Cherries
(After the painting by Eva Gonzalès)
by Gerard Wozek

A frilled linen cap conceals the crown
of the domestic's chestnut hair. The rest
held back by a simple bow that begs
to be torn away to reveal her luster.

The ash stained stripes of her servant's gown
seem to imprison her. She's frozen,
desolate against a backdrop of Impressionist fog
choking out any impulse beyond her duties.

Starched sleeves rolled up to scrub the tarnish
of the day, she deftly holds the paring knife
that will remove the pit and stem of each cherry.
A fruit she will not taste, but only imagine.

Her hand stays poised above five red spheres.
Orbs that reflect a source of illumination, a light
that cannot be found in eyes that search
beyond a captivity binding her to servitude.

She might have preferred to unseal a letter
from a furtive lover, accept a sailor's plea
to join him on a voyage. Or like Gonzalès,
render a universe, with oils and brushstrokes.

Poet's Comments

For several weeks I visited the quiet gallery on the upper north end of the Impressionist section at the Art Institute of Chicago where I was able to quietly meditate and take notes on the Eva Gonzalès painting, *Girl with Cherries*. The painting is hung between two of Manet's larger than life masterpieces and shares a kinship with them in terms of a dramatically lit human figure held against a somber and dark background. Directly observing the portrait created by Gonzalès, noting the fluid brushstrokes and melancholy colors, it became more clear that there was a sort of yearning within the subject, a kind of mourning that seemed to seep right through the painting and was more evident when viewing the image in person rather than through the museum's online image (Gerard Wozek).

Writing Invitation: Searching the visual for answers. Create a list poem or prose reflection that's composed of questions and/or answers. Alternatively, create an abstract poem or prose piece in which you use a list of directives.

Upon viewing a Caravaggio painting in Florence, the 19th-century French writer Stendhal (nom de plume of Marie-Henri Beyle) wrote about his extraordinary response to the act of deep-looking: "My head thrown back, I let my gaze dwell on the ceiling. I underwent the profoundest experience of ecstasy I had ever encountered. I had obtained that supreme degree of sensibility where the divine intimations of art ... merge with the impassioned sensuality ... of emotion" (Barnes *Nothing*). Ecstatic writing. In *Art Objects*, Jeanette Winterson reported that she "Saw a painting that had more power to stop me than I had power to walk on" (3).

The term we have for this sensation is relatively new: "In the late 1970s Dr. Graziella Magherini, a psychiatrist working in Florence, coined the term the *Stendhal Syndrome* to describe the sense of disorientation, temporary amnesia and panic attacks that would overwhelm visitors to the galleries of Florence—a sickness she connected with the ability of artworks to bring to the surface repressed emotional experiences" (Cheeke 170).

Just as Stendhal explained his bodily response to artwork, *duende* is a Spanish term of "heightened state of emotion, expression, and authenticity." It's the spirit of evocation, as in an emotional response to art. And, these experiences are directly proportionate to your capacity to receive. Even Winterson reminds herself, "I have to work for art if I want art to work for me" (6).

Regarding why most published ekphrastic creative writing is written to the fine arts, Spiegelman explains: "With a painting or sculpture we have an external, unchanging field to which we can return for verification. Because most paintings now reside in public spaces ... a poet can observe them, retreat for contemplation, and then reimagine or recreate them. Readers may respond in kind. The spatial permanence of painting, when compared to the temporality of music, makes for an anchor, if not exactly a safe harbor, when we are at sea in a changing world" (8). What are your thoughts? Do you find comfort in the "spatial permanence" of particular works-of-art?

Writing Invitation: Create a piece of writing that catapults the reader a sense of being in the physical presence of the artwork. Strive to capture the essence of the artwork in your writing.

Excerpt of Ekphrastic Nonfiction: Patricia Hampl, too, in her memoir, *Blue Arabesque* treats the ineffable experience of the Stendhal

Syndrome ekphrastically: "Then, unexpectedly, several galleries shy of my destination, I came to a halt before a large, rather muddy painting in a heavy gold-colored frame, a Matisse.... *Woman Before an Aquarium*. But that's wrong: I didn't halt, didn't stop. I was stopped. Apprehended, even. That's how it felt. I stood before the painting a long minute. I couldn't move away" (2).

During museum visits, I suggest that ekphrastic writers ponder curatorial decisions (what art to include, how to frame it, how to hang it, how to light it). An essential dimension to the museum experience involves the arrangement of the artwork in a gallery space. For example, how do the various pieces interact with one another and complement each other? Since the proximity of colors is influential, curators will pay close attention to how hanging one piece next to another will affect its optical properties.

Writing Invitation: Given many sculptures in a single gallery, consider how they relate to each other. Write associatively about their similarities as well as their disparate elements, and then create a suite of poems or prose vignettes.

Let us consider viewing three-dimensional museum art and environmental effects. Stand far from it and see it in the context of the space. Does it stand out, or does it blend in with the architecture? Next move near to see the texture, note color, and notice how light reflects differently in places. How is it illuminated—by natural light, by the placement of artificial light? Are shadows a function of the viewing experience? Walk around it. Does it suggest motion or stasis? How does it move and change as you move and change your angle? What is your relationship with the object? Does it tower over you? Is it displayed on a pedestal? Is it set on the floor? Is it roped off? These methods of display affect your perception of it.

Given a sculpture, note its shape—is it organic or geometric? If the sculpture has human qualities, is it anatomically correct or not? Do you suppose that the shape references something from the artist's mind? For example, creating a head that's larger than average can feel disarming. Remember that sculpture can exist in a series, so do you see all parts in that series, a couple, or a single piece? Notice the sculpture's reflective and matte properties. Finally, what are the tactile qualities of a sculpture? While touching museum sculptures is usually forbidden, many sculptors welcome the handling of their work in private collectors' homes and in outdoor spaces, which are intentionally created with audience interaction in mind.

Writing Invitation: What else happens during the experiencing of a sculpture in the museum? Do you perceive your own shadow? Do others in the space detract or embolden your art-viewing experience. Is there silence or sound within that space? Are people rapt or inattentive?

Does the physical proximity to the artwork have a direct correlation to the writer's aptitude or ability for ekphrasis? Such was the case for poet Frank O'hara. As one of the Museum of Modern Art's curators, O'Hara has been referred to as the "art world's favorite poet." *The Collected Poems of Frank O'Hara* includes ekphrastic poems on the art of Hieronymus Bosch, Jackson Pollock, Gustave Courbet, Piet Mondrian, and Josef Albers, as well as odes to artists such as Joseph Cornell, Grace Hartigan, Mike Goldberg, and Willem de Kooning.

Ekphrastic Freewrite: (After Leonardo de Vinci's *Portrait of Lisa Gherardini*)

Other artists in this room go unnoticed: Rosa, Giordano, Bacicco, Procaccini, Romanelli, Fetti, de Cortone, Castiglione, Strozzi, de Ferrari, and Rosselli, most of which the guard had to give me permission to look at (the ribbon partition with which to cue the Mona Lisa gawkers subsequently prevented admirers from these other works). The authorities could no longer control the crowd's desire to flash-photograph *Mona Lisa*. So now they have the 500-year old portrait encased in a bullet-proof and flash-accommodating thermoplastic. All people crowd around her like paparazzi and flash, flash, flash themselves posed near her. They know nothing about her, her plight in life and death, know nothing of him—yet here they gather. Take one minute to get the right shot, and their cameras go *click*. They never look directly at her, will never recall the somber hues, her hands, that mouth's ambiguity. They remember nothing of the experience as they skip home to reveal their prized shot.

Museum curators sometimes have untenable obstacles in acquisitions. Case in point, a curator in Florida was recently featured in the newspaper:

> "Time is running out," Aimee Rubensteen said. She is looking for people who want to donate any object (photographs, letters, immigration documents) from the pre–World War II era, during the Holocaust, or after. She informs people that the museum's goal is to save history. "I tell them that I'm here to advocate for the object," she said. "I'm here because if you think this object is important we need to preserve it (Switalski).

Writing Invitation: Explore an artwork that springs forth in you the notion of lost history or saved history. Use an objet d'art, an everyday object, or a museum piece as a starting place for your freewrite.

Sometimes the art in general is affecting and, therefore, fixating on one particular artwork is antithetical to your creative writing piece. For example, it is not definite which sculpture influenced Rilke's well-know

Archaic Torso poem. As Hollander wrote, "Now, even if we knew precisely which of two or three archaic *kouroi* in the Louvre Rilke was addressing in his celebrated and influential 'Archaic Torso of Apollo' it could not matter that much in dealing with the poem. The actual ecphrasis [sic] in it ... could apply to any one of a number of such paradigmatic pieces" (35).

Excerpt of Ekphrastic Nonfiction: In *Letters on Cézanne*, Rilke himself virtually answers the readers who are anxious to know which sculpture was the subject for his poem: "[I]t's remarkable what an environment they create. Without looking at a particular one, standing in the middle between the two rooms, one feels their presence drawing together into a colossal reality" (26).

Excerpt of Ekphrastic Nonfiction: Texture in a work-of-art is best experienced directly, as described in Michael White's memoir, *Travels in Vermeer*: "Over the centuries, a fine eggshell craqueleur has developed across the entire surface ... the essence of the girl projected through the cracked, eroded surface seems undiminished. In fact, she seems all the more moving to me, all the more precious for her ability to transcend the ravages of age. Reproductions are useless, I suddenly think" (31).

Writing Invitation: Visit a gallery or museum with a pair of binoculars so as to scrutinize the artwork close up without tripping an alarm or vexing a security guard. Cogitate on the details. Write about this heightened experience of magnified art. Alternatively, employ the help of a docent (a museum volunteer who's trained to offer insight about the artwork in a particular exhibit) to give you a tour, or purchase an audio guide to draw your attention to highlights and provide information on the art, the artists, and the time in which the artwork was made. Also, these resources are helpful for artwork on loan from private collectors which are often commissioned for specific exhibits and rarely cataloged online.

There are obvious benefits to firsthand art experiences. During the museum visit, you can get the context in relation to other pieces, behold the textures, view the whole piece (some reproductions focus on just a single detail), behold its size and scale, delight in the precision of color, physically inhabiting the gallery in which the curator's decision (regarding the color of the walls, the lighting, and placement) are a large part of that enterprise, as well as the direct or indirect interactions with other museum visitors. On the other hand, unlike in museums, reproductions you can hold in your hand, thereby inspecting it from other angles. Also, images of artwork are more accessible, and they are transportable—fitting framed artwork in your backpack proves more difficult than dropping in a postcard.

There is no substitute for experiencing art personally. Being in the presence of beauty! Museum visits afford you time for contemplation, study, reflection. Nonetheless, if you do not have access to museums or galleries, the Internet provides a myriad of ways that you can enjoy the fine arts. For instance, online, you can interact with Pieter Brueghel's 1559 painting of 100 proverbs, *The Topsy Turvy World*. (See the interactive webpage for Netherlandish proverbs.)

Art Conservation

Have you ever thought about art conservation? These experts are educated, skilled, precise, and they specialize in all subspecialties of the arts, such as easel paintings, frescos and wall paintings, archeology, and three-dimension artifacts like bones and feathers. American Institute for Conservation defines it this way: "Conservation is the profession devoted to preserving cultural material for the future. By melding art with science, conservation protects our heritage, preserves our legacy, and ultimately, saves our past for generations to come." Conservationists will only perform an act of conservation that can be reversed. For example, in the process of inpainting, they might decide to use watercolor, which ages differently than the original paint. And, another reason for visiting museums is that sometimes you can watch an art conservationist at work, for some institutions make their workspaces available to the public.

In a museum what do we expect to see? How do we evaluate what we are seeing? Pre-conservation? Post-conservation—what is gained, what is lost? Do we take a clean canvas for granted? How has the artwork aged? For example, aging art changes when artists have used paint that they themselves made versus mass-produced paint. Varnish layers, for instance, are typically renewed every thirty years. Why not allow the artwork to age naturally? What are your thoughts about conservation?

Suggested Viewing: For an introduction to art conservation, see images of all the panels in the Sistine Chapel before restoration and afterward.

Writing Invitation: Major American museums now have pages on their websites dedicated to art conservation. Some sites publish their conservation reports, which are a treat to read for their extended ekphrases. Read conservation reports and make a pastiche of the ekphrastic moments.

In the "Color Blind" article in *The New Yorker*, the Margaret Talbot writes, "Scholars have known for centuries that Greek and Roman marble figures were routinely covered in bright paint. Why does the myth of their whiteness persist?" This article begs the question, what do art conservationists know about what we see better than we know? They have a behind-the-scenes view.

Recent headlines on the J. Paul Getty Museum website "Behind the scenes at the Getty":

1. Getty and University of Arizona Partner to Conserve Long-Lost Willem de Kooning Painting. Over thirty years after it was stolen from the University of Arizona, a de Kooning will be conserved at the Getty.
2. Snail Mail: A Letter from Édouard Manet. A charming watercolor provides insight into the French artist's private world.
3. Child's Portrait Sheds Light on a Violent Episode in Renaissance History. The hidden story of a marble bust.
4. Science Reveals New Clues about Mysterious Ancient Greek Sculptures of Mourning Women. Why and how were these sculptures made? Science finds an answer.
5. The Surprising Detective Work of a Drawings Curator. Unsolved mysteries of old master drawings.

Writing Invitation: Take any of these headlines, or research others, and write the story behind it.

Artists at Work

Besides viewing art, what is the most memorable thing that you have encountered in a museum or art gallery? Another byproduct of museum visits is that you never know if you are inadvertently stepping into an artist's studio. At the museum, the real action might exist outside the frames, with fellow viewers. Whether it is interacting with other patrons, eavesdropping on a scholar giving a private tour, or observing a group of students making charcoal sketches of what they see, be open to serendipity during your visit. If you are lucky, you can observe an artist at work, for some artists' studios are museums themselves.

Ekphrastic Freewrite: (After Pieter Brueghel's 1565 painting, *Winter Landscape with Bird Trap*)

When people lean in to look closer at the painting, an alarm is tripped. In the Brueghel room here at the Kunsthistorisches Museum in Vienna: a small winter landscape is being rendered in front of our eyes. Behind the ropes used to separate viewer from art, an easel and box of paints. Part of the easel's mechanism is a bamboo stalk that runs across the canvas on the vertical. I lean in closer—the paint's still wet, it smells of oils. The painting left to dry, the paint box with mixed hues, the original masterpiece two feet away. The painter takes a rest on the nearby sofa; she chats with a security guard. She approaches her canvas to begin again. The maulstick steadies as she paints minute details. Her work is frenzied—head turning left, turning right, paint, paint, then the rinse, then to the bamboo again. Her painter's smock, a laboratory coat—buttoned white. What do we make when we make a replica? Technique and form, craft, and artistry right before our eyes. A reminder that these pictures were created by artists standing at their easels, candlelight and barren hovels. All that's left of the artist is the art. Paint fumes circle the gallery—some here are mute to it, and some here are moved.

Suggested Reading: William Carlos Williams' poem, "Thirteen Ways of Looking at a Blackbird"

Writing Invitation: Write a multi-part piece in which you discuss the same subject from numerous angles. For instance, find a mosaic whose pieces form an image that you admire. Consider the perspective of each tile, finding associations along the way.

Excerpt of Ekphrastic Nonfiction: In the memoir, *Leap*, Terry Tempest Williams had a similar experience. Regarding Hieronymus Bosch's triptych housed in the Prado Museum, *The Garden of Delights*:

> There is a Japanese woman who is painting *El jardín de las delicias*. Her name is Mariko Umeoka Taki. She has been working on her reproduction for four years.... She has her easel set up to the side of the triptych and is working on the bottom center quadrant of the Garden of Delights. I introduce myself to the painter. I ask her why she has chosen this particular painting to copy. "Because I need it," she replies matter-of-factly. "I feel it from the inside" (19–20).

Artist's Studies

At times in a museum, a curator will choose to display some of the artists' studies, in which spectators can appreciate the evolution of the making of a single artwork. To see how the art changed, where the genius moments occur, and where the missteps. To stand in a room surrounded by studies of the same scene is to appreciate part of the artist's process.

Excerpt of Ekphrastic Fiction: Since we as museum-goers are viewing the final product, we often forget the myriad of things that must have gone wrong. Were blunders made? In Julian Barnes' novel *A History of the World in 10½ Chapters*, this sentiment is echoed: "We must remember him in the confinement of his studio, at work, in motion, making mistakes" (134).

Writing Invitation: Study a series of paintings by one artist and write about that person's treatment of the scene. How does it morph? Does it advance or retreat? What is improved upon, what is diminished? What do you learn about yourself when you see a collection of artists' studies?

Ekphrastic Freewrite: (After Pablo Picasso's 1897 four studies for the painting *Science and Charity*)

The four constant characters: doctor, supine and convalescing patient, the nun at her bedside, and her child. The door behind the doctor comes and goes, as do the window shutters. The doctor's position alters from sitting toward the viewers or toward his patient. The nun loses her habit, then finds it—the woman: from sitting upright in bed to lying gravely and pale-faced. The medium seems to alter: oil paints with and without detail and colored pencil sketches. In one of the studies, the girl rends free from an adult's clasp and runs into the room. But in the other three studies, consistency: in the arms of the nun, her outstretched arms reaching for Mom. The doctor marks the patient's pulse. A nun offers tea, something which a weak hand cannot accept. In the final: the child, through four canvases of reaching out her arms in vain, has given up. The babe learns by watching and restrains herself. The doctor can reach the ailed, but her babe cannot. The brown shutters are closed, and their color drips down the walls. The red horizontal line of the woolen blanket is destined to run parallel but never touch, like a red cross. The third study: the child runs into the room, the doctor doesn't touch the sick woman, and the nun is a maid. The fourth canvas, the smallest and painted in loose strokes, is the closest rendering to the final. Like dress rehearsals, the natural desire of the director allows for the players' truths—means of discovery, learning what the players require of the painter. The scene, taking on a life of its own. Art being art in its actualization. Picasso, a mere vehicle through which these characters find life. Picasso was directing the characters into a scene, allowing for a suitable ending, but allowing the players to assert the needs of their characters.

Writing Invitation: Given a display of numerous studies in the service of a final artwork, write a play about the progress of either the artist or the subjects portrayed.

Artist's Series

Some artists aim to embark on a project of more than one artwork. Claude Monet's "Rouen Cathedral" and "Haystacks" already have been mentioned, but what other artists' series are you familiar with?

Ekphrastic Freewrite: Another example of a series of paintings on a theme is the four primal elements by Giuseppe Arcimboldo. Here is a freewrite on just one painting in that series: (After Arcimboldo's 1566 painting, *Fire*):

The bust is a composite of fire-associated things: burning logs and flames for scalp and hair. A bundle of wick for forehead, flint for nose and ear, pressed wax for face, a tiny burning candle for eye, a larger burning ochre candle for the sternocleidomastoid muscle. Cannon and pistol make up the shoulder. A bundle of match sticks for the mouth. What is the significance of such a fiery side profile? A bust made of stalks of flame, of heat. When the heat gets out of control, we call the combustion destructive. Flammable has a negative connotation as does cannon and pistol and logs left to redden and soar. Sore.

Suggested Viewing: Pablo Picasso's series of paintings, "Las Meninas (Conjunto)"

Suggested Viewing: Ruth Oosterman's watercolor series, "Collaborations with my Toddler"

Suggested Viewing: Jacob Lawrence's painting series, "The Migration Series"

Suggested Viewing: Chino Otsuka's series of photographic self-portraits

Writing Invitation: Choose an artist's series of work and make a suite of linked poems or prose pieces. Alternatively, find the symbolism in an artwork.

In addition to studying one artist's series, it can be instructive to compare and contrast how one artist treats the same subject in different works-of-art. For example, Vincent van Gogh's 1888 painting of chairs: *Gauguin's Chair* with a candle holder, a lit candle, and two books, and *Van Gogh's Chair* with a pipe and pouch of tobacco. Notice the characterization of the two men through the choices of which objects to lay in each seat. A story of friendship and camaraderie told in two still-lifes.

Excerpt of Ekphrastic Nonfiction: Jericho Parms in her book of essays, *Lost Wax* also finds poetic fodder in these men and their chairs:

> In 1888, Vincent van Gogh painted two of these well-known works while in the company of Paul Gauguin at Arles. *Vincent's Chair*, housed in London's National Gallery, vibrates with van Gogh's signature golds and blues and depicts a single straw chair positioned on a wood slab floor. A crumpled handkerchief with tobacco and the artist's pipe rest in the seat. Conversely, *Gauguin's Armchair*, exhibited in Amsterdam's Rijksmuseum, is darkly ornate (51).

Suggested Viewing: Jean-Michel Basquiat's paintings and drawings of heads and skulls

Suggested Viewing: Paul Gauguin's post-impressionism, primitivism, and modern art periods

Writing Invitation: Try looking at artwork from an artist's particular period of development and compare and contrast those periods in a creative way. For example, Goya had at least three: his period as a court painter for Charles IV, his politically rebellious period, and his dark stage. Pit one against the other? For instance, write one line of description from one piece in one period, the second line of description from one piece from the next period, in which you are weaving descriptions based on a single artist (in which many artworks are treated).

Art as Artifact

How familiar are you with the textile arts? Imagine if you could not see Millsent Connor's embroidered silk on linen but could only touch it. What would your fingers reveal? Merely imagining the tactile journey of contact with this type of art could lead a person to consider the Braille alphabet.

Suggested Reading: Raymond Carver's short story, "Cathedral"

Let's consider art as a handheld artifact, an object in which its private life can be a matter of intrigue. Art can be lost, found, stolen, sold, faked, and altered. Moreover, let us not forget that canvases can be cut from their frames, quickly rolled up, and carted off.

Ekphrastic Freewrite: Was Gustave Courbet's *The Preparation of the Dead Girl* manipulated for material gains? Seventy years later the title was changed to "The Preparation of the Bride" and the painting was revised. Though, x-ray images eventually uncover the truth behind Courbet's original scene. (After Gustave Courbet's 1850 painting, *The Preparation of the Dead Girl*):

Thirteen women surround the dead, darkened-in by service. The two in the back lay a white sheet down on the bed on which to receive the corpse. Those huddled in the back recite prayers, others stack the table of food. The one in the foreground kneels with a basin of water for her dead feet. Another steadies the corpse in the chair. See her hand on the girl's shoulder? See how the girl's head rests on the shoulder? A woman's duty to undress and dress the dead, for the girl to be received in afterlife as she was in life: virginal, clean, and prepared for receiving visitors who'll remark on the curls of her hair, the pressed dress. Courbet never finished the canvas. I imagine it was a businessman who cloaked her, lifted her head, gave her red locks, and put a vanity mirror in her once

Millsent Connor's 1799 embroidered silk on linen, *Embroidered Sampler* **(gift of Edgar William and Bernice Chrysler Garbisch, 1974).**

limp hand. How easy it is to mew a girl from corpse to bride. And the women tend to her: someone to wash her feet and someone to hold her up. On that side of the door, a grave, or a man—either way, she's in. Courbet's girl perhaps illustrating how marriage and death are one and one needn't always have a röentgenogram and the pass of decades before the sting's revealed.

Writing Invitation: Compare and contrast two versions of an artwork. Surmise who might have bowdlerized the piece, how, and why. Relate this to some aspect of your life.

Stolen Art

It is estimated that over 50,000 artworks are stolen annually. Having been stolen indeed launched the stardom of the *Mona Lisa*. A lost Caravaggio was recently found languishing in an attic, and another family discovered that for generations, a Leonard da Vinci painting had adorned their walls. The 1990 theft at Boston's Isabella Steward Gardner Museum remains an open case. Empty frames still adorn the walls. After the most prolific art thief known stole from nearly 200 museums, the loot, unbeknown to him, was tossed in a river by his accomplices. He, like the man who stole *Mona Lisa*, did it for the love of art.

Actual news headlines that concern stolen art:

1. Mona Lisa: The Theft that Created a Legend
2. Lost Caravaggio Painting Found in Attic Could Fetch $171 Million at Auction
3. How a $450 Million Leonardo da Vinci Was Lost in America— and Later Found
4. Gardener Museum Theft: An Active and Ongoing Investigation
5. The Secrets of the World's Greatest Art Thief
6. L'Origine du Monde: Mystery Courbet Nude Uncovered
7. Munich's *Scream* Is Stolen from a Crowded Museum in Oslo

Writing Invitation: Take any one of these headlines, or research others, and write the story behind it.

Ekphrastic Freewrite: Of all the museums I wanted to visit in Scandinavia, the Munch Museum in Oslo was top on this list. So, I set out on my own to explore that wet town, and there was a nagging feeling in my gut. First I meandered to the National Museum, but it wasn't yet open. Now I shall trek to the Munch Museum, I thought. *No,* a voice said, as my feet refused to lead me there. So, to the sculpture park instead—a few miles there and back, on foot and in the drizzle. Now, again at the doors of the National Museum. I noticed the peevish guard who said nothing to a couple who proceeded through with large knapsacks. I found myself in an entire room dedicated to Munch. Wow, a version of the *Scream*, a version of the *Virgin*, the *Dance of the Dead*, wow *Ashes*, wow a bust of Munch himself. So now I was determined to go to the museum dedicated to the master. Even though I had a few hours to spare, even though I'd long to go, even though I'd fallen dead in love with this fanatically morose artist, even though, even though—the voice said *no, your legs won't carry you there, you shan't go.* Later that afternoon on the BBC, "a heist at the Munch Museum this afternoon." Both the *Scream* and the *Virgin*, gone. Two masked people sauntered in. No one said a word. No one moved. The guard sat where he sat, a pistol shoved in his face.

Writing Invitation: Imagine that you could lift a painting off the wall or shove a sculpture into your bag. What would you do once you had it in your possession? Where would you take it? What would you do once you were alone with it?

Censorship

Unfortunately, the topic of censorship is relevant when discussing any discipline of art. There are numerous types of censorship, including religious, governmental, and self-censorship.

Once upon a time, photographers would be dispatched by the military to record significant events in and about America. Here is an example of how competing agendas resulted in military censorship: In 1942 photographer Dorothea Lange was hired to document the "evacuation" and the "relocation" of Japanese-Americans. Once she completed the assignment and shared her art, the military personal intuited from the photographs that Lange was more sympathetic to the plight of those she photographed than towards the government. The pictures and film were captured and locked away for decades (Lange).

As an example of governmental censorship: *Immersion* (also known as "Piss Christ") is a 1987 photograph by Andres Serrano. Per the artist's description of his creative process, he collected his urine, dumped it in a glass tank, acquired a small plastic crucifix, submerged the object, and took a photograph. One particularly potent byproduct of the protest of that artwork was the National Endowment for the Art deciding to disallow grant money for any individual visual artist. Also censored during this time was Robert Mapplethorpe's sexually explicit book of photography, *X Portfolio*.

Museum Resources

If you enjoy learning, you'll relish in the resources available at most museums. Before you go, research the possibility of attending a lecture, viewing a special traveling exhibition, joining a tour, taking a class, purchasing an audio guide, and meeting the artists. Museum shops, too, are brimming with resources for the art lover.

Overheard in the Galleria dell'Accademia in Florence, a guide to her students regarding Michelangelo's four unfinished stone columns, *Prisoners: Bearded Slave, Awakening Slave, Young Slave, Atlas Slave*: "An observer must complete the sculptures with his own imagination." Is this sage advice? Do you suppose that's what the artist intended? What are other approaches the imagination can take?

Ekphrastic Freewrite: (After Edward Hopper's 1932 painting, *Room in Brooklyn*)

On display at the Tate Modern Museum, it hangs in the corner of the gallery. A window on one wall, two windows perpendicular. On the far left, a woman sits in a rocking chair, and she stares out the window—her back to the viewers. As I stand in this gallery with the others, like a scene within a scene, I notice in front of me, and therefore closer to the actual painting, a patron in a wheelchair. So now, I see the back of him seated in a mobile chair, gazing at a picture of the back of a seated woman. And I wonder if he sees what I do, the dueling difference between the footed and the footless, the seated and the standing, the ones who gaze down at this portrait, or the ones who gaze up.

Writing Invitation: Art viewing is a shared, social experience. Invite your muse to shepherd you around a museum or gallery and begin a personal essay there in which you explore the difference between the individual and the collective art experience.

Excerpt of Ekphrastic Fiction: Historically, for museum-goers, a painting worked in tandem with news of the day. Again, let us read an excerpt from *A History of the World in 10½ Chapters*, in which Barnes describes the social pleasure of encountering art together in a common place: "Those who saw Géricault's painting on the walls of the 1819 Salon knew, almost without exception, that they were looking at the survivors of the *Medusa's* raft, knew that the ship on the horizon did pick them up (if not at the first attempt), and knew that what happened on the expedition to Senegal was a major political scandal" (132–133).

Writing Invitation: How does the grouping of artwork in a gallery or a museum affect you? The combination of artwork in one room creates a mood. Write from the embodiment of a particular mood you experienced in an art exhibit.

Ekphrastic Freewrite: (After Daniele da Volterra's 1564 bronze bust of Michelangelo)

At the Galleria dell'Accademia in Florence, the bust of old Michelangelo goes scarcely noticed in this room lined with prisoners busting from their stones and *David* presiding over them. It's not the artist himself we were concerned with, but the artwork he left behind. Aren't you curious to look into the eyes of the great master? How on his pedestal you must gaze up at him as you would a saint. He has aged nicely, with hair and bronze that turned black. His gaze pensive, perhaps gesturing to his work that stands like a demigod in this long corridor. Meanwhile, legs and torsos emerge from columns of stone—he merely was revealing the beauty that he knew was encased in that stone, pristine white and begging for release.

Writing Invitation: That art outlives its maker is the wish of most artists? It was the popularity of the art and not the likeness of the artist that seemed to matter. But seeing Michelangelo's bust is as close as viewers would ever get to facing Michelangelo. Isn't that something—to stare into Michelangelo's "face"? Identify an artist who has both created art and who is the subject of art.

Excerpt of Ekphrastic Fiction: Salman Rushdie in his novel, *The Moor's Last Sigh* names the pictorial company with which the central painting is keeping, similar to the technique of painting the chair by painting what is not the chair:

> My mother painted *The Scandal*, I don't need to tell any art-lovers, since the huge canvas is right there in the National Gallery of Modern Art in New Delhi, filling up a whole wall. Go past Raja Ravi Verma's *Woman Holding a Fruit,* that young bejeweled temptress whose sidelong gaze of open sensuality reminds me of pictures of the young Aurora herself; turn the corner at Gaganendranath, Tagore's spooky water-colour *Jadooga (Magician)*, in which a monochrome Indian version of the distorted world of *The Cabinet of Dr Caligari* stands upon a shocking orange carpet (101–02).

Let's consider conceptual art and imagination. Sometimes, reading the artist's statement or the artwork plaque affixed to the wall can offer insight, helping the viewer to see beyond sight. Regarding Jorge Macchi's 1993 artwork, *Pillow and Glass*, the Tate Modern Museum plaque reads, "He works with everyday and ephemeral objects. This piece comprises a domestic pillow covered in a paisley pillowcase that has been wrapped in a shattered sheet of glass. He carefully controlled the shattering process so that the fractures coincide with the pillowcase's design. Themes of chance and violence." These concepts weren't precisely evident in the artwork; that is, until you read it. That little bit of information regarding his creative process was the nexus that lead me to consider chance and violence in other situations. Here is a brief freewrite on that conceptual art:

Ekphrastic Freewrite: (After Jorge Macchi's 1993 mixed media art piece, *Pillow and Glass*)

Similar to the fresh break of thin ice under one's shoe, see what the head has accomplished. A slight and careful weight and before you know it, you're resting your head on cut glass ready to shard-up and nick you, imminent violence upon a rest, a wakeless moment waking to blood and screams. But you've done this to yourself. You rested here without being mindful of the transparent risk.

Regarding accessibility, art museums are beginning to incorporate technology as a means by which art can be made accessible to individuals who are visually impaired. For instance, Madrid's Prado Museum, Rome's Ara Pacis Museum, and the Smithsonian have included 3-D replicas of some of their masterpieces wherein individuals can touch a canvas that has raised features, including fabric and other textures.

Writing Invitation: Settle on one piece of art that you have seen firsthand. Now, write about having that same experience with a visually impaired friend. Alternatively, visit a museum that offers the 3-D replica feature and see what creative writing you can make of that tactile adventure.

Creative Writing

The Carousel by Sonia Gechtoff delights me, though there is no companion ekphrastic poem or prose piece included in this book. What do you see? Beyond the literal image of two young boys beside a carousel, I see friendship and play. Sometimes, our affinity for an artwork can be as simple as, "Looking at this image contributes to my happiness."

Creative Process

Do people daydream anymore? Sitting still and casting their gaze out the window, lost in that temporary fugue-state feeling? Art-viewing can spark our creative writing just as inkblots have been used in psychologists' offices as a portal into a person's mind. Art making and art enjoying are two types of play. "Imagination is more important than knowledge," asserted Einstein. Who deigns to disagree with Einstein?

Any comprehensive lecture on the creative process will include the imagination, flow, meditation, the unconscious mind, Freud and Jung's psychologies, surrealism and automatism, brainstorming, clustering, free-association, freewriting, stream-of-consciousness, the deep-image, other types of springboards, and the like. As it pertains to ekphrastic writing, it is advisable to see where the artwork might take you, rather than how you might declare supremacy over the artwork. For, as Paul Valéry declared, "There is in you what is beyond you."

Joseph Campbell in describing the artist posited,

While his conscious mind stands amazed and empty before this phenomenon, he is overwhelmed by a flood of thoughts and images which he never intended to create and which his own will could never have brought into being. Yet despite himself he is forced to admit that it is his own self speaking, his own inner nature revealing itself and uttering things which he would never have entrusted to his tongue. He can only obey the apparently alien impulse within him and follow

146

Sonia Gechtoff's 1968 painting, *The Carousel* (image courtesy New Orleans Auction Galleries).

where it leads, sensing that his work is greater than himself, and wields power which is not his and which he cannot command (310).

Similar to the *high* that athletes experience, being creative can usher the writer (and the artist) into a *flow* state, defined by poet Jane Hirshfield as, "the moment willed effort falls away and we fall utterly into the object of our attention" (4). Flow is the goal, as "nothing is more injurious to immediate experience than cognition" (Jung).

Jung also opined about the spirit of *extraverted art*, where the writer abandons intention by wholly submitting to the object's demands. In this way, ekphrastic writers subvert their conscious agendas for the plethora of possibilities insisted on by an object, including the ease with which the writer can leap from an object to the universe (Campbell 311).

Suggested Listening: Mihaly Csikszentmihalyi's TED talk "Flow, the Secret to Happiness" *check this*

Especially for individuals new to creative writing, what is a technique that helps them to express their imagination on the page freely? I have found that most of my students respond well to the method of freewriting, which I was introduced to by a writer named Peter Elbow, author of, among many other books, *Writing Without Teachers*.

Elbow joins a long list of individuals that, together, have helped to demystify how people can be creative. First was the father of American psychology (and Henry James' brother), William James who described the flow of ideas as "stream-of-consciousness." It was Sigmund Freud's free-association techniques that illustrated access to the unconscious brain processes and signaled to people that we lack control over vital aspects of our mentality. French writer Apollinaire launched surrealism, with André Breton cultivating the movement seven years later with his manifesto, in which he defined surrealism as "pure psychic automatism" across disciplines, with "automatic writing" specific to literary artists. Concurrently, Carl Jung's theory of the unconscious mind was gaining traction. "The creation of something new isn't accomplished by the intellect but by the play instinct," Jung wrote. Ken Macrorie's 1951 essay, "Words in the Way" introduced Elbow to the method of freewriting. A decade before *Writing Without Teachers* was published, Judson Jerome, in his book, *The Poet and the Poem*, called the conscious type of thinking that people do when they are awake "straight thinking." This form of cognizance relies on external reality and intention. Inversely, Jerome's "stoned thinking," is attained through exercising the unconscious mind and relies on intuition and chance. From Richard Hugo's 1979 book, *The Triggering Town*, we learn it is the trigger or initiating subject that gets us to the page, but it is the bullet, or the true subject, that announces itself after we have busily scribbled down the first subject. Finally, the contribution of Natalie Goldberg's essay "First Thoughts" in her seminal 1986 *Writing Down the Bones* and Anne Lamott's "Shitty First Drafts" from her 1994 *Bird By Bird* emboldened the discussion. What all these thinkers agree on is this: writer's conscious intent and the writer's creative process are antagonistic.

Suggested Reading: Pattiann Rogers' poem, "Discovering Your Subject"

The distinction between writing and rewriting is beautifully shown in this excerpt of the "Freewriting Exercises" essay from Elbow's book: "The most effective way I know to improve your writing is to do freewriting exercises regularly.... The idea is simply to write for ten minutes.... Don't stop for anything. Go quickly without rushing. Never stop to look back to cross something out, to wonder how to spell something, to wonder what word or thought to use, or to think about what you are doing" (3).

Elbow continues: "The main thing about freewriting is that it is *nonediting*. It is an exercise in bringing together the process of producing words and putting them down on the page. Practiced regularly, it undoes the ingrained habit of editing at the same time you are trying to produce. It will make writing less blocked because words will come more easily" (6).

Writing Invitation: Take a quick glimpse at an artwork and freewrite (that is, writing quickly and without interruption) on your immediate response. Next, spend more time with the artwork and create a second freewrite. Excavate your loved lines from each freewrite and begin drafting a single piece of writing from those lines.

Suggested Reading: Frank O'Hara's poem, "Why I Am Not a Painter"

Some students of writing might disagree, but poet William Stafford in his essay, "A Way of Writing" pronounced that "A writer is not so much someone who has something to say as he is someone who has found a process that will bring about new things he would not have thought of if he had not started to say them. That is, he does not draw on a reservoir, instead, he engages in an activity that brings to him a whole succession of unforeseen stories, poems, essays, plays...." What are your thoughts?

Deep-Image

Take a look at Corot's landscape. What do you notice? Does it intrigue you? Do you feel invited into the scene? Is the place familiar to

Jean-Baptiste-Camille Corot's c. 1830 painting, *Houses Near Orléans* **(courtesy the Open Content Program at J. Paul Getty Museum).**

you? When the associative poet (that is, a writer whose work is driven by loose associations) selected this image from which to respond, the muse directed her to two distinctly different poems. Read each one, noticing the rich imagery and surprising associations:

House Near Orléans
(After Jean-Baptiste-Camille Corot)
by Judith Skillman

An august day—
no grasshoppers,
no black flies *en plein air*,
only stone-lipped eaves
and mustard-yellow fields.

A *samedi* like the others,
gift of the countryside outside Paris
after his father
gave up trying to make him a draper.
He wears the cornflower shirt,

linen stained ochre and umber
beneath a mortar and pestle sky.
Here he narrows the path,
curves it to shadow
as easily as gut strings

a violinist arrests with horsehair bow.
He does not say
O eternal summer,
come wearing your fragrant dress...
The path brightens

close to his easel. A glint of nacre
slices the topmost chimney.
A solitary shadow can court him,
coax him out from the studio
to find another bride.

Poet's Comments

After staring at Corot's painting for a few days that stretched to about three weeks, I felt as if I'd been captured. The first poem, "House Near Orléans," came in fragments. While doing some soft research, I learned that Corot's father did not want him to be a painter. This was not in and of itself surprising; what seemed more exciting was the fact that his father wanted him to follow the footsteps of a draper (cloth merchant), which is artistic in its own way. At the point I collected the fragments together, the lines "He does not say / *O eternal summer,* / come wearing your fragrant dress..." entered the poem from elsewhere, and I felt connected to the painting less as a victim (in that I "had" to write about it, or wanted to write about it but didn't know how) and more as an accomplice to the beauty of that vacant countryside (Judith Skillman).

Pinned to the Luminous
(After Jean-Baptiste-Camille Corot's *House Near Orléans*)
by Judith Skillman

We stare at the sky for so long it grows pearlescent. Until we are prisoners of the place. No one can enter the stone houses—*c'est interdit*. The path calls us to shade. We hover in the underbrush, double back, take to the furthest realm of disarray, return to a fixed station, as of the cross. René Char's Yvonne is not yet here, nor is the long stroke of summer lightning, nor the black flies, nor the grasshoppers. We stay and remember, lucky inmates. I for one walk the fields. The others are too shy, too reticent to trample such grasses and prefer to remain mute, spellbound and straightjacketed in a scentless *été*. The vigil begins when the chimneys cease to breathe. A certain ardor in the lush habitat lifts our eyelids, like a lover determined to show that he is not dangerous. We listen for a moment or a *siècle*. The spell cast by midi keeps us suspended, in bondage to the austere, yet inside the frame we twirl and whirl like reprimanded children. The stars will bloom tonight in soundless, scentless aspects of the *personnes dignes* we must become in order to return to such an *inviolé* countryside.

Poet's Comments

The prose poem "Pinned to the Luminous" emerged in a day. It felt as if I were taking dictation, as poet Anna Akhmatova describes so well in her book of selected prose, *My Half Century*: "X asked me whether it was difficult or easy to write poetry. I answered that when somebody dictates it to you it's easy, but that when there is nobody dictating—it's quite impossible." After writing this poem, I felt a great sense of release. It was as if I had truly entered the frame and been in the very countryside where Corot had set up his easel. The experience was mystical—as if I'd been inside both the place and the process of this heretofore pristine and forbidding, albeit beautiful, work. The place became populated with "us"—which included Yvonne, a woman from a René Char poem, various children, and adolescents seduced by first loves (Judith Skillman).

What ensnares the observer's attention and triggers a chain of associations? Discuss why the first poem required delineation, but the second poem required the prose form? Which associations most thrill you? Are there signature moments in each poem that hearken back to the single author? Given the image, what do you notice in terms of the poet's ekphrases? Which conventions did she employ?

In *Modern Painters*, Ruskin quipped about the susceptibility of the poets' imaginations:

> Hence it is, that poets, and men of strong feeling in general, are apt to be among the very worst judges of painting. The slightest hint is enough for them. Tell them that a white stroke means a ship, and a black stain, a thunderstorm, and they will be perfectly satisfied with both, and immediately proceed to remember all that they ever felt about ships and thunderstorms, attributing the whole current and fullness of their own feelings to the painter's work (350).

Do you find this assessment accurate, inaccurate, ironic, or humorous?

How can we access our imagination? In the article "The Heart and the Eye," J.T. Bushnell describes the differences between the brain's higher region ("left brain") and the lower region ("right brain"). The higher region is "in charge of secondary processes such as facts, math, logic, language rules, moral judgment—in other words, conscious thinking." While the lower region is "responsible for primary processes such as sensory input, movement, selective memory, and emotional response—the more automatic systems." In other words, this lower region drives our instinct, gut responses, and associative connections. To summarize how the two halves work concurrently: "As our upper brains are busy converting language into meaning, our lower brains are forming quick and automatic associations between the thing being described and the nature of the description."

The term "deep-image" comes from the school of thought that the experience of creating imagery formed from the unconscious mind (the deep place rather than the superficial conscious mind) can be the basis of meaning in a literary work. And, these deep-images can be garnered by anyone who is practiced at free-associating and who is proficient at leaping back and forth from the unconscious mind to the conscious mind quickly. Are you the type of writer who makes creative use of associations? And if so, how do you accomplish that? As Robert Bly wrote in *Leaping Poetry*, it's the processes of leaping back and forth from the conscious mind to the unconscious mind (1). Deep-imagery, cultivated in the unconscious mind, is subsequently unencumbered by realism, as compared to images spawned from the conscious mind and chained in reality. In the section of this book on technology and ekphrasis, I will discuss this idea again in terms of a notional image versus an actual image.

Let's deep-dive into the brain; imagine a division between the hemispheres:

Left	Right
Immediate awareness	Awareness not directly accessible
Better at language communication	Better at visual imagery
Motivated by what it knows	Motivated by what it experiences
Sees exactly what it expects	Open to the connectedness of things
External reality and awake state	Intuition and dream state
Dominated by the censor	Directed by freedom
Intention, will, proscription	Accidents, chance, speculation
The conscious mind	The unconscious mind
Portion of the iceberg above the waterline	Portion of the iceberg below the waterline

Given the differences between the two parts, can you deduce that to be imaginative, we need to be able to summon the right brain? It is true that during our waking hours, we toggle back and forth from the left brain to the right brain. Take, for example, the fact that our ability to recall images happens effortlessly and rapidly, as compared to our ability to communicate in words. To illustrate this type of leaping, as well as the fact that that the visual precedes the verbal, take a moment to answer this question: Where do you keep your sweaters? Articulate your answer aloud.

So, what's your answer?

Hanging in a closet? In a plastic bin under your bed? Folded in a dresser drawer? Before you answered out loud, did you picture that specific sweater location? Asked another way, which came first, the image or the words?

Your imaginative writing will spring forth from given stimuli that you find most provocative. Ekphrastic writers find infinite possibilities from what they see, but that can require some excavating. How deep and how far is up to you; the farther you dig, the further you will go.

Excerpt of Ekphrastic Nonfiction: To whom or what do artists have an allegiance? "The imagination is always right," insisted Ruskin (336). In the readers guide to *Guide to Girl in Hyacinth Blue*, Susan Vreeland speaks on her relationship with her muse: "This is the province and privilege of the writer, to let those concrete things that move us feed our imagination until we find meaning in them" (4).

Verbal Imagery

Does any experience we have begin with one of our bodily senses? Physical sensation portrayed in literature is physically stimulating. Author Joseph Conrad explained,

> My task which I am trying to achieve is, by the power of the written word, to make you hear, to make you feel—it is, before all, to make you *see*. That—and no more, and it is everything. If I succeed, you shall find there according to your deserts: encouragement, consolation, fear, charm—all you demand; and, perhaps, also that glimpse of truth for which you have forgotten to ask (Updike 199).

What do you know about the power of sensory observations? Well, it has something to do with verbal imagery.

There are nine modes of imagery: visual, auditory, olfactory, gustatory, tactile, kinetic (objects in motion), kinesthetic (humans or animals in motion), organic (bodily experiences such as thirst, hunger, pain, intuition, and physical exhaustion), and synesthesia (fusion of two different sense experiences). Since senses comprise so much of the human experience, it's typically agreed that the mark of successful literary writing relates to the writer's aptitude for verbal imagery. W.J.T. Mitchell explained, "Effective rhetoric is ... two-pronged strategy of verbal/visual persuasion, showing while it tells, illustrating its claims with powerful examples, making the listener *see* and not merely *hear*" (Faigley et al. x). Are these goals that you have for your own creative writing? If imagery is a struggle for you, I suggest you read Robert Olen Butler's *From Where You Dream*, in which he challenged writers to record an event that evoked emotion and to begin writing about that event "moment to moment through the senses" (28).

Writing Invitation: Select an artwork to freewrite on in which only descriptions of smells, taste, sounds, and tactile stimuli are created. In other words, rather than allowing the visual to dominate your writing, notice what discoveries result from focusing on your other senses.

Poetry

What is the role of the poet? Aristotle maintained: "[I]t is not the function of the poet to relate what has happened, but what may happen—what is possible according to the law of probability of necessity ... for poetry tends to express the universal." What are the ways in which you agree or disagree with Aristotle? Is poetry vital in your community?

On occasion, I have heard individuals describe both a visual artist and his work as "poetic." How can a piece of visual art be poetic? Does it need to incorporate poetry onto its canvas for that classification? Does it need to exploit poetic devices such as rhythm, symbolism, or metaphor in order to be called "poetic"? So, if a visual artist can be poetic (poet-like) and visual works-of-art can be poetic (poem-like), then what painterly qualities, for example, can be said of poets and poems?

Are the critics of ekphrasis misinformed, and it was really the painters who envied the verbal talents of writers? Alpers in *The Art of Describing: Dutch Art in the Seventeenth Century* teaches us that,

> To call a picture descriptive at the time was unusual since description was a term commonly applied to texts. From antiquity on, the Greek term for description, *ekphrasis*, was the rhetorical term used to refer to a verbal evocation of people, places, buildings, or works of art. As a rhetorical device *ekphrasis* depended specifically on the power of words. It was this verbal power that Italian artists in the Renaissance strove to equal in paint when they rivaled the poets (136).

How do both artists and writers create work that's both specific to their experiences (either personally or invented) and general enough for universal appeal? The art of presenting specificity is a concern for artists of all types. Keep in mind, though, "Our senses note only particulars. We never see color, we see particular *colors*; we never just touch, we touch *something*" (Nims 11). Goldberg, in *Writing Down the Bones*, explores the power of naming and specificity: "Things, too, have names. It is much better to say 'the geranium in the window' than the 'flower in the window.' 'Geranium'—that one word gives us a much more specific picture. It penetrates more deeply into the beingness of that flower. It immediately gives us the scene by the window—red petals, green circular leaves, all straining toward sunlight" (70).

Excerpt of Ekphrastic Nonfiction: Here, in William's *Leap*, is an example of precision of language and specificity: "I take down my binoculars and let them dangle around my neck. The guards are staring. I open my notebook and make a checklist of all the birds seen so far in *El jardín de las delicias.*

Swifts
Scarlet Ibis
Great White Egret
Little Egret
Wagtail
Blue Rock Thrush
Cuckoo
Spoonbill...." (17)

As stated in the introduction, the primary genre for ekphrasis has been poetry. One reason is the ease of designation. When a poem (which is often shorter than prose) takes an artwork as its subject and dedicates much time to describing the artwork, it is natural to call the work "ekphrastic poetry." Contrarily, while prose might feature an artwork and treat that subject descriptively, rarely does an entire prose piece revolve around a work-of-art. So, while there might exist some ekphrastic moments, it would be unwise to call the writing "ekphrastic prose." Research for this book uncovered only a handful of books, stories, and essays that could rightfully be called entire works of ekphrasis.

Excerpt of Ekphrastic Poem: Look at the opening lines of Patricia Hampl's ekphrastic poem, "Woman before an Aquarium," which was influenced by Henri Matisse's painting of the same name (to which Hampl also wrote a memoir): "The goldfish ticks silently; / little finned gold watch on its chain of water..."

Writing Invitation: Notice how Hampl evokes sound with "silently" along with the "watch" metaphor. Move beyond visual imagery, and determine which sounds exist inside an artwork. Alternatively, describe the absence of sound.

What is poetry, and how does it differ from prose?

1. Poetry from the Greek *poiesis*, "making" or "creating."
2. This definition from Plutarch, "Painting is silent poetry, and poetry, speaking painting."
3. And, from Horace, "Ut pictura poesis," translated as, "as in painting, so in poesy."
4. Samuel Taylor Coleridge wrote that poetry is "the right words in the right order," though, isn't that also true of prose writing?
5. Poetry is more refined, structured, and rhythmic than prose and is organized in stanzas (that is, through the employment of line breaks). However, many poets dispense with line breaks and stanzas, and prose writers sometimes use rhythm and unconventional structure in their work.
6. Poet Mina Loy espoused: "Poetry is prose bewitched, a music made of visual thoughts, the sound of an idea."
7. If you are writing something where each line focuses on lyricism and imagery, and you do not need to employ entire sentences to get your point across but rather your writing relies on pithy, powerful sounds and pictures, then you are more than likely writing poetry.
8. T.S. Eliot eloquently wrote that "Poetry is not a turning loose of emotion, but an escape from emotion; it is not the expression of personality, but an escape from personality."
9. "Painting is Poetry which is seen and not heard and Poetry is a painting which is heard and not seen," clarified Leonardo da Vinci.
10. Butler differentiates two genres thusly: "Fiction is a temporal art form. Fiction exists in time. Poems, by contrast, are very condensed objects, virtually exempt from time. A poem may capture a fleeting momentary impulse; and the length of a line is usually a part of its essential form, so the poem is also an object on the page" (39).

What is your definition of poetry? What specific literary devices distinguish your writing as a certain genre? Do you create hybrid works? Be open to artwork that might beg you to create cross-genre writing.

Suggested Reading: Aristotle's *Poetics*

In all genres of creative writing, figurative language can be used to connect ideas in fresh and surprising ways. Some types of figurative language are ripe for use in ekphrastic poems:

metaphor	metonymy
simile	allegory
allusion	onomatopoeia
personification	hyperbole
paradox	understatement
symbolism	overstatement

Excerpt of Ekphrastic Fiction: Consider how well this extended ekphrastic simile from Julian Barnes' novel is functioning: "The figures on the raft are like the waves: beneath them, yet also through them, surges the energy of the ocean. Were they painted in lifelike exhaustion they would be mere dribbles of spume rather than formal conduits" (136–137).

Excerpt of Ekphrastic Nonfiction: In his essay, "Listening," John Edgar Wideman divides William Sidney Mount's *Walking the Line* into three comparable parts:

> The artist composed his picture as a kind of triptych: a dominant, highlighted central panel, balanced by two wings. The left-hand panel stretches outward towards the viewer and a light source exterior to the painting.... The right wing recedes to a shadowed alcove where the even darker mass of the negro man is planted in a corner, the area most distant from where the painting positions the viewer (Hirsch 67).

Suggested Viewing: Francis Bacon's diptychs and triptychs paintings

Write Invitation: Find an artwork with two or three panels and use figurative language to compare them. Attempt to link the parts through comparisons that yield a larger narrative.

The quality of sound is one level on which we measure poetry. Poetry is best experienced in the mouth, for the pleasure of both the mouth and the ears. Reading a poem, then, should feel like a line-by-line discovery. How well do you evoke sound in your poems? Do you compose your poem aloud during the creative process in order to select the best mode of sound, such as assonance, consonance, alliteration, rhyme?

Suggested Reading: André Breton's poem, "La Liberté d'Amour"

Writing Invitation: Locate artwork that incorporates elements of repetition. Write a type of formal poem that utilizes repetition (for example, sestina, villanelle, ghazal) or write a poem with parallelism. Alternatively, find artwork that stirs in you an interest in working with sound.

Writing Invitation: Discover artwork that concerns music and write a lyric, a blues poem, a chant, or a ballad. A musical composition influenced by art, and aptly called, "Pictures at an Exhibition," is a suite of ten pieces composed for piano by Russian composer Modest Mussorgsky in 1874.

Suggested Reading: Siglind Bruhn's nonfiction book, *Musical Ekphrasis: Composers Responding to Poetry and Painting*

Here is the corresponding poem influenced by Millsent Connor's embroidered silk on linen, *Embroidered Sampler*. Notice how the poem of couplets begins with ekphrasis and is extended through association, all while weaving and redoubling the imagery:

Mourning, Thread on Silk
by Nicole Cooley

Clouds scalloped white as the collar of a girl's Sunday dress—
banner below the sky: *Millsent Connor, Her Work Aged Ten Boston 1799.*

In her sampler, silk on linen, everything is paired. Woman stands
in a doorway. Woman walking on a path. Two men. Animals:

a horse and a dog. Double rows of pink potted flowers. Two houses
starred with branches. Two birds backstitched into the air. I picture the girl,

a daughter, bent over cloth in a kitchen chair, alone. A first small knot
will be a rose along the border. Her mother is seven days dead.

Lace filling stitch: now this girl threads red brick to build a house
she will never live in. There are no daughters in this new world. Also

no mothers. Only women dressed in white, waiting. Reversible stitch:
I can't understand the symmetry so I invent a story. All knots.

All tying off of thread. When I imagine a world—single
satin stitch—why do I always return to mother and daughter?

To the word *bereft*? To the daughter after a mother's death?
Silk on linen. I backstitch to this girl, to her past, to doubled

blooming plants, as she sits dizzy and untethered, studying
her work. In silence. What does it mean to be *bereaved*

and why do I imagine her so? Bereft meaning also: *deprived or robbed.*
Yet we are all of course untethered. Fishbone stitch. We all wait

for grief. We all walk out on a path to nothing. Meanwhile in the kitchen,
a girl wishes herself two. Silk and linen. Spill of dirt.

Writing Invitation: Unearth artwork that treats death, dying, bereavement, or grief. Create a series of epitaphs, an elegy, an ode, or an eulogy.

Both the visual arts and the literary arts are opportunities for multicultural exchanges, and a preponderance of the arts embrace others' cultures as well as highlight their own in the process of making art. Though, the openness of artists has not always been celebrated. I discovered a poster from the 1950s anti-communist regime that broadcast this caution: "Beware of artists. They mix with all classes of society and are therefore the most dangerous."

Suggested Reading: Cynthia Macdonald's 12-part tanka, "Mary Cassatt's Twelve Hours in the Pleasure Quarter," which takes cultural cues from the artwork and uses those cues as elements of the poetic form.

Writing Invitation: Identify an artwork in which another culture is represented. Research the poetic traditions of the culture and incorporate some aspect of that knowledge into your piece. For example, write in the Japanese tradition of the tanka or haiku. Alternatively, find artwork in which a culture you are not familiar with is represented, or write a poem that incorporates another language.

Excerpt of Ekphrastic Nonfiction: From Guy Davenport's essay collection *The Geography of the Imagination*, whose excerpt was influenced by Grant Wood's painting, *American Gothic*, here is an example of an author using references to other cultures: "We can see a bamboo sunscreen—out of China by way of Sears Roebuck—that rolls up like a sail: nautical technology applied to the prairie. We can see that distinctly American feature, the screen door. The sash-windows are European in origin, their glass panes from Venetian technology as perfected by the English..." (12).

Writing Invitation: Explore artwork that concerns a political subject, an aspect of social justice, or a disenfranchised people. Write an event, insult, or protest poem, or write a satire or parody.

Suggested Viewing: Irma Stern's painting, *Watusi Policemen*

Writing Invitation: Discover art that depicts your cultural traditions. Are you compelled to write a lyrical poem, a narrative, or a personal experience? Alternatively, find art that illustrates some problem that exists in your society.

We have seen two ekphrastic poems on the same image by a single poet. Now, here is one of two poems by different poets that took influence from Sandy Skoglund's *Babies at Paradise Pond*. Notice the not-knowing beginning, the use of simile, and the surprising philosophical musings:

Babies at Paradise Pond
(lithograph by Sandy Skoglund)
by Kim Addonizio

I don't know what to make of these scary babies
Pale babies naked on their backs flailing in the grass
crawling & staggering baldly around

like abortions swarming in a dream, full-grown & dead-eyed
like newly molting cockroach nymphs flushed out of hiding

like a medieval brochure for Baby Limbo
On the Banks of Pristine Paradise Pond:
As Close as They Can Get to the Beatific Vision!

They look like dolls dropped from outer space
by a giant petulant girl creature with twenty-six arms

throwing up her twenty-six hands all at once, then running out of the galaxy
& slamming it behind her

A picture of so many babies should be happy & maybe it is for some people
if they don't look too closely
which is the only way I know how to truly be happy
Things look so much better in the subaqueous glow of the bar
   on a third glass of wine
I love the world most when I can barely make out what's going on out there

The little dog down at the edge of the pond might be licking that baby
or eating it

Even the grownups are scary, gazing out over the water
toward the dispirited trees & the invisible source of the light

Creepy pre-birth or post-death light
Spaceship tractor beam of the many-armed mother
picking up all the toys

Oh as usual all I can see is time & death
Everything is already lost
& not coming back

    This second companion poem to Skoglund's image is conversational in tone, which creates a sense of intimacy. Note the use of internal repetitions (within lines) and internal rhymes. While it would be natural to compare this poem to the one we just read, as with translations of literature and musical covers, it might be prudent to simply enjoy another poet's take on the same image rather than evaluating each one given the other:

Border Vermillion
(photo, Sandy Skoglund, *Babies at Paradise Pond*)
by Laura McCullough

Wanting to write about innocence, I sidled up to chaos, the tumble

of wounded children inside myself, generations
of trauma rolling downhill in hysterical laughter. A playground
of hidden shame, grief, abandonings. When I looked

at the broken and unformed children inside of you, their inherited stories,
the ones inside of me wanted to take their hands, say,
I forgive. But these children aren't to be trusted, unreliable narrators
of their ethereal, purgatorial lives. They bite. Mine,
as well as yours. I'm sitting now at the base of a green hill, my back
to the mysterious pond of the future, arms wide, yelling,
You can do it, but can you forgive that I don't trust anyone right now?
All of us like ambulatory babies run amuck.
Wanting. Wanting. Wanting. No sense of the other. Innocence can be
dangerous when coupled with selfish need.

And with fear. I'm thinking, of course, of you.
And of myself. How willingly you lied to get what you wanted. How willing

I was to deceive myself: it wasn't possible; I declared,
I believe in you. Who knew goodness hides a shadow? Everyone. The Greeks.

The heart has many chambers, and the line

between the lips and face grows less distinct with age, perhaps like borders
between love and loathing, and the heart

a dark pond under the surface of which something roils. Lips made of soft tissue
are not unlike baby skin, and the twin tips
of the cupid's bow is disarming, yet charm only goes so far when deviousness
is discernible underneath. Once a man told me
he could see the wounds in my past by the way I held my mouth, a tightness

in the lips that belied possible cruelty.
In my dreams I have three babies, but with only these two hands, there is constant

fear: one of them is bound to drown.

I hope that the lessons gleaned from studying different poets' approaches to the same image is as easily as feeling welcome to enter the ekphrastic conversation. For example, read Peter Cooley's poem and Anne Sexton's poem, both called "The Starry Night" influenced by Vincent van Gogh's painting, *The Starry Night.* Also, the DeCillis & Gillet anthology, *Mona Poetica,* boasts nearly fifty writers who have written ekphrastic poems on Leonardo da Vinci's painting, *Mona Lisa,* including William Blake and Christina Georgina Rossetti, as well as visual artist Agnes Martin. Now, would you like to contribute to the conversation by writing your own poems to *The Starry Night* and *Mona Lisa*?

Nonfiction

Let's consider nonfiction in the visual arts. Beyond veracity, have you experienced nonfiction in art that's similar to nonfiction in literature, wherein it feels artful and imaginative, but it is factual, verifiable? Can entire works-of-art be nonfiction or only certain aspects? Under the auspices of nonfiction, there is confessional art, art that depicts historical events, realistic landscapes, and photojournalism, to name a few. Rilke wrote, "One is tempted to explain the work of art in this way: as a profoundly interior confession that is released under the pretext of a memory, an experience, or an event, and that can exist on its own when thus detached from its creator" (Baer 140).

Here are Dorothy Allison's thoughts on the function of art: "I took the notion that art should surprise and astonish, and hopefully make you think something you had not thought until you saw it." What are the ways in which you agree and disagree with Allison? Take Sally Mann's photography of her three children: what qualities of that image render

SALLY MANN *Emmett, Jessie and Virginia,* **1989 Silver gelatin print, 8 ×
10 inches, (20.3 × 25.4 cm) and 20 × 24 inches, (50.8 × 60.9 cm) Edition
of 25. © Sally Mann. Courtesy Gagosian.** *Image courtesy of the Museum of
Fine Arts, Houston*

it artful? Perhaps the essence of the Mann image is, as Rilke said, that
"Things look back at us once we have learned to look at them, enabling
a mutual recognition process that gives way to human self-awareness"
(Strathausen 27).

Writing Invitiation: Discover art that echoes the spirit of these
words by Jane Hirshfield: "You cannot leap beyond human consciousness
without first going through it; but if you gaze deeply enough into being,
eventually you will awaken into the company of everything" (140).

Memory: Is remembering an activity? Is forgetting an activity? How
do we forget—for voluntary and involuntary reasons? In *Memory* by Jonathan K. Foster, he describes that the brain's process involves encoding
information (receiving stimulation), storing those memories over a period
of time, and retrieving (recalling) that stored information (25). Freewriting can be a method by which the writer calls up latent memories, for
it is often when we stop trying to force memories that memories freely
announce themselves.

Recall the function of mirror neurons: Given real pain and pain that's imagined, the brain, in terms of stimulating pain receptors, knows no difference. The same can be said of memories: "there is no completely reliable way of distinguishing between 'real' and 'imagined' memories" (Foster 72–73). The painter Salvador Dali wrote, "The difference between false memories and true ones is the same as for jewels: it is always the false ones that look the most real, the most brilliant."

Writing Invitation: Pair the notion of "seeing is believing" with "seeing is not believing." Or pair "the longer I look at the artwork, the more I trust" with "the longer I look at the artwork, the more I distrust." Alternatively, select artwork and compose ekphrastic nonfiction in which everything is a lie.

Let's consider Marcel Proust's "Involuntary memory" wherein a benign action such as dumping pebbles out of your shoes can elicit a vivid memory. Also, his notion of "creative wrong memory" can be highly useful to the nonfiction writer. Rather than feeling stymied about the things you cannot remember, start by listing those things that are blurry in your memory and build the narrative by conjoining what you can envision with what you cannot quite recall.

Writing Invitation: Discover art that stirs within you interest in exploring "creative wrong memory." Here are some ideas for merging the known with the unknown in your freewrite: know/don't know, remember/don't recall, understand/never understood, believe/can't believe, see/never saw, and hear/didn't hear.

Is your voice not merely yours alone? In addition to the personal, some theorists believe that as a species, we hold collective memories and ideas. Jung posited, "[W]e have an intuitive, inborn knowledge of the collective stories of human experience." Can you imagine that beyond the individual, private experiences, our brains might also house a collective domain, cultural memory? Do you subscribe to ancestral memory? How might these beliefs inform the works-of-art that you attend to and the words that you ascribe to those experiences? Moreover, Jung held that "The impact of an archetype ... stirs us because it summons up a voice that is stronger than our own" (Campbell 321).

Writing Invitation: Given that Jung insisted that we hold the knowledge of the collective stories of the human experience, discover an artwork that either represents for you the collective unconscious or that stirs within you a need to write from the place of ancestral memory.

Here is the ekphrastic flash-nonfiction piece which was informed by the image, *Radha, the Beloved of Krishna*, in which the image seemed to spark a personal memory for the writer. What craft elements can you appreciate? Might this piece be called metaekphrasis?

Radha
by Sayantani Dasgupta

I learned about Radha from my grandmother. She was a wonderful storyteller, and I, at four, was hungry for tales of gods and beasts, princesses and talking parrots. Radha is a goddess. She is the beloved of Krishna, not perhaps his wife, but very much his consort and best friend. Unlike some of the other Hindu goddesses though, Radha, neither marches on enemies nor vanquishes demons. She has a practical job. She is a milkmaid. Did she and Krishna become friends because of his legendary love for butter? He stole, she admonished, so on, and so forth? I like to imagine that they fell in love because unlike others, he truly saw her work, the churning, churning, churning, the hard labor, the painstaking repetition. He acknowledged her work, and through it, he acknowledged her.

Indian art is rife with depictions of Radha and Krishna as a couple. I like this one where she is by herself, her hands and words caught in mid-sentence, perhaps giving directions, perhaps caught by the artist in a moment of self-reflection.

My grandparents were married for sixty-five years until his death. Right until the day he stopped working, my grandmother followed the same routine every evening. She would wash her face; rub in moisturizer; dab talcum powder to stay dry in Calcutta's monsoon-sticky heat; brush, coconut-oil and pin her hair; and change into a fresh sari. Once, I asked her, why. She said, "For your grandfather. He likes to see me this way." It was the first time I understood it means something to be seen.

Were my grandparents best friends? I can't answer that. I never saw them hold hands, or kiss, or hug. They were traditional in many ways. But I know my grandmother never deviated from her evening routine, and my grandfather supported her other loves—writing, music, solo traveling. Seeing, seeing, seeing.

One byproduct of ekphrastic writing can be self-investigation: a means of unconscious reflection whereby we are sparked by art which begets our own art. As Winterson wrote, "True art, when it happens to us, challenges the 'I' that we are" (15).

Excerpt of Ekphrastic Nonfiction: An illustration of nonfiction and the treatment of the photographic image, in which the privilege of not being temporally confined can be appreciated, is Judith Kitchen's ekphrastic memoir, *Half in Shade: Family, Photography, and Fate.* Notice especially the intersection of the past tense and future tense: "How did he ever get to be somebody's uncle? Here he is, sitting like any good six-month-old.... His christening dress covers his tiny clubfoot so here you can't tell that he'll never walk right" (18).

Writing Invitation: Select a piece of art from your own collection (a photograph or an artwork that hangs on your wall) and, again, allow your writing to unite any duality (or duplicity) of your choosing: known/unknown, remembered/forgotten, comprehensible/incomprehensible, believing/the incredulous, seen/not seen, or heard/never heard. Alternatively, read Jane Kenyon's poem, "Otherwise," and compose a "what could have been" flash-nonfiction piece.

Consider the confessional mode as a rhetorical device. What is more important to readers: what writers say or how they say it? A writer can take a confessional tone without actually confessing much of anything, right? One issue insofar as the reader-writer relationship is concerned is reader entitlement. For example, if readers know definite things about writers' backgrounds, and then those writers refer to the contrary in one of their writings, do we as readers feel slighted? It is problematic when readers assume a level of allegiance to the truth of the writer's life, wouldn't you say? "Confessional" poet Anne Sexton announced, "I often confess to things that never happened." Also, writer Victor Hugo insisted, "When I speak to you about myself, I am speaking to you about yourself. How is it you don't see that?"

Writing Invitation: Find an artwork that seems to be a companion to William Carlos Williams' poem, "This is Just to Say," and write a piece in which you apologize for something you have done or something you have never done.

Besides using the fine arts to prompt you to the page, any object will do. For example, if you aim to write a memoir about a friend who died, study his urn, your correspondence with him, his baseball cap, or photographs. Both art and writing can probe our past, thereby teaching us our mysteries.

Writing Invitation: Artist Wassily Kandinsky expressed that "Everything that is dead quivers. Not only the things of poetry, stars, moon, wood, flowers, but even a white trouser button glittering out of a puddle in the street.... Everything has a secret soul, which is silent more often than it speaks." Uncover the secret soul in an artwork and let that discovery reveal things about you or the story you are compelled to tell.

Writing Invitation: Write a series of letters to a single artist. The tone can be praiseworthy, confrontational, accusatory, or questioning (to name a few options). Read Rilke's *Letters on Cézanne*.

Writing Invitation: Locate an artwork that begs you to write within a specific structure or framework. Ideas include the use of repetition and refrains, the use of the outline format, the heavy use of a modals (would, will, could, can, should, shall), the exclusive use of fragments, or use of the cause/effect construct.

Suggested Reading: Pam Houston's novel, *Contents May Have Shifted*

Writing Invitation: Consider the Irish proverb, "There's nothing so bad that it couldn't be worse," and recall a tragedy from your life. Now, compare it with a piece of art in which something "worse" is depicted. Compose a piece that treats both subjects.

Excerpt of Ekphrastic Nonfiction: Here is an example of how the nonfiction writer Jericho Parms unites ekphrases with personal recollections, in which she moves seamlessly from artist Degas to her childhood memory: "Degas's bronze is polished, near black. The light catches the horse's muscular limbs, like white wax on obsidian, the patent leather shoes I wore as a girl in the city, or the riding boots I packed when we traveled west to Grandfather's ranch..." (3).

Excerpt of Ekphrastic Nonfiction: Here is another illustration from that same memoir, *Lost Wax*, in which the author relayed moments of art observation and personal musings:

> I would sit before a small reproduction of Matisse's *The Red Studio* that hung in my parent's bedroom.... For the longest time, I thought Matisse's studio must be a room in a dollhouse—somewhere the Queen herself might reside. Awash in Venetian red, the canvas depicts what the artist must have seen before him as he worked—a still-life of propped paintings and sculptures (87).

Excerpt of Ekphrastic Nonfiction: The uniting of artist-related facts with the autobiographical can be as effortless as situating one sentence next to another, as in this example from Mary Gordon's "Still Life": "Bonnard painted from memory. I am afraid of my own. It has proved undependable" (58).

Writing Invitation: Discover art that prompts you to make connections to your own life, and utilize the pleasure of moving back and forth through time. Flashback to yourself as a child. Flash forward to yourself as an older person. Recall specific life events, rites-of-passage, times of joy, or sorrow. Given the infinite works-of-art with which you could engage, consider what the compositions, details, the artist's life or the tools and techniques remind you of.

Excerpt of Ekphrastic Fiction: Rushdie's protagonist in *The Moor's Last Sigh* talks about the real subject of his mother's artwork: "And the painting they found on her easel was about me. In that last work, The Moor's Last Sigh, she gave the Moor back his humanity. This was no abstract harlequin, no junkyard collage. It was a portrait of her son, lost in limbo like a wandering shade" (315).

Writing Invitation: Find an artwork that most viewers believe is a fictional person but that you believe is you; it is a portrait that you never sat for.

Writing Invitation: Compare an actual family photograph to one that was never taken, but might have been. Describe both photographs— the real (actual) and the imagined one (notional)—in detail.

Suggested Viewing: Vanessa Bell's 1943 interior painting, *The Memoir Club*

Writing Invitation: Philosopher Alfred North Whitehead elucidated, "We think in generalities but we live in detail." Think about where you were when some major national or international event occurred. Locate artwork that relates in some way to that event. Write an essay that draws a parallel between an event in your life and the way that event is depicted in art.

Writing Invitation: What art hung in your childhood home? Which images have been imprinted on you? What is your most beloved artwork? Embark on a series of freewrites on that single work-of-art. Write every day for at least seven consecutive days. It is curious to see that, even though we might feel that we have exhausted a subject, more can be revealed to us the more we are poised to receive it.

Writing Invitation: Ponder Aristotle's words: "Since the poet is an imitator just like a painter or any other image-maker, he must necessarily imitate things one of three ways: the way in which they are; the way in which they are said or thought to be; or the way they ought to be." Settle on a single artwork. Freewrite three times on this single art in the vein of Aristotle: how the artwork is, how the art is thought to be, and how the artwork ought to be. Alternatively, look at three artworks with similar subject matter (people in an interior, for example). Compare and contrast and then compose one piece that unites objective with subjective observations.

Suggested Viewing: Johannes Vermeer's painting, *Woman Reading a Letter*

Writing Invitation: Identify an artwork that appears to be a tribute to a loved one (or a beloved animal, object, or place). Compose a love note that would accompany the artwork. Alternatively, find art in which travel, correspondence, or time is its subject, and compose a corresponding travelogue.

Writing Invitation: Carroll in *Read This If You Want to Take Great Photographs* wrote, "Very often, nothing kills an image more than keeping your distance" (19). Discover artwork that sparks in you a feeling of distance. Freewrite on this feeling and what in the artwork elicits it.

Fiction

In addition to ruminating on artwork to help drive us to the page, using the visual arts as a vehicle to assist us in finishing a non-ekphrastic work-in-progress is another method by which writers can benefit by viewing art. Once you have become more familiar with global fine arts, it will be easier for you to find specific work to assist you with your specific goals. For instance, what are the ways in which an individual artwork can help you with building a character? Or, what artwork can assist you with the conflict, complications of conflict, crisis, and resolution in a story?

Fiction is any narrative that springs from the imagination, and "is ultimately the art of human yearning" (Butler). It is your responsibility to locate the story in artwork: As explained in this book's introduction, your ekphrastic story can concern the artist, the artwork, or the act of viewing the piece. Allow for organic moments of discovery, though. If you are receptive to the story, the story will find you, although it might not be the story you had ever intended on writing.

Let's consider storytelling in the visual arts: Locating stories in art might be the most accessible way to compose ekphrastic fiction. Which artwork are you familiar with that conveys story? Many literary subgenres of fiction can also be found in the visual arts: magical realism, historical fiction, speculative fiction, and gothic fiction, to name a few.

The world's first complete visual story, composed by King Ashurbanipal of the Neo-Assyrian Empire (c. 668–627 BCE), was a series of stone reliefs that told a story of his war and was composed visually (rather than in a language) so that the illiterate could enjoy the story as well. Also of note is the c. 113 AD story-monument in Rome, Italy. The Trajan's Column commemorates victory in the Dacian Wars, and it is composed of thousands of characters and complex scenes and reaches over 100 feet. Both visual artists and literary artists can delight in the craft elements of this stone tale (Hedgecoe).

Writing Invitation: Art-making is a complex series of decisions. In the choice of hues, in the objects portrayed, in the brushstrokes. Write a fiction piece on the art of writing fiction. Alternatively, write an ekphrastic story that's conscious of its limitations as an ekphrasis, in which readers might see the artwork and hold opinions about the narrative and its details. Let voice drive the piece.

Writing Invitation: Write either a dramatic monologue about a subject who knows he/she is immortalized in an artwork or in which the subject has no idea he/she is the subject for art.

Writing Invitation: Use the detail in an artwork that depicts another time, and write a story in that particular time as authentically as possible.

Writing Invitation: Use an artwork to activate a story but write the opposite of what you see. What is the opposite of an interior? The opposite of a decorative vase? The opposite of a smoking cigar?

Writing Invitation: Spot art in which someone is depicted as speaking, or in which you can imagine that someone is speaking. Create a dialogue that answers, among other things, who is speaking, who is listening or responding, and what is the occasion.

Writing Invitation: Identify at least three works-of-art that make prominent an object that you can relate to. For instance, a doll, a type of machine, a musical instrument, or a basket of flowers. What do the objects in this artwork imply about how space is used and by whom? Use these objects to create an interior or exterior scene.

Here is an ekphrastic flash-fiction piece that's a response to the Marie Denise Villers' painting, *Marie Joséphine Charlotte du Val d'Ognes*. Note the treatment of the absence and how the repetition builds. How does the form and content of this prose piece relate to the form and content of the artwork?

Record
(After Marie Denise Villers)
by Lynn Crawford

I lose my close family and a distant aunt gets me a position at the castle. Not a real position. Not scrubbing floors, washing pots, or changing bedding. Not caring for children, embroidering and taking long walks with the sisters, or listening to the mother. No handsome young man eyes me. I am allowed. To stay. Not a person of interest.

At first I float, sadly, craving an anchor. Then begin watching others, carefully, hoping no one feels the intrusion.

Not one of them notices me, so I look at them more. Separately and together. And learn who creeps out of bedrooms late at night, who spits in the stew, who rides a horse at the same time daily to a remote, private, wooded area, who dispatches letters to the next estate. Every day I watch, fact find, learn. Every day I sketch my view, piling up reams of documentation, (whispers, smiles, screams, skirts, tears, throats, kisses, furrowed brows). And learn a valuable lesson: sometimes it is better to document than participate—it brings a special form of power.

Writing Invitation: Select an artwork in which you can appreciate a shifting points-of-view. Write a story in which you start with one point-of-view (the artist's, for example), and then you switch to one figure's point-of-view, to an object's point-of-view, and back again.

Writing Invitation: Having trouble fleshing-out one of your characters in a non-ekphrastic piece of fiction? Discover that person in a piece of art and begin with a literal description. Alternatively, construct a narrative from the point-of-view of a minor character depicted in a work-of-art.

Writing Invitation: Having trouble with a setting in a work-in-progress? Select an artwork in which you can study an interior or exterior landscape. Locate your story's setting in a picture and begin with simple descriptions.

Writing Invitation: Divulge something about one of your characters by having that character refer to a masterpiece. Let that character's description be idiosyncratic or plot-revealing. Alternatively, write a story in which multiple characters react to the same piece of art. What would each see? What would each person overlook or ignore? What memories or projections into the future might emerge in each character's encounter with the artwork?

Writing Invitation: Imagine you found a particular artwork in a thrift shop. Why hadn't someone already purchased it? Imagine the life it had before you found it. Who owned it? What role did that artwork have in the person's life? Imagine why it was discarded.

Let's consider implicit action in the visual arts. As a writer, do you assume the artwork's stasis or do you imbue the object with action? While most ekphrastic writing seems to settle on inertia, imagining kinetic and kinesthetic possibilities of art can lead to surprising moments.

Excerpt of Ekphrastic Nonfiction: Take for instance this illustration of action in Terry Tempest Williams' *Leap*: "I begin counting cherries in Bosch's Garden. I lose track, they are in such abundance. I stop at sixty. Cherries are flying in the air, dangling from poles, being passed from one person to the next, dropped into the mouths of lovers by birds, worn on women's heads as hats, and balanced on the feet as balls" (8).

Writing Invitation: Write about the dramatic situation in a piece of art. Halt the action. Extend the action. What ought to be happening in the artwork? How does this contradict what is happening? What happened before this scene? What happens next?

Excerpt of Ekphrastic Fiction: In Anita Brookner's novel, *A Misalliance*, we have an example of the emotional tenor of the character being mirrored in a work-of-art:

> But she knew, without a hint of sentiment, that her life might just as well be over, and although she had stared so recently at that image of Bacchus and Ariadne in the National Gallery and had willed that ecstatic moment of recognition into being—so immediate that Bacchus' foot has not had time to touch the ground he leaps from his chariot, so shocking that Ariadne flings up a hand in protest— nothing now would happen (15–16).

Excerpt of Ekphrastic Fiction: Similarly, Margaret Atwood, in the short story, "Death by Landscapes" from her collection *Wilderness Tips* creates an ekphrastic scene wherein her character's emotional state is revealed:

> She looks at the paintings, she looks into them. Every one of them is a picture of Lucy. You can't see her exactly, but she's there, in behind the pink stone island or the one behind that. In the picture of the cliff she is hidden by the clutch of fallen rocks towards the bottom, in the one of the river shore, she is crouching beneath the overturned canoe. In the yellow autumn woods she's behind the tree that cannot be seen because of the other trees, over beside the blue sliver of pond; but if you walked into the picture and found the tree, it would be the wrong one, because the right one would be further on (146).

Writing Invitation: Something or someone is inside a painting but is not a part of the painting itself, but an extension of a landscape beyond the artist's construct. Is the object or person lost or hiding?

Excerpt of Ekphrastic Fiction: Susan Vreeland, in her story "Olympia's Look," from her collection *Life Studies,* has her character look to an Édouard Manet's painting, *Luncheon in the Studio* in order to find someone (León). But, for what? Friendship? "She went back into the dining room to consider *Lunch in the Studio.* In it, Léon appeared as a bright, fashionable young man in a straw hat leaning against the table" (76).

Writing Invitation: Imagine a character whose only friend exists in a painting. Name the artwork characters, if you do not already know who is depicted in a particular art piece, and have your literary character refer to her or him by name, as if there's a familiarity between them.

Excerpt of Ekphrastic Fiction: In Willa Cather's novel, *The Song of the Lark,* which refers to the painting of the same name by Jules Breton, we have an example of a character who has an affinity for an individual art piece, in which the author can illustrate the emotional state of a character via the description of her relationship to the painting:

> She imagined that nobody cared for it but herself, and that it waited for her. That was a picture, indeed. She liked even the name of it, 'The Song of the Lark.' The flat country, the early morning light, the wet fields, the look in the girl's heavy face—well, they were all hers, anyhow, whatever was there. She told herself that that picture was 'right.' Just what she meant by this, it would take a clever person to explain. But to her the word covered the almost boundless satisfaction she felt when she looked at the picture.

Writing Invitation: Albert Camus, in *The Myth of Sisyphus,* wrote, "The gods ... had thought ... that there is no more dreadful punishment than futile and hopeless labor." He continued, "If this myth is tragic, that is because its hero is conscious. Where would his torture be, indeed, if at every step the hope of succeeding upheld him?" And, finally, Camus finished his essay with, "One must imagine Sisyphus happy." Identify an artwork that depicts something tragic or heinous, but imagine instead that the subject is happy.

Excerpt of Ekphrastic Fiction: A few years ago, *The New Yorker* published an ekphrastic story, along with its companion photograph. "Labyrinth," by Roberto Bolaño and translated from the Spanish by Chris Andrews, runs 6,500 words. For the first 1,900 words, the story is almost entirely an extended ekphrasis of the photograph. The story begins: "They're seated. They're looking at the camera. They are captioned, from left to right," and the narrator names the individuals. Even though we as readers of the story and viewers of the printed photograph can see that there's no photo credit, the narrator says, "There's no photo credit." And, we can wonder if overstatement, irony, or humor is going to be implemented throughout the story. The next few lines read, "They're sitting around a table. It's an ordinary table, made of wood, perhaps, or plastic, it could even be a marble table on metal legs, but nothing could be less germane to my purpose than to give an exhaustive description of it." But then, for the next 1,820 words what the narrator does is give an exhaustive description of the picture. The picture, its subjects, the viewing of, and then commenting on it, are all part of the story's complex components.

Writer and photographer Eudora Welty in *One Time, One Place* likens picture-taking to fiction writing: "I learned quickly enough when to click the shutter, but what I was becoming aware of more slowly was a story-writer's truth: The thing to wait on, to reach for, is the moment in which people reveal themselves.... I learned from my own pictures, one by one, and had to; for I think we are the breakers of our own hearts" (McQuade and McQuade 141). Have you ever broken your own heart? What artwork might illustrate that pain?

Every artwork has elements of fiction, some of which can be proven, most cannot. Writer Richard Marius implored, "Writing is not a matter of obeying rules; it is a matter of observation and imagination." And, the same can be said of the visual arts.

Ekphrastic Freewrite: (After Sandro Botticelli's c. 1475 painting, *Spring*)

In a citrus grove in spring, the wind distributes the pollen, then gestation happens and hence, flora sprouts from her mouth. Spring personified as the maiden carries a bunch of flowers and petals. Mercury as Wind on one side of the canvas. The three Graces, intertwining all 30 fingers, signify love for humanity. In the center, Venus cloaked in a white gown and red wrap. Cupid hovers above her and aims his arrow carelessly. All bodies are symmetrical and serene. The translucent gowns, see the curves and see their faces like friends. We must relish spring but not adhere to it. In winter, the mind was at home with the cold white mornings and the short days smelling of decay and endings. Do not let spring fool you, she begs, relish in all the elements: Talk to the wind so no one will hear you, look to Cupid's aims if you've lost direction, gaze at Mercury, for when he appears, it's only an illusion. The fruit and flowers depicted in this painting couldn't have existed in nature at the same time. But the artist could not consider realism, the way grass grows upward and green, and how some nights the wind gusting through your window is a little blue man. As for Venus, she can name the flowers and fruit, but she can never describe to you their colors.

Writing Invitation: Jean-Auguste Ingres' painting of a person with five extra lumbar vertebrae is called, *La Grande Odalisque*. Take a close look at that artwork and write the story of the artist's precision or mishap.

Ekphrastic Freewrite: (After Jacques-Louis David's 1804 painting, *The Coronation of Napoleon*)

What did the painter think when the little man demanded that he include his mother at the ceremony? She thought her son arrogant and had boycotted the event. There she is, in the galley nearest to Napoleon, wearing a proud smile. How odd that we can construct history by our lying. How do you construct your reality to suit yourself? How much of the "manipulation" of facts gets penned down as "history"?

Writing Invitation: Recognize the fictional elements in a piece of art and write a nonfiction piece in which falsehoods exist.

Writing Invitation: In the service of your story, take one artwork, and have a couple of characters each describe that single artwork and compare and contrast their responses. For instance, how would your protagonist and antagonist each describe a painting in which any of these professions were portrayed: gardener, banker, clergy, dance teacher, physician, hairdresser, or factory worker?

Let's consider context: Imagine a picture of a single flower, for example, but if the photographer panned out, would your experience of the flower change knowing that it sprouted from a drain pipe, was laid across the chest of a dead child, was floating in an alpine lake, or was in an enormous field of flowers?

Writing Invitation: Settle on an artwork that depicts one or more characters and imagine panning out beyond the edges of the piece. What do you see? Perhaps you see more of the character's life? Is that character the villain, the hero, the victim? Latch onto one character and see that character's full story beyond the frame.

Josse van Craesbeeck's c. 1645 painting, *Card Players* (gift of J. Paul Getty Museum).

Regard this interior scene by Craesbeeck. What strikes you? Do you find the scene relatable? Do you see a story? Are you entranced by one particular detail, or would you be pleased to consider the entire image in writing your ekphrastic response? Also, here is the companion flash-fiction piece. Notice how the writer focuses on a single detail and then pans out temporally. Which modes of imagery can you appreciate? Could you imagine an entire book of ekphrastic flash-fiction influenced by a single painting?

Merry Company
by Kim Barnes

When he has forgotten all else—his name, his age, his three wives deceased, the faces of his living daughters, and his sons lost to war, that he is missing one finger, severed by his docking knife, that he had pitched that piece of himself to the chickens—even then, when he can't remember his country or his county, he will lie on his death bed and remember being a child in that same room, sitting beneath a tavern table on the chilled stone floor, the square of light shafting in through the open window, bringing with it the stench of dung and catkins. Around him, the smell of tobacco and wine, the sound of grunting as the cards were dealt, the quiet lute leaned against the wall with its risen belly full of nothing but air and how badly he wanted to touch it, how he sucked on his biscuit instead. He remembers the small mirror slipped beneath the table and into the folds of a skirt, the quick brown reflection he understood himself to be. He doesn't remember the voice or the leavened body of his mother, whose lap he had slid from, but he remembers her smell: yeast and marigolds. He didn't yet know she would disappear that night with the man he recognized only as a pair of stained boots set hard against the floor and stinking of urine, but he recalls stretching his own legs to admire his new shoes, which, in a matter of months, he would grow out of, squat over, fill with his own excrement, and drop down the well of the uncle who had ridden across the county to claim him, who took him home, tied him like a shoat pig, and greased him with castor. He won't remember helping to bake the village breads nor beheading the stewing hens, the avuncular ax brought down again and again, and then brought across his uncle's throat, the miles he walked in bloody stockings until he found that tavern, that room, stepped inside, and began to live, firing his oven beneath the chestnuts' ancient shade—sour desem, spiced peperkoek, sweet mastellen—marrying, fathering, growing old, and now dying in that same square of light that holds all that he sees, all that he knows, all that he will remember until even that moment is gone.

Flash-Fiction Writer's Comments

The boy caught my focus immediately. I had great fun researching the time (17th Century Flemish Baroque) and using the aesthetics to heighten the language. I also drew upon Josse van Craesbeeck's work as a prison baker; the sub-genre called the Merry Gathering/tavern; the allegory of five senses the painter is focused on (as well as the colors); the period's fascination with the 'crude and vulgar' peasants.... Kind of manufactured an inventory and went with it! (Kim Barnes)

Creative Writing Overall

While most of this book's discussion has revolved around art-influenced writing, it is fascinating to learn about artists who were influenced by literature and artists who were interdisciplinary. Here are some notable pairs:

1. Read Lord Tennyson's poem, "The Lady of Shalott" (part IV) and view the painting that it inspired, John Waterhouse's, *The Lady of Shalott*.
2. Read Miguel de Cervantes' *Don Quixote* and view Paula Modersohn-Becker's painting, *Miguel de Cervantes*.
3. Read the 1860 children's book by Reverend Charles Kingsley, *The Water-Babies* and view the painting that it influenced, John Covert's *Water Babies*.
4. Read Michelangelo's poem, "When the Author Was Painting the Vault of the Sistine Chapel" and view his painting on the ceiling of the Sistine Chapel.

Let's revisit notional ekphrasis: How often is notional ekphrasis based on notional art? Well, it is not often that a writer would describe an artwork that does not exist, though this is undoubtedly an option and a challenge. Take, for instance, mythology. Global mythologies—African, Asian, Greek, Native American, Norse, and Roman—have long influenced artists. A preponderance of mythology-informed art concerns Greek myths, which treat gods, goddesses, and heroic humans, as well as Roman myths, which revolved around origin, destiny, and social mores. When we engage with art that's based on lore or myth, we can include or exclude the notional aspect of the artwork.

Suggested Viewing: Sandro Botticelli's painting, *The Birth of Venus*

Suggested Viewing: Romare Bearden's collage, *The Return of Odysseus*

Suggested Viewing: J.M.W. Turner's painting, *Ulysses Deriding Polyphemus*

Suggested Viewing: John Flaxman's sculpture, *Shield of Achilles*

Suggested Viewing: Lavinia Fontana's painting, *Venus and Cupid*

Suggested Viewing: Francis Bacon's lithograph, *Oedipus and the Sphinx*

Writing Invitation: Identify artwork that takes mythology as its subject. Challenge the myth, expand upon the narrative, or create a combination of a classical myth with your narrative for a modern twist.

Tension—In all art, there is tension, either in the subject, in manner, or from audience expectation. How exactly is tension created in ekphrasis? Tension is created if there is image-word conflict, as in words contradicting the image. How the subject is treated can lead to tension—sympathizing with the perceived villain in the artwork, for example. Tension is also created for the audience by artists or ekphrastic writers when they challenge assumptions or values in the art they respond to.

Diction—Mark Twain made this startling comparison: "The difference between the almost right word and the right word is really a large matter—'tis the difference between the lightning-bug and the lightning." Now that you have been introduced to the general language of the tools and techniques of the general visual artist, you, presumably, have a newfound vocabulary to utilize.

Are you always on the search for provocative diction? Even if a person abhors art viewing, much can be done creatively with the nomenclature associated with the visual arts. Dive unabashedly into the specific language of visual arts to collect what you might need to build creative writing poems. Case in point—"pentimenti." It's Italian for "repent," and it refers to marks that remain after artists correct their drawings. By tracing the journey of artists' pentimenti, you can appreciate their creative processes, make inferences about the accidental and essential errors, and so on. Borrow *Descriptionary* from your local library and begin making your own list of beloved art-related terms.

Syntax—Creative writer, how surprising or innovative is your syntax? In *The Triggering Town* Hugo suggests, "If you want to change what's there, use the same words and play with the syntax: This blue lake still has resolve. / This lake still blue with resolve" (38).

Titling—How an artist titles a piece can be revealing. The Dutch painter Frans Hals often gave his pieces banal titles: *Portrait of a Woman*, *Portrait of a Man*, and *Laughing Boy*, which were indeed paintings of just what he called them. What you see is what you got, in terms of his approach to titling. How often have you wanted some insight and turned to the artwork's title, only to be disappointed by its "Untitled" state? Conversely, some artists offer titles that give another dimension to their pieces.

A few years ago, I attended a gallery opening in Seattle. I was particularly smitten with a painting that depicted what I perceived to be three individuals in the back of a 1950s taxi. The hues were somber, suggesting nighttime or the general emotional atmosphere. Two individuals were pressed cheek-to-cheek in a loving embrace. Far on the other side of the seat was a younger woman who was applying lipstick to her reflection in a compact mirror. What was the narrative? I imagined it had something to do with three people en route somewhere, or perhaps they did not even know each other. I could have had a myriad of interpretations, but for one thing: the contextualizing title that the artist gave. Rather than *Untitled* or *Three on a Seat*, the artist gave a title that marked the painting's point-of-view. The title, I was stunned to read, was *Mom and Jack*. Given this title, I redirected my gaze to the young woman seemingly content to ignore the affectionate couple next to her. But, with that particular title, I gathered there was a strain in the relationship among all three figures.

Suggested Viewing: Alexander Petrov's painting, *Mom and Jack*

Excerpt of Ekphrastic Fiction: Again in Rushdie's novel, one of the characters considers different titles for a single artwork: "'I have called it *The Artist as Boabdil, the Unlucky (el-Zogoybi), Last Sultan of Granada, Seen Departing from the Alhambra*,' said Vasco with a straight face. 'Or, *The Moor's Last Sigh...*'" (160).

Writing Invitation: Consider what you would make of a particular artwork if you did not have the benefit of its title, and the importance thereof (context, abstraction, point-of-view)? Alternatively, re-title numerous artworks and see where the fluidity of naming gets you.

A fusion of form and content—Per Aristotle, there are "three differences which distinguish artistic imitation—the medium, the objects, and the manner." Regarding manner, an ekphrasist can choose to respond to the artist's style. In the essay, "The How and the Why" by Marjorie Welish, she explains that the best directive for students of ekphrasis "is not '*Describe* abstract painting,' but '*Construct* a verbal artifact commensurate with the visual one'" (Foster and Prevallet 122).

Writing Invitation: Explore artwork that begs you take notice of its composition. Think about the arrangement of forms, as well as the negative spaces within the frame. Construct a concrete poem (typographical) or a projective verse piece that emulates the artwork's composition.

Earlier, we saw the images of a pair of sculptures by George Rodriguez, *Tia Catrina & Uncle Sam*. Here is the corresponding ekphrastic flash-fiction piece. Are you familiar with concrete poetry? Have you ever seen a fiction writer handle that method? How does the shape of this piece reflect the artwork that influenced it? How do the writing's shape and other typographical nuances complement your reading experience? Notice also the incorporation of Spanish words, as well as an attention to diction and characterization:

Tia Catrina |||| Uncle Sam
(After George Rodriguez's *Tia Catrina & Uncle Sam*)
by Michael Mejia

SHE: Ay, cariño, tu never ring anymore, except on nights when the wind howls, every light gone dark. Then your coin drops from dusty moonlight, glazing the barren hill, some hunched dogs, a pistol's muzzle, fingerless hands of nopal. All the empty homes here: a lineup of skulls. The last time, you kept shouting *listen, listen to me*, and I cried my eyes all the way out—pero te amo, cariño. Sí, todavía te amo.

SHE: We could lie close as we used to, amor, two mountains at a pass, riverbanks joined in the current, the mud we make, the dark roil: beatings of one tumbling heart, the wounds and bruises of that old, slow collision. One body, close to burning, burning, on a rock, in the sand, nowhere not us, and speaking in tongues. Why turn your back, turn back, to you, alone? Rest here, amor. Somos tu corazón.

HE: I never remembered my dreams after that first coming to. Waking in darkness: the dawn chorus and one sharp voice—fresh timber. No time! No time but for the making of it. A sloped field to clear, wresting stump and stone, the setting of fenceposts, wattle and daub. A barn, a well, an outhouse. By the fire, her pale hands washed my feet. God's firmament all quiet again. Only the rumble of wheels passing by—

HE: No nodding, you. Hoist them dungarees with a fresh hide belt. Make for the emptiness that broadens shoulders. Red rock and pasture. See: a mountain of their skulls. Well, I'll be your uncle, Monkey. Rope and barb wire today. Dude up on Sunday. Say a prayer as you drive each nail. See you in the funny papers! Those guns going off: it's a holiday.

SHE: [Wanders the desert, trailing a
zagging lizard, finds her old vecinos
resettled beneath saguaro, ocotillo,
their sunken faces all smiles.]

SHE: I can't hear you from over here, amor, so I'm throwing a few rocks, little love notes, memoranda, memento mori. We'll wait for you beneath the bridge. No olvides! There's a little baby under here, our sisters and cousins. Still breathing. They could use a drink, but you know, we'll wait. We always will. One day you'll look our way again. With love. It's certain. Press yourself up against this fence a minute. Look again the way we do.

HE: They'll watch from the highest windows, their holdings blooming across the valley, up the hillside, down to the sea. The map *is* the territory! But they'll accept better offers. They'll open lines of credit, dam them up, trickle off a bit to them and thine. Outside the red line only, hear? No surprise they'll keep making it, making it up, to the top and over. World beaters: no secrets in their blood, no tint. Pure as water from the tap, mostly.

In art, the way materials and subjects relate is paramount. In creative writing, it is called "form and content" or "form follows function," in which there is an implicit connection between the subject and the method by which the subject is treated. A type of instruction might read: "Adapt the techniques of the painter in the storytelling" (DeGhett 102). Consider the curated creative writing for this book: Is it notable that many poets use couplets? As an exercise, try to arrive at reasons for why the ekphrastic writer would use pairs of lines for ekphrastic poetry.

There are many parallels between the visual arts and the literary arts. In poetry, specifically, we consider the function of the line and also in the visual arts the function of the line is a topic of discussion and study. What can you make of that connection?

Writing Invitation: Allow the artwork's textures to inform your writing. Given that "Visual textures help to make a drawing more gripping by breaking up large areas of tone with a certain pattern" (De Reyna 55), find a drawing with various textural techniques and let those textures inform your writing. Be sure to include tactile imagery.

Writing Invitation: Consider rhythm in artwork and rhythm in poetry. What can you make of that parallel? In the textbook, *Living with Art*, Gilbert explained, "Visual rhythm depends on the repetition of accented elements, usually shapes" (148). Now, find artwork in which rhythm (or patterns) are created or broken. Use that visual rhythm to inform your writing; in other words, aim for a composition that's rhythmic.

Here is the poem influenced by Piet Mondrian's painting, *Farm near Duivendrecht.* Look closely at the image and contemplate the form and content relationship. Notice the poem's contextualizing title—an astute reader would spend much time on what is conveyed in that title and how it sets the tone for the poem. How is the first-person point-of-view functioning? How does this poem differ from the poem that you would write, given the same image?

While I Am Walking in Light Rain on Palm Sunday, a Mirror Appears on an Illinois Street
(After Piet Mondrian's *Farm Near Duivendrecht*)
by David Wright

Though it is April, and it is morning, and this asphalt
is not canvas, and I am expecting nothing beautiful,

there it shines: rainwater glazing the ground, a motor oil
sheen collecting clouds from the sky over Duivendrecht.

The farm you have sketched again and again for years
(have painted a half-dozen times while the Great War

bisects bodies into cylinders) arrives upside down.
Canopies of trees interlace branches to dome and shelter

the house, the barn. Its several indistinct birds now alive
in the Illinois sky. They glide across and beside still waters.

In my copy of your copy of the stream there is no man in blue
who kneels by the bend and wishes for the water to be clear.

You have said we are only line and color, assembled angles
and curves. Any object we recognize obscures the beautiful.

What we need is a purer mirror, a place where we see only
absences. I believe that you believe beauty resides in nothing

we recognize as a thing. But I am no theosophist. I cannot stop
losing sight of the darkness we make from the plastic world.

Today, though, I can follow this liturgy you score straight
in dark lines, dance in this refraction of easel as sky.

How else could a body skip through the Dutch countryside
during war, shoes splashing cloud-cover into concentric circles?

How else could I make my way through bare treetops, never
falling through the empty world? Thank you, for showing me how

to stay a whole shape, to keep from dissolving to ash when I step
into what might, otherwise, be a light, a fire, an actual sun.

Poet's Comments

I had a draft I liked. Then I took a walk and there was, suddenly, a draft that I loved. It's an example of how an experience of a painting and a lived experience can become one another at times (David Wright).

Gertrude Stein

The writing of Gertrude Stein is particularly fascinating to study on numerous levels related to ekphrasis: As another person whose life included the sciences, the visual arts, and the literary arts, Stein sat at the helm of the Lost Generation of expatriates in Paris between the two wars. Stein and her sibling Leo were early patrons of artists Picasso, Matisse, and Cézanne, to name a few. It's no shock then that Stein's poetry and prose became shaped by the art she saw. Stein's approach to art in the service of her writing was novel; her muse was driven by the challenge of building a verbal construct that echoed the artist style of art and also the utilitarian dimensions of everyday objects.

Marjorie Perloff in her article, "The Difference Is Spreading: On Gertrude Stein" offers us insight about Stein's creative process, as well as her literary innovation as compared with her contemporaries:

> Stein herself insisted that *Tender Buttons* was entirely "realistic" in the tradition of Gustave Flaubert. "I used to take objects on a table, like a tumbler or any kind of object and try to get the picture of it clear and separate in my mind and create a word relationship between the word and the things seen," she recalls in "A Transatlantic Interview—1946" with Robert Bartlett Haas. What she no doubt means is that reference remains central to her project even if representation does not. Unlike her contemporaries (Eliot, Pound, Moore), she does not give us an image, however, fractured, of a carafe on a table; instead, she forces us to reconsider how language actually constructs the world we know.

Excerpt of Ekphrastic Poetry: Here are some lines from the section, "A Piece of Coffee" from Gertrude Stein's *Tender Buttons: Objects—Food—Rooms*: "A single image is not splendor. Dirty is yellow. A sign of more is not mentioned. A piece of coffee is not a detainer. The resemblance to yellow is dirtier and distincter. The clean mixture is whiter and not coal color, never more coal color than altogether." What are your thoughts on Stein's approach to objects? Have you ever considered how you're constructing the world verbally?

Similar to stream-of-consciousness, where the individual's conscious experience is regarded as a continuous series of occurrences rather than as disconnected events, a signature style of Stein's was the abandonment of grammatical and syntactical conventions for the propulsion of present-moment sensory experience. Broadly, it was her exposure to cubism in visual art that informed her cubist approach to writing. Because she had sat for Picasso almost a hundred times, I imagine that they discussed his technique in the studio as he painted her.

Cubism is an art movement that's characterized by a separation of the subject into geometric forms (cubes included) in abstract arrangements rather than by organic shapes. Additionally, in cubism, multiple planes are exposed at once. For instance, with a side profile of a human head, one eye and one ear are obscured. The cubist artists seek to honor multiple views at once. Hence, side profiles with both the eyes and the ears arranged on the face in unexpected ways. This intriguing ambiguity holds excellent creative possibilities for writers, specifically, wherein they can parse out narratives with shifting points-of-view.

Suggested Viewing: Pablo Picasso's abstract painting, *Woman with Mustard Pot*

Suggested Reading: Richard Shelton's poem, "From a Room"

Writing Invitation: Consider cubist poetry's similarity to cubism in visual art. When things are rearranged, this fresh arrangement, in which compelling juxtapositions happen, can result in new ways of seeing. Use imagery from an artwork laden with specifics such as the naming of colors, textures, and patterns. Begin with a single quatrain, and then continue reworking the pattern of words for at least three more quatrains, using poet Richard Shelton's cubist technique as a guide.

Excerpt of Ekphrastic Fiction: Additionally, Stein's writing was also informed by her friend, Paul Cézanne. Specifically, her first book of fiction, *Three Lives* was influenced by his *Portrait of Madame Cézanne*. Notice the syntax. This is from the section, "Part I. The Good Anna": "Life went on very smoothly now in these few months before the summer came. Miss Mathilda every summer went away across the ocean to be gone for several months. When she went away this summer old Katy was so sorry, and on the day that Miss Mathilda went, old Katy cried hard for many hours. An earthy, uncouth, servile peasant creature old Katy surely was" (8).

Writing Invitation: Discover an artwork in which you see syncopation that might yield a syllabic poem. Consider Gertrude Stein's cubist fiction and the concept of form-follows-function.

Excerpt of Ekphrastic Nonfiction: Here is an excerpt of a multi-page extended ekphrasis that Rilke included in his *Letters on Cézanne*. In ruminating on the portrait of Madame Cézanne in an armchair, you can see the focus is on fabric patterns and how that becomes a metaphor for the sitter. As an exercise, compare and contrast Rilke's musings with Gertrude Stein's, in which two writers treat the artist's techniques in their own writing:

> A red, upholstered low armchair has been placed in front of an earthy-green wall in which a cobalt-blue pattern ... is very sparingly repeated; the round bulging back curves and slopes forward and down to the armrests (which are sewn up

like the sleeve-stump of an armless man). The left armrest and the tassel that hangs from it full of vermilion no longer have the wall behind them but instead, near the lower edge, a broad strip of greenish blue, against which they clash in loud contradiction. Seated in this red armchair, which is a personality in its own right, is a woman, her hands in the lap of the dress with broad vertical strips that are very lightly indicated by small, loosely distributed flecks of green yellows and yellow greens, up to the edge of the blue-gray jacket, which is held together in front by a blue, greenly scintillating silk bow (79–80).

Community of Artists
and Writers

Have you built an artist community for yourself? As Aristotle wrote, "Art is an activity of the spirit." Let's discuss art as a social act, wherein artists of all types can cultivate their artistry by producing and sharing. Case in point: Rilke's propinquity to visual artists meant he could learn from them, which in turn nurtured his art. In her introduction to his *Letters on Cézanne*, editor Clara Rilke relayed that "he did not learn how to look at pictures until he had met and talked with artists; that previously he had searched many a painting for a narrative or lyrical content instead of regarding it as an artwork" (ix). There is no substitute from learning firsthand what artists themselves can teach you.

Suggested Viewing: Paula Modersohn-Becker's painting, *Portrait of Rainer Maria Rilke*

Because we know so much about poet Rilke's creative process, mainly due to his record of his and sculptor Auguste Rodin's multidisciplinary friendship, we have great insight about the influence that artists can have on each others' aesthetic development. When Rilke was employed as Rodin's secretary, the sculptor revealed to the poet that he engaged with each piece of marble without any preconception. The artist's tutelage included looking as a meditative act, and the friends wondered if writing could be approached in that same manner. They drew up a list of things around Paris that Rilke could gaze upon, in the spirit of art-making. Inspired, Rilke adopted Rodin's method for his poem writing. As a result, Rilke's dinggedichte (*thing-poems*) were products of detached gazing and included a panther (seen at Jardin des Plantes), a swan, a gazette, a unicorn (notional), flowers, paintings (by Cézanne), and sculpture. This is an illustration of a mode of ekphrasis wherein the writer adopts an artist's approach to art-making: To see through Rodin's eyes by physically and emotionally emulating his approach to sculpture. "The principle of my

Marie Denise Villers' 1801 painting, *Marie Joséphine Charlotte du Val d'Ognes* (courtesy the Mr. and Mrs. Isaac D. Fletcher Collection, bequest of Isaac D. Fletcher, 1917).

work is a passionate subordination to the object..." Rilke wrote (*Testament* 8). Moreover, Ulrich Baer in *The Poet's Guide to Life* wrote, "The power of Rilke's writings results from his capacity to interlock the description of everyday objects, minute feelings, small gestures, and overlooked things—that which makes up the world for each of us—with transcendent themes" (x).

Suggested Reading: Rainer Maria Rilke's poem, "Der Panther"

Writing Invitation: Instead of finding artwork of animals on which to gaze, visit a zoo or aquarium and write as some artists do, *en plein air*.

In Paris, concurrent to the Rodin-Rilke partnership, the dawn of modernism in the art world, the literary field, and psychoanalysis was breaking. The "avant-garde" writers and artists at that time celebrated "new psychology," forged essential relationships, and spawned artistic movements such as futurism, cubism, dadaism, and surrealism, which resulted in work that defied past conventions.

The Lost Generation is another example of a community of artists of various disciplines whose art was shared and shaped by one another. The visual arts up until that time celebrated wholesome value and mastery of craft: art that mirrored life—for example, a viewer could appreciate the painting of a girl's face with precision. Thus they could easily conclude what was "masterful." The buzz among the thinkers of the time included an exploration of the human psyche, with Sigmund Freud and his dream interpretations, the ego and id, and the theory of sexuality, as well as Carl Jung's conscious and unconscious minds, archetypes, and the collective unconscious.

Suggested Viewing: John Singer Sargent's painting, *Daughters of Edward Darley Bolt*

But then an art exhibit traveled to New York City in 1913. The Armory Show was a success in that thousands of viewers came, but the show was considered shocking, an "abstract invasion," for this was the American public's first view of modern art. The show was controversial as it obliterated the puritan point-of-view through the distortion of the human form. If you had grown accustomed to seeing only realism displayed in art, with a nod to puritan values, imagine your shock at seeing abstraction for the first time. The show was seen as an artist revolt against the academy, for a new standard emerged, as did a new definition of art. This show precipitated a profound effect on artists, art collectors, and the art market in general that still resounds today.

Suggested Viewing: Marcel Duchamp's abstract painting, *Nude Descending a Staircase*

Suggested Viewing: Wassily Kandinsky's abstract landscape, *Improvisation No. 27*

So, friendships between artistic individuals at that time yielded new types of art and artistic freedom heretofore unknown—the freedom of the imagination and the freedom of frankness (creativity with clarity). Art for its own value, liberated from the stronghold of the academy. Finally, modern art grew more abstract, and literature grew more concrete. Besides the dawn of modernism being a cross-disciplinary exchange, it was also a cross-cultural one: People in America were learning more about European art, and people in Europe were learning more about American literature.

Also at that time in Paris, surrealism had its birth. Surrealism, both an artistic movement and a literary movement, the cornerstone of which is play and chance, was founded in 1924 by writer André Breton. He was particularly intrigued by Freud's dream theory, and he thought that dreams could help unlock the mystery of a person's unconscious mind. As discussed previously, Breton's method for exploring the unconscious was free-associating and automatic writing (freewriting), which he referred to as "thought's dictation ... independent of any aesthetic or moral preoccupation" (Jung, *Man and His Symbols* 257). Besides automatism Breton practiced "dedoublement, or detachment ... of the mind from the body [which would] guarantee that automatic writing would reveal the hidden order of the writer's subconscious" (Freeman 101–102).

The surrealists, then, created various games of automatism, which enticed their players into a hypnopompic state. These games included automatic writing, automatic drawing, exquisite corpse art-making, and collage, among other games, which enabled the players to liberate and explore the unconscious mind. Stream-of-consciousness and a celebration of chance and randomness were regular practices of the surrealists, in which they chose not to interfere with the vital work of the unconscious mind consciously. Letting go of that control, though, is not something everyone can do.

Suggested Viewing: Leonora Carrington's surrealist paintings

Tenets from the Surrealist manifesto included, "the absence of any control exercised by reason," unlocking of the dream state, "spontaneous creative production without conscious ... self-censorship," and the "interplay of word and image association" (98). In *Third Mind*, Anna Balakian wrote, "The surrealist poet in his use of words was approaching the painter's technique, and that is how a closer bond was established between poetry and art than ever before" (Foster and Prevallet 164). In other words, treating the artist's style (or manner) has become another important facet of ekphrasis.

As promised earlier, here is the companion poem to Lo Ch'ing's painting, *Post-Industrial Society Has Arrived*. I have placed this poem in this particular section, for it is the most surrealist poem of the bunch. What constitutes a surrealist poem? You will have to decide for yourself, though, given some background on Stein's aesthetic, along with the mode of the "interplay of word and image association," making the surrealist designation for this poem seems about right. Some points of discussion include the poet's use of the "at" sign, the repetition of contemporary neologism (the invented "@agirl"), the illustration of exuberance, and the sound resonance:

Post-Industrial Society Has Arrived
(After the painting by Lo Ch'ing)
by Vidhu Aggarwal

@agirl, chasing her cloud formations into the maze.

@! @! @!

atomic clouds! clouds of barista macchiatos!

Welcome to compulsion!

@agirl, force of nature, where are you?

O maze, O labyrinth, O vortex of my capitalistic yearnings,
    gulping down the girl, the force—
the disappearing labor force, the electromagnetic force, the strong nuclear force,
the force of gravity!

@agirl, how your material being floats inside the maze, inflation adjusted!
@agirl, there is nothing to hold you, but you are caught, no?
@agirl you are not jobless. No! You generate
loads of foam. Rapturous clouds drift out from your very being!
    The foam has purpose!
The foam

obscures the absolute shrinkage of the goods. I don't see the goods.
    I don't see the gods.
I only see vistas

suspended inside the service sector. Skyscrapers cutting into view,
    into the cloud foam, into
the red blazing sunset of the free market.

@agirl, where are you?
@agirl, are you the swirling caryatid, a grey cyclone holding up a lone
skyscraper, your shadow raking the electrified edge of the field?

Or are you a haze of particles
circulating fervently within the tiny atavistic temple
atop the highest vista

where trees hang out? I mean "topiary" because even the trees are trained.
Who trained them? A refrain of engineered trees, emanating
from the tiny red temple, buzzing though trapezoids
of privatized hissing vistas, through the maze, through the signs of our time.

@agirl, are you a damsel? Do damsels float? Do damsels require job training?
Do damsels still spread

their accelerated skills and frothy distress signals into the post-industrial age?

Collaboration

When I asked the painter Emerson, "what can writers learn from visual artists?" He answered that "wonderful things happen when you get involved in a discipline outside your own. One thing leads to another. It's a worthy experience, the engaged mind." What are your thoughts? How often have you engaged your mind by way of learning from visual artists?

Since *collaborate* means "with" and "work," technically, ekphrastic writing isn't collaborative. Ekphrasis is usually predicated on the artist already having completed the artwork to which the writer will turn for fodder. Regardless, ekphrasis can help to bridge communities. What opportunities do you have for collaboration?

The interactive street art mural by Candy Chang, "Before I Die"... is an example of a concept art piece that, when introduced into a community, became a collaboration of ideas. According to the artist's website, Chang wished to start an existential conversation among her neighbors in New Orleans, prompting those to confront rather than avoid discussions of death. She covered an abandoned house with chalkboard paint and offered the prompt, "Before I die I want to _____," as well as chalk with which to write their response for all to read. That one act in that single neighborhood ignited a chain reaction. Now, thousands of "Before I Die" walls have been created in dozens of countries.

Collaboration Invitations

1. Select a writing partner and each person chooses an artwork. Together, write a single call-and-response piece. In other words, one piece of writing, two works-of-art, and two voices.
2. Assemble a group of writers, select a single artwork, and ask each person to freewrite on it. After freewriting, the writers choose one to three favorite lines. Transcribe these lines onto slips of paper, come together as a group, and settle on an order for the verbal collage.
3. Collaborative tabula rasa—when both the writer and the artist begin together with respective blank canvases. The writer writes on a sheet of paper, a wood panel, or a canvas and then offers that surface to the artist. Making decisions driven by the words, the artist paints or draws on that surface, either allowing some or all of the words to remain readable or obscuring them entirely. Once the paint has dried, the surface can be returned to the writer for contribution and a back-and-forth can continue indefinitely. Concurrently, the artist paints on a sheet of paper, a wood panel, or a canvas and then offers that surface to the writer. So, two surfaces are exchanged concurrently.
4. Collaboration between painters and writers: First, the writers create one page of text of any genre with some stipulation on the

structure. For example, "Emphasis should be placed upon the development of a persona and the interaction of the individual within a specific place." The artists, then, are randomly assigned a writer's composition. They are then instructed to use the writing as an influence, but with specific parameters, such as "element of surrealism must be included; only half of the painting can be realistic."

5. For over a decade, visual artist Joan Miró and poet Paul Éluard worked together to create the book, *À Toute Épreuve* ("Reading for Anything"). Pair up with an artist and together make a single work or an entire collection of text-images. Explore resources at your local arts center and create a comic or graphic novel together.

Suggested Reading: Art Spiegelman's graphic novel, *Maus: A Survivor's Tale*

Suggested Reading: Marjane Satrapi's graphic novel, *Persepolis: The Story of a Childhood*

Excerpt of Freewrite on Collaboration: Collaboration between young writers and photographers. The creative writing students who oft wrote with and about abstraction were paired with photography students whose task was to find something concrete and create their art from that specific thing. The poet kids of mine gathered with the photography kids of Kurt's to explore chance, perspective, and play. What changes when we move our eyes to look in a new way? Kurt said that anything that can be photographed exists, which is so curious because my kids can pull things out of thin air: victory, glory, beautiful, soul, dreams, despair. All these vast happenings can and do exist in my kid's poetry, but one can never photograph victory. Sure, there are objects which represent victory, and those things can be photographed, apprehended. But really, the thing they are after—victory for example—is an abstraction, and abstractions just cannot be captured by a lens and shutter. How to merge the two worlds? The two together create a skillful and talented "I." But the photographer is always distanced from emotion, not to get at the wreck itself, or even the story of the wreck, but the wreckage, the objects that convey the narrative of railroad ties buckling, the iron rusting, the train tipping over, and the evidentiary plunge into a lake. Does every artist need a respondent to complete the work? For the camera always comes between the photographer and what's being photographed. So, who is in control over what we see? The balance between nearness and distance? Who does the developing? Who brings in the light?

Further Reflections

In Rosa Bonheur's painting *The Horse Fair*, we can count at least twenty horses and as many human figures. What do you notice about the composition? Do you feel that having an affinity for horses is necessary before you could successfully engage with this artwork ekphrastically? Here is the companion persona poem, in which the writer adopts the voice of the artist, with details that hearken back to ninetieth-century life:

The Horse Fair
(Rosa Bonheur b. 1822 Bordeaux)
by Jana Harris

My masterpiece, I told Mlle. Micas,
will be the talk of the Paris Salon.
Standing in the plaza, I sketch horse
after horse, the disc of the jaw, a thicket
of forward slashing parallel legs. Oh
those well-muscled moons of the rump,
and the high tide sea of manes.
In two quarter time a chaos of hooves
hammers dust into June's chestnut leaves.
At the end of the Boulevard, a ghost
of the *Hospice de la Salpêtrière*
when it housed mad women chained
like these ungovernable beasts: *Rosa,*
they'll send you there if you don't cease
trampling flower beds, bossing and hitting
with fists, if you don't learn to read or master
a needle and thread.... I could draw
before I could walk and when I sketched
une alouette, Mere wrote A; *Boeuff;*
Cheval-cheval-cheval.
Renard, Oie, Salamander, Alouette;
portraits of animals were all I would render.
Pushing one of Papiche's artist pencils like a bit
between my smallest brother's lips,
we played Horse Fair for hours.

Rosa Bonheur's 1852–55 painting, *The Horse Fair* (gift of Cornelius Vanderbilt, 1887).

Tourists stop, study the easel of someone
they take for a boy. Oh joy, what mischief:
over here on the right I will paint my mare
with me astride hatless in spatterdash and blue
flapping smock, back to the crowd. On the left,
again my sorrel Margot, but riderless as
I first saw her. An excellent balance, the eye
catches her coming and going—if,
like Mlle. Micas, you know what to look for.
Later at my studio, a rented barn, Margot
and my menagerie around me,
I stipple dust, Mlle. enters,
tall as a crane and wordless, stares
drop-jawed at my canvas, the widest remnant
the shirt-maker would trade for a pastoral with sheep.
As Mlle. lays a *petit four* atop the frame, white
sugar rains on the dapples of grays
Romanesque enough to pull her coach
when the Empress presents *moi* the *Ordre National.*

Papiche's words rise from the grave: Rosa,
like a son to me; I will teach you everything I know.

Poet's Comments

I did LOTS of research; that's all her, Rosa. That's who she was, even her sorrel
horse's name, Margot (Jana Harris).

Research—How much, if any, research will you conduct during
your ekphrastic journey? Nowadays, not only is there ready information
about artists online but also about the artwork. Will that hamper

your production if you embark on research before first engaging the art with your imagination? In addition to scholarly research, you must decide how much credence you will give the facts of the art. For example, is it permissible to call a painting a photograph because that choice was imperative to your writing? Clearly, it is a woman donning a green hat in the canvas, but the muse insists "black hat." How much do readers, in general, expect in terms of truthfulness? This can be problematic in ekphrastic writing, for our readers (who can also become viewers of the artwork) might hold their own opinions. While some readers are unforgiving, hopefully, most recognize the art-begets-art spirit of ekphrastic writing. In "Notes on Ekphrasis," Corn argues that "Without the original image, though, we are forced to trust the poet's description as being accurate, and we are unable to know where it is not." Nevertheless, it is allegiance to the imagination that's the creative writer's sincere pledge.

Revision Invitation: Try another genre? If your piece is not reading well as poetry, try losing the line breaks and see where prose might get you. The same can be said of words that are not being served by the prose form. Perhaps, though, your words beg a composite structure. If you are unfamiliar, here is a reference suggestion: *American Hybrid: A Norton Anthology of New Poetry*, edited by Cole Swensen and David St. John. Decisions that could enliven your piece might consist of hybrid approaches to content, organization, structure, and visual elements. Be fanciful—be innovative.

Suggested Reading: Paisely Rekdal's *Intimate: An American Family Photo Album*

Revision Invitation: Take your list of descriptive clauses and rearrange them, as description order usually is not imperative, only as a matter of how the eye is being instructed to move about the artwork. Alternatively, try describing the artwork without any modifiers. Use the descriptive force of the verbs and nouns.

Scaffolding—As stated before, a piece of writing that starts as ekphrastic might not end that way. From *The Triggering Town* we learn, "A poem can be said to have two subjects, the initiating or triggering subject, which starts the poem or 'causes' the poem to be written, and the real or generated subject, which the poem comes to say or mean, and which is generated or discovered in the poem during the writing" (4). Hugo continues, "The initiating subject should trigger the imagination as well as the poem. If it doesn't, it may not be a valid subject but only something you feel you should write a poem about" (5). In other words, do not confine yourself too strictly to the artwork. Allow it to provide the reason for the start of your writing, but it does not have to be the reason for you to continue to develop your creative writing.

Metaekphrasis—Must the ekphrastic writing evoke the image? Or, can the ekphrastic piece exist independently from the artwork from which it sprang (Rusk 78)? Here is an argument against the need to see what influenced the writer: "In one sense, the *availability* of a painting represented by a poem should make no difference to our experience of the poem, which—like any specimen of notional ekphrasis—is made wholly of words" (Heffernan, *Museum of Words* 7). Let's revisit this term that I coined: Recall that metaekphrasis is a mode that we can adopt if it is decided that the artwork is not integral to the final version; the artwork was merely a springboard. In the end, we must decide if the influence of the visual arts on our writing is necessary to broadcast.

Dramatic occasion—Must poems and prose have a dramatic occasion? Is ekphrasis evidence enough? The mode of ekphrasis, says Corn, "can provide a special angle."

Methods of titling—To identify the artwork or not? Naming the artwork is also a way of giving your writing a dramatic occasion. Some writers use the artwork's title as the title of their own ekphrastic writing. Using an epigraph in which the artist and the specific piece are named is another option. Nowadays, some writers are using the term "ekphrastic" in their title. Is this method of titling redundant, similar to reading a sestina called "Sestina"?

Modes and titles—Ekphrastic writing sometimes evokes the artwork other times does not:

> The ekphrastic elements are apparent, and the writer names the artwork.
> The ekphrastic elements are apparent, but the artwork goes unnamed.
> The ekphrastic elements are not apparent, but the writer names the artwork.
> The ekphrastic elements are not apparent, and the writer does not name the artwork.

Evaluating Ekphrastic Writing

Must we speak of the poem, essay, or story in terms of the image it was influenced by in order to comprehend the writing's ekphrastic and literary qualities fully? In which terms do we speak when we evaluate the quality of ekphrastic work? Here are some points to ponder, though you will notice that some contradict each other:

1. "Successful ekphrastic poems vary widely, but generally the writers move beyond the artwork they see before them, to associations that arise from it" (Rusk 78).
2. Evaluate the emotional resonance of ekphrastic writing. Is it superficial, deep, flat, round? Poet Richard Wilbur wrote, "one does not, merely by referring to the dying god or what not, evoke a legitimate emotional response"(Jerome 193).
3. "Ekphrasis, when it's compelling, opens out" (Rusk 75).
4. Corn's "Notes on Ekphrasis" ends with, "[L]ocate the act of viewing visual art in a particular place and time, giving it a personal and perhaps even an historical context…. In such poems, description of the original work remains partial, but authors add to it aspects drawn from their own experiences— the facts, reflections, and feelings that arise at the confluence of a work of visual art and the life of the poet."
5. Is ekphrastic writing full of imagery? By definition they are image-based writings, so do they fail if they neglect to evoke the central image? If the reader is left seeing nothing, has the writing inherently failed its ekphrastic foundation?
6. Ekphrastic writing is not about description itself but about an artful experience that might beget an artful quest. This, I believe, is what makes a piece of ekphrastic writing "successful," absent description or, as a naysayer teacher once said, "a knowledge of theoretical discourse."
7. The poetry editors of *Ekphrasis* have this caveat on their website: "Acceptable ekphrastic verse transcends mere description: it stands as transformative critical statement, an original gloss on the individual art piece it addresses."
8. "Word and image neither translate nor illustrate each other, but work inseparately as single compositions" (Swensen).
9. When you write ekphrastically to artwork by a long-dead, famous artist, the good news is that the dead hold no opinions (or do they?). However, their adoring fans most certainly do. On the other hand, when you write ekphrastically to artwork by a living artist, the bad news is that they can voice their opinions; in which case, your artistry could be affected. "Many failures of ekphrasis come from the writer's urge to recreate, and share with readers, a particular aesthetic blessing" (Rusk 78).
10. For some people, writing with artwork in mind is merely an exercise in looking and describing. It might be a tough decision, but you should be clear about your work-in-progress. Does your

piece transcend the writing invitation? If not, your writing might be a mere exercise. If so, it needs no revision.

11. In the end, you must decide: Does it profit you to write ekphrastically? If it feels forced or your engagement with the arts is inauthentic, your writing will reflect that.

Ultimately, technical aspects of ekphrastic poetry, nonfiction, and fiction fall under the same scrutiny as non-ekphrastic text. The only difference is its subject matter or its impetus.

Some ideas about presenting your ekphrastic work:

1. Broadcast your influence? Ultimately you will need to decide how necessary is it that the companion images be seen with writing they influenced.
2. Subvert your influence? If publicizing the artwork that influenced your writing was only done to assuage the imagined curiosity of your readers, perhaps that is not reason enough.
3. Create an audio recording of the ekphrastic writing, played on a loop, along with the projection of the text and a projection (if you've been granted approval, and you've correctly credited the creator) of the art in a gallery space, in which you don't even have to be present—for you've created an art installation.
4. If you have created a collaborative piece with another student, invite the campus for an unveiling of the artwork along a recitation.

Creating a book—There are no inherent conventions of assembling a book of ekphrastic poems (for instance), though reading samples of great work is invaluable. The first entire collection of ekphrastic poems that I discovered was Peter Cooley's *The Van Gogh Notebook*, which was like a beacon in my life as a graduate student.

Insofar as ekphrastic prose is concerned, as explained earlier, it is rare to see an entire essay, story, memoir, or novel that revolves around art. The excerpts that I have quoted in this book are from a solid list of authors who did just that, however. For the most part, the inclusion of the images and how to navigate the text around those images is something a writer must consider in assembling a book.

Regarding publishing her ekphrastic prose along with original photography, the author of an ekphrastic memoir, Judith Kitchen offered these words in my interview:

> Description was actually what I hoped to avoid, or at least reduce. So much non-fiction is descriptive, and especially when it comes to photographs. We are at a stage in the technology where the photograph, instead of acting as confirmation

or illustration, can be a part of the text. Can make its own statement at the time when that becomes necessary. So, although I sometimes describe, I usually resort to describing parts of the photograph: small details that might be overlooked by a viewer; something that might have been mentioned by someone in the photo; something that takes me outside the frame of the photo, possibly into memory or speculation. What I hoped for was an integration of the photograph and the text—a place where one cannot function without the other—a bit the way a good poem about a painting needs the reader to know the painting through the content of the poem, to see the painting in fresh ways because of what the poem brings to it (Baugher, "An Interview").

Recent strides in technology have allowed for such discussions regarding images accompanying works of literature. Though, as alluded to in the list of what might make successful ekphrastic writing, not all writers hold that the art should attend to the text. As an analogous comparison, let's consider choices that translators (of poetry) and their publishers must make: After the translations are complete and ready for publication, the translator must decide how best to represent the work. Should the reader accept the translations as gospel and thus have no need for the original?

On the other hand, consider both versions sitting on the recto and verso (facing) pages. This accomplishes a couple of things: first, the reader has a point of reference. The curious reader will at least glance at the original, while others will have their own ideas of how the translation is precise, poignant, or problematic. Second, with the original version present, this can enlighten those ignorant of the foreign language, thus bridging the gap between cultures. Also, having the two side by side can inspire readers who may have never considered translating themselves.

In the case of ekphrastic writing, only artwork that you own or that you have permission to present can exist in tandem with your writing. Making a reference to the artwork by offering the link to the place where the digital image legally lives is the only other ethical way to present it.

Art/Life—What are your ideas for art immersion? Collaborating, inter-art scholarship, interdisciplinary learning? In-person art viewing includes neighborhood art walks (gallery openings) and museum visits (usually with suggested donations). There are numerous benefits to visiting artists' studios and public galleries: you can see not only new art and meet other people interested in art viewing, but you also have the opportunity to meet the artists themselves, and perhaps make friends with whom to collaborate. Remote art viewing includes art books (libraries, second-hand shops), websites (museum-run have the best quality images), and taking an art history class. Try volunteering to be an artist's model or visit art supply stores, many of which offer art workshops.

Is viewing art a type of universal language? Images can transcend time, space, and culture. It's ecstatic writing, to be sure. Are you ready to join the chorus of ekphrastic voices across the globe? Let's end this section by celebrating two particular works-of-art that have informed great literature: Vermeer's *Girl with a Pearl Earring* and Fabritius's *The Goldfinch*. In the many ekphrastic writings responding to these two pieces, the descriptions are decidedly different. Are you surprised?

Johannes Vermeer's c. 1665 painting, *Girl with a Pearl Earring* (courtesy Mauritshuis, The Hague).

Excerpt of Ekphrastic Nonfiction: From Michael White's memoir, *Travels in Vermeer* (regarding *Girl with a Pearl Earring*): "The lovely sympathy in her hazel irises, the lush eroticism of her lips, her mouth. She is the clapper, I am the bell, and she rings through my whole body" (31).

Excerpt of Ekphrastic Fiction: From Tracy Chevalier's novel, *Girl with a Pearl Earring*: "The baker's daughter stands in a bright corner by a window.... She is facing us, but is looking out the window, down to her right. She is wearing a yellow and black fitted bodice of silk and velvet, a dark blue skirt, and a white cap that hangs down in two points below her chin" (90).

Excerpt of Ekphrastic Nonfiction: From Michael White's memoir, *Travels in Vermeer* (regarding *The Goldfinch*): "It's the Carel Fabritius's trompe-l'oeil miniature, *The Goldfinch*.... It's a painting of a domesticated goldfinch on an elaborate perch attached to a whitewashed wall, and the contrast between the off-center, startlingly realized bird and the softly glowing wall behind is striking" (30).

Excerpt of Ekphrastic Fiction: From Donna Tartt's novel, *The Goldfinch*:

> Why this subject? A lonely pet bird? Which was in some way characteristic of his age or time, where animals featured mainly dead, in sumptuous trophy pieces, limp hares and fish and fowl, heaped high and bound for table? Why does it seem so significant to me that the wall is plain—no tapestry or hunting horns, no stage decoration.... Chained to his perch? Who knows what Fabritius was trying to tell

us by his choice of tiny subject? ... And if what they say is true—if every great painting is really a self-portrait (765).

Is the spirit of making ekphrases similar to when we were children with picture books and the images invited speculation, urging us to await with bated breath what would happen next? With ekphrasis, we can extend that speculation, thereby honoring the child we once were and the child that's within us still. Ultimately, though, there is no recipe for responding creatively to visual imagery. *What pleases you about the artwork* is my suggestion for beginning your engagement. Creative musings on art are never conclusive.

Carel Fabritius's 1654 painting, *The Goldfinch* (courtesy Mauritshuis, The Hague).

Additional Instructional Applications

In Mary Cassatt's painting, *The Child's Bath*, a brunette woman with her hair in a bun, is seated on a cushion on the floor of a room. On her lap is a child, naked except for a white cloth draped over her lap. The woman's face is close to the child's as they both look down to regard the basin of water. Earlier, you read the ekphrastic poem by Peter Cooley.

The power of description is a tool that students will use throughout their lives, and composition and rhetoric have infinite applications in classrooms of students of all ages. The teaching and learning of any subject can be enhanced through the lens of the visual arts. Some topics include children's literature, the politics of imagery, multicultural studies, environmental studies, sociology, and S.T.E.M. This section focuses on the use of ekphrasis in teaching, so I will be addressing teachers of all levels directly.

Suggested Viewing: Sister Wendy's (Wendy Mary Beckett) Story of Painting

Children's Literature

Picture books without words welcome reader participation, and picture books with words combine the art of storytelling with illustration. Teaching how the visual arts and language arts intersect in children's books is another form of image-word inquiry. Aside from imagistic or graphic decoration, image-word relationships in books for children are worth studying, for the images function in a way that extends the story's meaning beyond the words.

Let's review the different genres in children's literature: Mother Goose books and nursery rhymes (sound-driven); books fostering aesthetic development (rhyme, rhythm, and other repeat patterns); books cultivating social-physical development and cooperative play (animal, moral, and folk tales); toy books (tactile experiences); alphabet books (concrete images paired with abstraction); and books targeting cognitive development (counting and concepts).

While the stories remain fixed, sometimes new illustrations are introduced with subsequent editions, which ultimately can echo the current zeitgeist. For instance, it is fascinating to compare and contrast the different illustrations associated with these two stories: *Little Miss Muffet*, illustrated in 1900 by Kate Greenaway, illustrated in c. 1932 by E. Bachmann,

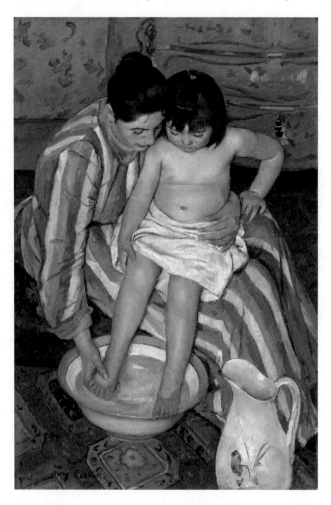

Mary Cassatt's 1893 painting, *The Child's Bath* (courtesy the Robert A. Waller Fund).

and the imagery related to the 2011 publication by Miles Kelly Publishing, and *Jack Sprat* and its corresponding c.1833 wood engraving, illustrated in 1910 by Margaret W. Tarrant, and illustrated in 1966 by Raymond Briggs.

In Western societies, we typically read artwork the way we read a page of text, from left to right. Knowing this, illustrators tend to situate the protagonist on the left. Other typographical decisions include page and book orientation, size and shape of pictures, placement of words and images, and whether they're adjacent, on opposite pages, or if they overlay or infringe on each other's design in some way (image placement can obscure the words and word placement can confuse the image, for instance). Tension may or may not exist between what the words say and what the illustrations depict. In some cases, the picture would make little sense without the words.

Here is a book whose recto and verso pages offer illustrations from different points of view:

Suggested Reading: John Burningham's picture book, *Come Away from the Water, Shirley*

Common artistic styles found in picture books include realism (art representing the natural world with lifelike detail), cartoon art (exaggerations, caricatures), expressionist art (in which there is experimentation with line, color, space), impressionist art (color-driven, dreamlike, emotive), surrealist art (presentation of juxtapositions, thereby making thought-provoking and bizarre connections), and folk art (where utilitarian objects are ornamented).

Beyond decorative and illustrative art, when you consider image-and-word relationships in children's literature, it is a list similar to the modes and methods of ekphrasis. For example:

Images illustrate the words
Images replace the words (e.g., rebuses)
Images explain the words
Words are indicated in the images (e.g., alphabet and counting
    books)
Words comment on images
Images comment on words
Images supplement the words (e.g., historical, cultural context)
Images standalone, irrespective of the words presented

Ekphrasis for Children

For children, as well as adults, artwork can be an entry into the imagination and memory. Numerous children's books present actual physical gateways into fantastical realms. Who hasn't enjoyed breeching the portals of Alice's looking-glass (Lewis Carroll), the children's wardrobe (C.S. Lewis), and Milo's tollbooth (Norton Juster)?

Suggested Activity: Make inkblots with your students and then have them engage verbally with their creations.

Over a hundred years ago Rorschach himself "called for better training on how to see" (Searls 25). As a warm-up, ask students to close their eyes and answer these questions: Describe the classroom: describe the floor, the walls, the furniture. How many tables, chairs, students, books? How many windows? What (if anything) is written on the board or displayed on the screen? What (if anything) is posted to the wall? Describe the outfit of another person in the room.

Instructing young children—Guide students to responding intuitively during in-class discussions of art. Some students will express a natural tendency to see patterns and meanings in shapes. Others may have a difficult time with the freedom or limitless possibilities of this type of inquiry (that is, interacting and responding to art). When this happens, I invite you, their teacher, to deflect their questions. For example, "Can I turn it around? *It's up to you.* Should I try to use all of it? *Whatever you like. Different people see different things.* Is that the right answer? *There are all sorts of answers*" (Peot, 4).

While it's been many pages since you have seen the image of pumpkins in a garden, here is Chapman's ekphrastic poem, which is a nice first ekphrastic poem to introduce to young students for the relatability of the gourd. Notice the six-line stanzas play with and against the "three pumpkins" of the title. Ask the students about the references to numbers and vegetation. Can they locate internal rhyme and alliteration? What else do they enjoy about the poem? Now, show them the image and discuss the marriage of word and image.

Three Pumpkins

(Yayoi Kusama)
by Robin Chapman

Yellow and black, they rise
from black soil tessellated
by leaf-shape into black background print—each edge of leaf
catches the yellow light
of which they're made—

three squashes, I would say,
shaped like delicata mashed
into pattypans, fat lobes
lolling upwards in sinuous

shapes, black circles tracing
their arcs, condensing to spots

spilling into stripes in my eye—
and the stems cut to dry—
two stippling patterns,
two colors to tell us, in circle
and line, the season of harvest,
late autumn, before snow.

Abundance stored up glows
inner orange in the mind,
and the artist who has painted
naked bodies with polka-dots
turns from prints to pumpkin
installations—in this photograph

they rise like beanstalks four,
six, eight feet high, sprung
to 3-D, large enough to house
the Pumpkin Eater's wife,
advancing from the trees
like giants, playing with size

to stretch the landscape, raise
the faraway trees to tower-height.

Poet's Comments

I chose this image because I'm a gardener, attracted to vegetable shapes, and because I am working on a collection of gardening poems. The poem, as I sat down to describe what I saw, took on a roughly three-beat line, then a six-line stanza shape, then rhyming echoes that all influenced word choice along the way—gradually I found myself in multiple worlds: my American garden, the world of Japanese haiku evoking seasons, the world of Japanese prints with three repeating images, the cognitive science of how images call up memory for events bubbled-up, the experiment on relative size perception in the Ames Room, the story of Yayoi Kusama's avant-garde life, and how screen prints are made, followed by research, into her artistic methods. One change I made in drafting the poem was to appropriate the gardening shears for myself, rather than the farmer (who must have cut the originals for her models a quarter-century ago), and to incorporate the photo of her 3-D installation of the same polka-dotted shapes in 2009. The last change I made was to omit mention of the shears and instead pull in the artist's early practice of painting nudes with polka dots (Robin Chapman).

Ekphrastic Classroom Activities

Materials—Postcards of art purchased at museums, collected during your travels, collected at galleries, or purchased at stationery stores. Have at least three small art reproductions per student in your class.

Overview—Help your student to start to engage with the artwork by mandating literal descriptions. Then move into a discussion of the figurative description, personal associations, and meaning. Have everyone do a freewrite on the same image. Have volunteers share their writing, in which students can notice the unique qualities of each one.

Literal ekphrasis—Given a single artwork for the whole class to attend to, start the class discussion by having students describe aloud what they see (not what they interpret, no abstractions, no opinions, no explanations). Make it a challenge among the students who can point out the most minute details. Do this as a class exercise until all literal description has been exhausted.

Realistic art—Ask the students to engage with a painting in the style of realism. Pieter de Hooch's painting, *The Mother*, is one that I often use. Handout a copy of the image for each student to study. Walk them through the image in terms of concrete observations, making sure every object, figure, color, shape is mentioned. Have them cover up the image with a piece of paper and reveal the image millimeter by millimeter. What did they overlook? Next, what abstractions do they see? Finally, ask how the image resonates with them personally.

Abstract art—Distribute the same abstract image to each student and have them describe and respond to the piece. Depending on the age of the class, either ask them for their input aloud or have them partake in timed freewriting. Use artwork of your choice, or if you are unfamiliar with abstract artists, I suggest selecting artwork from any of these artists: Judy Chicago, Grace Hartigan, Hartmut Austen, or Charles Emerson.

Freedom of choice—Let the students drive the ekphrastic conversation by giving them autonomy in picking a picture. Display the images on a large table and ask students to chose one image that pleases them. Next, allow the students to study the image for a few quiet minutes. During this time, urge them to muse on all aspects of the image: colors, shapes, narrative, perspective, and so forth. Finally, ask the students to freewrite for ten minutes. Afterward, allow the students to voluntarily share their freewrites while exhibiting the image they used.

Show and tell—Involve the students by encouraging them to find museum-quality art, bring the image to class (physically or digitally), and introduce each other to those works-of-art. You can expand this exercise by having the students write an imagined history of the artwork, including the artist's background.

Photographic imagery—In lieu of physical postcards or other methods of sharing artwork, ask students to bring photographs of their family. One idea is to facilitate a discussion about how strangers know less about your family than you, as well as the notion that strangers can know more about your family than you. As the teacher, collect photographs from each student and then randomly distribute them to all the students. What image-engagement and writing invitations can you create?

Practice—The importance of practicing ekphrastic writing (or writing of any sort, for that matter) cannot be overstated. To be a better ekphrastic writer, you must write (and read) regularly. Think of it as building muscle and stamina.

Guest art teacher I—Invite someone from your school's art department to give your students a brief overview of how to look at art. Then, escort the students to the school's gallery or museum. Give the students 30 minutes to select an object and do a freewrite. Once everyone has completed the assignment, ask students to share their freewrites in front of their influences. Allow more than one student to select the same artwork and celebrate their individual responses. Remind students that many of their freewrites, after serious revision, can become polished ekphrastic writing.

Guest art teacher II—Ask an art teacher to teach some drawing basics. Then, pair up the students, distribute one image per pair, ask one student to close both eyes while the partner describes the image. Then, they do the exercise again, with the second student attempting to draw the image while the first student, again, describes the image. Did the description improve with the second articulation? How well did the artist render the verbal description? Keep the exercise fun and celebrate the creativity, both verbally and visually.

All-class collaboration—Select one artwork for the whole class to engage with. Have them freewrite on what they see and then what they do not see. Distribute strips of paper and have students transcribe a favorite line or two from their freewrite. Have the students come together with their strips of papers and direct them to make a collaborative story or poem. They will need to find a suitable order for the lines, and once they have, a title will need to be assigned. Have the students present the work aloud. Type up the collaborative piece, including all contributors' names, and distribute a copy to each.

Suggested Viewing: The art of photo-alchemist, Kensuke Koike

Image manipulation—Find museum-quality photography, print out the images on sheets of paper, and ask your students to experience manipulating the handheld artifacts to see how the viewing of each changes. With scissors in hand, crop the picture, focusing on one detail, or cut it on the vertical, horizontal, or diagonal. Remove all humans. Use a hole-punch and recreate the photograph from the tiny pieces. There are a plethora of ways to cut, paste, and otherwise manipulate images to make new ones.

Ingredients exercise—Create lists of ingredients for an ekphrastic assignment (wherein more structure allows for greater freedom). For example, find a landscape that illustrates a place you have never visited. Notice elements of repetition in the artwork and use a refrain in your poem, as well as three spondees, two slant rhymes, and assonance.

Suggested Discussion: Compare and contrast various artists' styles, techniques, and philosophies about their art-making.

Suggested Discussion: Given Alper's observation, "There is probably no artist or writer who meditated as continuously and as deeply on the relationship between seeing, knowing, and picturing the world as did Leonardo da Vinci," it's worth introducing the students to his art, writing, and philosophies as an example of an interdisciplinary visionary (46).

Writing Invitation: Create a persona poem or a prose character sketch influenced by an artwork.

Writing Invitation: Locate an artwork that features an object. Write poetry or fiction in which you use personification.

Writing Invitation: Research the art of Huang Yung-Fu, which adorns most of the surfaces of the Taiwan village of Taichung. As an old man, he swathed his village in colorful paint after the government threatened to demolish it. Alternatively, locate mural art, street art, or graffiti art in your own town. If you could cover your neighborhood in art, what would that look like?

Writing Invitation: Any object can illicit reverie and spawn a piece of creative writing. Ask the students, "Who in your life is a maker?" Allow their answers (factual or imaginative) to prompt them to the page.

Suggested Discussion: Examine visual arts and corresponding literary arts movements: Introduce students to both visual and verbal art from a single artist movement (for example, dadaism, fluxus, surrealism) in order to demonstrate the commonalities between the disciplines.

Writing Invitation: Discover artwork that concerns harmony or discord between two individuals. Write an epithalamium or another occasional poem.

Writing Invitation: Write about a fictional character whose job it is to create sculptural art for some specific audience.

Writing Invitation: Using the details of two or more works-of-art, weave those details together in a single piece of writing.

Writing Invitation: Painter Emily Carr lamented that people would ask her, "'Explain the picture,' but how can one explain spirit?" Unearth an artwork that celebrates the spirit.

Gender Politics of Imagery

Here is one opportunity to help students cultivate their critical thinking skills: Given pictorial depictions, how often are gender roles stereotyped? What is the "male gaze?" Why is it that a preponderance of famous art was created by males, but most of the portraits are of women?

Heffernan in *Museum of Words* observed:

> Ekphrasis ... evokes the power of the silent image even as it subjects that power to the rival authority of language, it is intensely paragonal. Second, the contest it stages is often powerfully gendered: the expression of a duel between male and female gazes, the voice of male speech striving to control a female image that is both alluring and threatening of male narrative striving to overcome the fixating impact of beauty poised in space (1).

Suggested Viewing: Balthus' portrait painting, *Alice*

Suggested Reading: William Carlos Williams' poem, "Portrait of a Lady"

Suggested Viewing: Balthus' painting, *Girl with Cat*

Suggested Reading: Christina Rossetti's poem, "In an Artist's Studio"

Suggested Reading: Francine Prose's essay, "Scent of a Woman's Ink"

Though we have not seen the corresponding image by Lilly Martin Spencer for a while, here is a poem that deals with gender politics, though with an unexpected twist:

Or, Didn't You Know That What You Really See Is Your Own Reflection?
(After *Young Husband: First Marketing* by Lilly Martin Spencer)
by Hedy Habra

Listen. Everyone thinks I've had it all, but let me tell you. Things aren't as they seem. Look at the pond's mirroring surface; it tricks you into thinking nothing perturbs its deeper layers, yet who knows how many mini tragedies unfold within its murky bottom? You say you wish you'd find a man like your dad. He was not the man you see now. It takes a lifetime. You need to slide stakes in slowly, overlook an occasional bending, praise the slightest effort.

I still recall that evening when I saw him through lowered blinds, pirouetting on one foot as he tried to open his umbrella under pouring rain, the overloaded basket dancing over his knee. Passers-by giggling at the sight of the broken eggs, the lettuce head and tomatoes scattered all over the glistening pavement, a painterly scene, I thought. I'll never forget his frown and clenched features. I understood it all. The forgetfulness. The items missing from the list. I knew I had to stop nagging.

And weren't my mom's words prophetic? And her olden days rigmarole about men are like children—*they need to be praised*, and her same old tune about a man *not wanting a smarter wife*? Things don't change that easily. Nothing happens overnight. Think of the pond. What you really see is your own reflection, the reflection of your desires.

Writing Invitation: Here are two ideas for a writing an ekphrastic gender-politics poem, essay, or story: contrast the fashion designs associated with female heroes versus male heroes, and explore the portrayal of stereotypical gender behaviors in art—females and maternity, domesticity, matrimony, and sexuality (as symbols of weakness) versus males as warriors, deities, religious leaders, thinkers, and machinists (as symbols of strength).

Multicultural Studies

How do images of any given culture affect social and cultural values? In the average museum, how often do we see images of cultures of which we're ignorant? What are some examples of cultural stereotypes in art? Raising cultural awareness in our pluralistic society has become profoundly important. Fortunately, finding cross-cultural pedagogy opportunities is relatively easy when dealing with the visual arts. Here are some items for arts engagement and cultural enrichment:

1. Introduce students to "traditional art," which is art that reflects the culture of a particular group of people's skills or knowledge and has been passed down for generations. Which traditional art has been important to the students' families?
2. What is the relationship between art and culture? How have world events been informed by art? How has art affected national, international, or global change? In the US, what effect has art had on social justice? Is art-making a type of freedom of speech? Is art determined by the intent of the artist or by the response of those who experience it? What social responsibilities should artists have?
3. Studying image-word productions across cultures is fascinating. For example, in Japanese, Korean, and Chinese cultures, poetry and art have historically been woven together. What cross-cultural or cross-discipline lessons might you create with these cultures in mind?
4. Identify art from a particular time and geographic location and have the students respond by writing in forms that are specific to that culture. For example, the pantoum (Malaysia), daina (Latvia), or lục bát (Vietnam). The assignment can be expanded to include historical events.

5. Aside from ekphrastic writing to the visual arts, symbolic objects, as well as everyday objects, can offer great fodder. **Writing Invitation:** Given these objects (or select your own), see what germinates for you: death mask of L'Inconnue de la Seine, tombstones at Père Lachaise, sculpture of Lady Justice, a wishing well, Venice's bocche di leone, a national flag, burden baskets, or the sculpture *Liberty Enlightening the World*.

6. Study various cultures' rites-of-passage ceremonies through the visual arts. Learn the rituals, the anthropological significance, and companion works of world literature, all while taking a visual trip through those passages from one social group to another.

7. Historically in some cultures, images, and the people who created them were synonymous with the supernatural. For instance, some tribal art, pagan art, and Haitian art had associations with magic, voodoo, hoodoo, and conjure. What lessons could you create that teach the power of the image along with social constructs and religious ideals?

8. Cultural relativism: Not all images are created equally, and unfortunately, not every human has had the freedom to create art. In history, artists have been excommunicated, exiled, and executed because of their creations. In some cultures, for instance, there exists a religious prohibition against images. Denmark's museum, The David Collection explains it thusly: "A conspicuous feature of art in the Islamic world is the limited use of naturalistic images of living beings. This is because Islam, like Judaism and in certain periods Christianity, practices a kind of prohibition against the making of images....The purpose of a prohibition against images was initially to avoid idolatry." It continues, "The result of restraint in the use of figurative depictions in time led Muslim artists, more than those in other cultures, to concentrate on abstract forms of expression. In traditional Islamic art, vegetal ornamentation, geometric patterns, and a fascination with script—calligraphy—reached unprecedented heights" (davidmus.dk).

9. As an extension of what we see and how that affects us in a way we might not be conscious of, regard the world map. **Suggested Viewing:** Look at the Gall-Peters projection map, which counters the typical perception we might have of the size, shape, and location of land masses on this planet.

10. Along with cultural studies, translation studies can be taught through the framework of ekphrasis. The artist who created the curated artwork, *Post-Industrial Society Has Arrived* also wrote

ekphrastically to his painting in his native language of Chinese (which he then translated into English).

Here is an excerpt of Lo Ch'ing's poem, 〈後工業社會來了之後〉 羅青

在末班地鐵一長串煞車聲之中
聽見了一鈎變形又發亮的弦月
基地台高舉刺蝟般的天線松針
刺破了漫天星斗散落虛擬人間

Here is the English translation of the poem, "Here Comes the Post-Industrial Society":

In the ear-piercing braking sounds of the last subway
A flickering Arabian-scimitar crescent is heard loud and clear

Cell towers camouflaged themselves into a plastic pine forest of porcupine
Pricking the canopy sky with sieving stars raining into immersive virtual realities

Technology and Ekphrasis

What influence does modern technology have on imagery, art, description, and creative writing? Will the fine arts become supplanted by the digital arts or artificial intelligence?

Visual Persuasion: Each of us in this modern world experiences image-inundation. Mass media successfully uses the art of visual persuasion in ways that can result in excessive consumerism, political propaganda, and appropriation. Technology has forever altered our relationship with the world of art.

Suggested Viewing: The artwork of contemporary hyperrealism artist, Carole A. Feuerman

Digital ekphrasis—Currently, many ekphrastic writers are not limiting their engagement of imagery to museum-sequestered art. Also, they are not limited by the constraints of physical sheets of paper. These days, technology-savvy ekphrastic practitioners are creating work that harkens back to children's picture books and involves a digital communion of word and image in a virtual space, wherein the placement of the writer's contribution and the placement of the artist's contribution—and the interplay between the two—drive production decisions. The interdependency of word/image can involve a single creator or can be a collaborative effort.

New media poetry, nonfiction, and fiction—"New media" is a term used in the visual arts and literary arts to define work that was created with technologies such as digital art, computer graphics and animation, video games, robotics, and 3D printing, to name a few. The presentation of these new media art forms is especially innovative in that it can be digitally interactive.

Let's look at some terms and concepts to better understand the current trends in technology and how those trends could have an effect on how we use imagery and description, which in turn could influence our approach to art—not to mention the potential evolving definition of *art*—and our verbal engagement with it.

Art accessibility—Historically, "art accessibility" meant that a person could readily access works-of-art physically and digitally. Today, though, it has a dual meaning: accessibility both in terms of viewing art and in terms of making art.

Digital arts—Included under this label are digital sketching and drawing, digital painting and watercoloring, digital sculpting/sculpt modeling, and digital photography. One benefit to working in the digital arts is that you can work faster, and in so doing (presumably) accessing and executing ideas more rapidly. There is no deciding which supplies to purchase, acquiring those supplies, preparing your materials, and setting up your studio. Your hands remain clean. However, what is lost is your connection to the medium. Do the soiled hands that made the physical artwork contribute to a feeling of intimacy with the art? Furthermore, you are not necessarily working through your mistakes on a screen; you are merely deleting what did not work and moving on. Does digital art lack the maker's personality because of the subjugation of those missteps? Have the digital arts diminished the quality of artists' ideas by allowing them to undo, to start over?

Generative art—Also called "computer art" or "algorithmic art," generative art is created with the use of a non-human autonomous system. Furthermore, it is purported that the system can execute its own artistic ideas, thereby becoming the sole creator. Types of generative art include architecture, music, visual art, and literature. All art, digital or otherwise, is an approximation. Although we might see Magritte's painting of a pipe, it's not a pipe after all.

Deep-learning—"Deep learning" is the term for a software approach to teaching technology. For decades, the database of languages has been growing, and that, coupled with language-processing algorithms and machine-learning research, has lead to AI synthesizing texts, from which it can perform reading comprehension and summarizing, as well as natural language processing. Additional byproducts of deep-learning include speech recognition and image recognition.

AI artistic style transfer—Once the computer system has been programmed to learn styles of various art movements (cubism, expressionism, impressionism, to name a few), a user can introduce a picture of a New York City street corner, for instance, and ask the program to translate that realist scene into cubism by applying that chosen artistic style. With just a click of a button, the computer style-transfer can mirror certain major artists' masterpieces.

Suggested Reading: The Federal Visual Rights Act of 1990

Suggested Research: Intellectual Property Rights (IPR) and Copyright

AI-generated notional images (based on text)—If you will recall, the deep-image is an image unconcerned with realism, as its imagery is spawned from the unconscious mind. Conscious mind imagery is based on realism, for it is a pictorial of something that can occur in the world: hummingbirds, pianos, and an Underwood typewriter share a room. The deep-image, on the other hand, takes as its source freedom from literal constraints: one dozen hummingbirds playing pianos in a symphony orchestrated by a typewriter. If we were to ask the computer to generate an image based on the orchestral scene described above, it would successfully offer up that output whose imagery was constructed from our imagination.

AI-generated actual images (based on text)—Computer programmers have created software that, given a simple sentence of description, a photorealistic image could be created. In this system, words are converted to generalized images, which are culled from a database of millions of images. The algorithm reads the words, "A large dog with a ball in its mouth" and outputs a general image of a dog holding a ball in its mouth. It is just a matter of time, though, when artificial intelligence can accept longer, more elaborate text descriptions, thereby generating more detailed images. As the technology matures, so will its specificity to image-producing. "Large dog" will become "a four-year-old female fox-red Labrador," for example.

AI-generated text (based on images)—Computer programmers have successfully created a neural network that enables computers to describe in a single sentence an image on the screen. A user can upload an image of a red bird on a tree branch, and based on that photorealist image, the computer's typed response is "A red bird sits on the branch of a tree."

Thought-generated media synthesis—In the end, the goal will be the facilitation of direct human thoughts translating to media synthesis. Given this scenario, verbal description will become irrelevant because it is predicted that the system will eventually circumvent the need to express our ideas (whether by conjuring in our minds verbal descriptions, expressing them orally, or writing them). In the future, might humans think up an image as precisely as possible, and the computer will respond with a pictorial translation of that image-thought?

Artificial Intelligence—One projection that I have concerns computer programs' capacity for assisting ekphrastic writers with the validity of their descriptions. When we use words to describe the literal, we are banking on readers seeing exactly what it is that we have in mind. However, do they? Once these programs can move beyond a single, simple sentence of description, then perhaps writers can introduce their extended descriptions into the AI program, which then could interpret the text and create the image output. This program could be another tool that the writer uses to create an effective description. Subsequently, it would be the computer, and not the instructor or reader, who's providing feedback about the effectiveness of the writer's verbal representation. In this way, technology could offer a real-time, objective response to a rhetorical prompt concerning description. Additionally, for the programs that output a text description given an image, young students beginning to learn the art of description can work parallel to the AI program and see if their words and those of the computer's align. Therefore, it could be a method of checking your work as you proceed through description exercises. Last but not least, art students as well can use this program to see how well their text-based images compare to those of the computer's.

The implications for these methods of image-generation are vast. As an ekphrastic writer and teacher, I wonder: Is description about to enjoy a new renaissance? Will ekphrasis become an essential form of rhetoric again wherein a new generation of students will be formally instructed on how to perfect it? Given this projection, then will ekphrastic writers who employ extended descriptions be celebrated for their verbal prowess? In other words, will the mode of ekphrasis be revered as a skill inextricably connected to technology? We shall see.

Final Words

Paul Valéry wrote, "One makes use of images in order to guide oneself, to please oneself, to heal oneself, to know oneself," and it's the question of where vision can lead a person that consumes me. There is an art and science to deep-looking. Once you have a sense of which type of art is compelling to you, and you learn how to read any given artwork, you can approach art-viewing as an intuitive act. Giving your full attention to artwork can be transformative, and it can feel dramatic, as in Stendhal's experience. When we are receptive to art, what might ensnare our attention may very well trigger a chain of associations. Art-viewing opens a world of speculation, surprise, and discovery, all of which can tempt us to the page.

Finally, I wish for you a life in which art resides within you and in which you feel, in the words of Fernando Pessoa, *always astonished.*

—J.J.B.

Bibliography:
Works Consulted

Ackerman, Diane. *A Natural History of the Senses.* Vintage Books, 1990.

Adams, Eddie. www.journals.sagepub.com.

Allen, Donald, editor. *The Collected Poems of Frank O'Hara.* Alfred A. Knopf, 1972.

Allison, Dorothy. "This Is Our World." *Seeing and Writing.* McQuade, D. and C. McQuade, editors. St. Martins, 2000, vol. 1, pp. 155–60.

Alpers, Svetlana. *The Art of Describing: Dutch Art in the Seventeenth Century.* The University of Chicago Press, 1983.

American Institute for Conversation website, 20 Dec 2018, www.culturalheritage.org/.

Aphthonius. *Progymnasmata.* www.people.umass.edu/dfleming/E388%20Aphthonius%20 Progymnasmata.pdf.

Aristotle, *Poetics.* www.fulltextarchive.com/page/Poetics/.

Arnheim, Rudolf. *Art and Visual Perception: A Psychology of the Creative Eye.* University of California Press, 1974.

Arnold, Dana. *Art History: A Very Short Introduction.* Oxford University Press, 2004.

Association of Writers & Writing Programs, Annual Conference. *Pedagogy Papers,* 2006.

_____. Pedagogy Papers, 2007.

Atwood, Margaret. "Death by Landscape." *Wilderness Tips.* Bloomsbury Publishing, Ltd., 1991, pp. 121–146.

Baer, Ulrich, editor and translator. *The Poet's Guide to Life: The Wisdom of Rilke.* Random House, 2005.

Barnes, Julian. *A History of the World in 10½ Chapters.* Vintage Books, 1989.

_____. *Nothing to be Frightened of.* Vintage Books, 2009.

Baugher, Janée J. "Art to Art: Ekphrastic Poetry." *Boulevard Magazine,* vol. 25 no. 1, 2009, pp. 111–114.

_____. "An Interview with Judith Kitchen." *The Writer's Chronicle,* vol. 47 no. 6, May/Summer, 2015, pp. 30–41.

Beck, Martha. "Half a Mind is a Terrible Thing to Waste." *O Magazine,* vol. 10, no. 11, 2009, pp. 57–60.

Bell, Julian. *What is Painting?* Thames and Hudson Limited, 2017.

Berger, John. *Ways of Seeing.* Penguin Books, 1972.

Berger, John, and Jean Mohr. *Another Way of Telling.* Vintage Books, 1995.

Bidart, Frank. *Watching the Spring Festival.* Farrar, Straus and Giroux, 2008.

Bierds, Linda. *The Ghost Trio.* Henry Holt and Company, 1994.

_____. *The Profile Makers.* Henry Holt and Company, 1997.

Billingham, Richard. www.saatchigallery.com/artists/richard_billingham.htm.

Blackburn, Julia. *Old Man Goya.* Pantheon Books, 2002.

Blakeslee, Sandra. "Deconstructing the Gaze of Rembrandt; Scientists Say a Vision Flaw May Have Aided His Genius." *The New York Times*, 16 Sept 2004, p. E00001.

Bly, Robert. *Leaping Poetry, an Idea with Poems and Translations*. Beacon Press, 1972.

_____. "What the Image Can Do." *Claims for Poetry*. Hall, D. editor. The University of Michigan Press, 1982, pp. 38–49.

_____. "A Wrong Turning in American Poetry." *Claims for Poetry*. Hall, D., editor. The University of Michigan Press, 1982, pp. 17–36.

Bolaño, Robert. "Labyrinth." *The New Yorker*, 23 Jan 2012, pp. 66–72.

Bosveld, Jennifer, editor. *Elastic Ekphrastic: Poetry on Art*. Pudding House, 2003.

Breton, André. *Surrealism and Painting*. Editions Gallimard, 2002.

Bridge, Helen. "Rilke and the Modern Portrait." *The Modern Language Review*, vol. 99, no. 3, 2004, pp. 681–695.

Brookner, Anita. *A Misalliance*. Vintage Books, 1986.

Brower, Reuben A., editor. *On Translation*. Harvard University Press, 1959.

Brown, Kurt. *Verse & Universe: Poems about Science and Mathematics*. Milkweed Publications, 1997.

Brown, Rebecca, and Mary Jane Knecht, editors. *Looking Together: Writers on Art*. University of Washington Press, 2009.

Buchwald, Emilie, and Ruth Roston, editors. *The Poet Dreaming in the Artist's House: Contemporary Poems about the Visual Arts*. Milkweed Editions, 1984.

Burroway, Janet. *Writing Fiction: A Guide to Narrative Craft*. Pearson Education, 2003.

Bushnell, J.T. "The Heart and the Eye: How Description Can Access Emotion." *Poets & Writers*, vol. 41, no. 1, 2013, pp. 48–56.

Butler, Robert Olen. *From Where You Dream: The Process of Writing Fiction*. Grove Press, 2005.

Byatt, A.S. *The Matisse Stories*. Random House, 1993.

Cameron, Julia. *The Artist's Way: A Spiritual Path to Higher Creativity*. J.P. Tarcher/Putnam, 1992.

Campbell, Joseph. "On the Relation of Analytical Psychology to Poetry." *The Portable Jung*. Random House, 1976, pp. 301–322.

Camus, Albert. *The Myth of Sisyphus*. Vintage Books, 2018.

Carroll, Henry, editor. *Photographers on Photography: How the Masters See, Think and Shoot*. Laurence King Publishing, 2018.

_____. *Read This If You Want to Take Great Photographs*. Laurence Kelly Publishing, Ltd., 2014.

Carson, Anne. *Autobiography of Red*. Vintage Books, 1998.

Cather, Willa. *The Song of the Lark*. www.gutenberg.org/files/44/44-h/44-h.htm.

Césaire, Aimé. *Lost Body*. Translated by Clayton Eshleman and Annette Smith. George Braziller, Inc., 1986.

Chang, Candy. *Before I Die*. www.cand16ychang.com/work/before-i-die-in-nola/.

Cheeke, Stephen. *Writing for Art: The Aesthetics of Ekphrasis*. Manchester University Press, 2008.

Chessman, Harriet Scott. *The Lost Sketchbook of Edgar Degas*. Outpost 19, 2017.

_____. *Lydia Cassatt Reading the Morning Paper*. The Permanent Press and Seven Stories Press, 2001.

Chevalier, Tracy. *Girl with a Pearl Earring*. Penguin Group, 2001.

Cohen, David. *Ambiguity and Intention*. www.interdiciplines.org/artcog/papers/ll, 2003.

Coldwell, Paul. *Printmaking: A Contemporary Perspective*. Black Dog Publications, 2010.

Concannon, Kevin. "Yoko Ono's CUT PIECE: From Text to Performance and Back Again." *Imagine Peace*, 2008, www.imaginepeace.com/archives/2680.

Cooley, Peter. *The Van Gogh Notebook*. Carnegie Mellon University Press, 1987.

Cooper, Arnie. "The Inspired Mind: A Window into the Writer's Brain." *Poets & Writers*. Jan/Feb, 2013, pp. 41–47.

Corn, Alfred. "Notes on Ekphrasis." *Poets.org*. 15 Jan 2008, www.poets.org/text/notes-ekphrasis.

D'Arcy Hughes, Ann. *The Printmaking Bible: The Complete Guide to Materials and Techniques.* Chronicle Books, 2008.

Davenport, Guy. *The Geography of the Imagination.* Pantheon Books, 1981.

DeGhett, Stephanie Coyne. "Paintings in Fiction: Ten Lessons from the Masters of Ekphrasis." *The Writer's Chronicle.* May/Summer, 2014, pp. 96–107.

Denham, Robert D. *Poets on Paintings: A Bibliography.* McFarland, 2010.

De Reyna, Rudy. *How to Draw What You See.* Watson-Guptill Publications, 1996.

DK Publishing. *Art: A World History.* DK Publishing, 1997.

Doherty, John. "Art Appreciation Activity—Questioning in Learning and Teaching." *Art Department, Sha Tin College,* 2015.

Dolin, Sharon. *Serious Pink.* Marsh Hawk Press, 2003.

Edwards, Betty. *Drawing on the Right Side of the Brain: A Course in Enhancing Creativity and Artistic Confidence.* J.P. Tarcher, Inc., 1979.

Edwards, Steve. *Photography: A Very Short Introduction.* Oxford University Press, 2006.

Elbow, Peter. *Writing Without Teachers.* Oxford University Press, 1998.

Eliot, T.S. "Tradition and the Individual Talent." *Selected Essays, 1917–1932.* Harcourt, Brace and Company, 1932, pp. 3–11.

Emerson, Charles. Painter/Instructor. Interview, 15 Sep and 22 Dec 2018.

Encyclopaedia Britannica, editors. *Hermann Rorschach, Swiss Psychiatrist,* 29 Mar 2019, www.britannica.com/biography/Hermann-Rorschach.

Eschner, Kat. *Hermann Rorschach's Artistic Obsession Led to His Famous Test,* 8 Nov 2017, www.smithsonianmag.com/smart-news/hermann-rorschachs-artistic-obsession-led-his-famous-test.

Faigley, Lester, et al. *Picturing Texts.* W.W. Norton and Company, 2004.

Farr, Sheila. "Unexpected Lessons: Corot to Picasso Show Paints a Portrait of Modern Art." *The Seattle Times,* 16 June 2002, pp. K-1, K-4.

Fautrier, Jean. "Head of a Hostage," *Tate,* 1943–4, www.tate.org.uk/art/artworks/fautrier-head-of-a-hostage-t07300.

Finch, Annie. *A Poet's Craft: A Comprehensive Guide to Making and Sharing Your Poetry.* University of Michigan Press, 2012.

Finnell, Dennis. *The Gauguin Answer Sheet.* University of Georgia Press, 2001.

"First Stories in Stone." *How Art Made the World.* www.pbs.org/howartmadetheworld/episodes/once/first/.

Fischer, Barbara K. *Museum Mediations: Reframing Ekphrasis in Contemporary American Poetry.* Routledge, 2006.

Forrer, Matthi, translator. *A Peasant Crossing a Bridge.* www.artic.edu/artworks/57271/a-peasant-crossing-a-bridge-from-the-series-a-true-mirror-of-chinese-and-japanese-poems?is_public_domain=1&page=34.

Foster, Jonathan K. *Memory: A Very Short Introduction.* Oxford University Press, 2009.

Foster, Tonya, and Kristin Prevallet, editors. *Third Mind: Creative Writing through Visual Art.* Teachers & Writers Collaborative, 2002.

Franck, Frederick. *The Zen of Seeing: Seeing/Drawing as Meditation.* Vintage Books, 1973.

Freeman, John. *New Performance/New Writing.* Red Globe Press, 2016.

Frith, Laverne, and Carol Frith. *Practical Poetry: A Guide for Poets.* Frith Press, 1998.

Fumo, David. *A Gentle Introduction to Neural Networks Series—Part 1,* 4 Aug 2017, www.towardsdatascience.com/a-gentle-introduction-to-neural-networks-series-part-1-2b90b87795bc.

Geske, Norman, editor. *The Art of Printmaking.* University of Nebraska Art Galleries, 1966.

Gilbert, Rita. *Living with Art.* McGraw-Hill, 1995.

_____. *Writing Guide and Projects Manual to Accompany Living with Art.* McGraw-Hill, 1995.

Goldberg, Natalie. *Writing Down the Bones.* Shambhala, 2005.

Gombrich, Ernst. *The Image and the Eye.* Phaidon, 1994.

Gordon, Mary. "Still Life: Bonnard and My Mother's Death" *Salmagundi,* nos. 146/147, Spring/Summer, 2005, pp. 33–79.

Griffin, Farah Jasmine. "Mamie Till Mobley's Gift of Grace." www.emmetttillproject.com/ farah.

Haggerty, Bill. "Icons of Photography: Eddie Adams." *Sage Publications,* 9 June 2009, www. journals.sagepub.com/doi/abs/10.1177/0956474809106669?journalCode=bjra.

Hagstrum, Jean H. *The Sister Arts.* University of Chicago Press, 1958.

Haines, John. *The Owl in the Mask of the Dreamer.* Graywolf Press, 1993.

Hampl, Patricia. *Blue Arabesque: A Search for the Sublime.* Harcourt, Inc., 2006.

_____. *Woman Before an Aquarium.* University of Pittsburgh Press, 1978.

Harris, Jana. *We Never Speak of It: Idaho-Wyoming Poems, 1889–90.* Ontario Review Press, 2003.

Haven, Paul. "Town Bombed in Spanish Civil War Remembers." *The Wenatchee World,* 27 Apr 2007, p. A9.

Hedgecoe, Mark, producer. *How Art Made the World* (DVD). Nigel Spivey, Narrator. BBC, 2006.

Heffernan, James A.W. *Cultivating Picturacy: Visual Art and Verbal Interventions.* Baylor University Press, 2006.

_____. *Museum of Words: Poetics of Ekphrasis from Homer to Ashbery.* University of Chicago Press, 1993.

Hirsch, Edward, editor. *Transforming Vision: Writers on Art.* Bullfinch Press, 1994.

Hirsch, Marianne, editor. *The Familial Gaze.* University Press of New England, 1999.

_____. *Family Frames: Photography, Narrative, and Postmemory.* Harvard University Press, 2012.

Hirshfield, Jane. *Nine Gates: Entering the Mind of Poetry.* Harper Perennial, 1998.

Hollander, John. *The Gazer's Spirit: Poems Speaking to Silent Works of Art.* University of Chicago Press, 1995.

Homer. *Iliad: Books 13–24,* Lines 600 through 603 of Alexander Pope's Translation. Harvard University Press, 1999.

Horowitz, Elizabeth. *Watercolor: A Beginner's Guide.* Watson-Guptill Publications, 2009.

Hughes, Glenn. *Imagism and the Imagists, a Study in Modern Poetry.* The Humanities Press, 1960.

Hugo, Richard. *The Triggering Town: Lectures and Essays on Poetry and Writing.* W.W. Norton & Company, Inc., 1979.

Hurley, Ann, Cole Swensen, and Peter Cooley. "Panel Papers." *American Writers Program Conference,* 14 Feb 2009.

Ionova-Gribina, Maria, photographer. *Natura Morta,* 2010–2013, www.ionovagribina.ru/ posts/6-natura-morta.

Jaranson, Carla. "What is Sumi-e? Traditional East Asian Brush Painting." *Sumie Society of America,* 2019, www.sumiesociety.org/whatissumie.php.

Jerome, Judson. "The Poet and the Poem." *Writer's Digest,* 1974, pp. 189–211.

Jung, Carl G. *Man and His Symbols.* Doubleday & Company, Inc., 1964.

_____. *The Spirit in Man, Art, and Literature.* Princeton University Press, 1966.

Kandel, Eric R. *The Age of Insight: The Quest to Understand the Unconscious in Art, Mind, and Brain, from Vienna 1900 to the Present.* Random House Publishing Group, 2012.

_____. "What the Brain Can Tell Us about Art." *The New York Times.* 13 Apr 2013. www. nytimes.com/2013/04/14/opinion/sunday/what-the-brain-can-tell-us-about-art. html?smid=fb-share&_r=0.

Keller, Lynn. "Poems Living with Paintings: Cole Swensen's Ekphrastic Try." *Thinking Poetry: Readings in Contemporary Women's Exploratory Poetics.* University of Iowa Press, 2010, pp. 97–123.

Kitchen, Judith. *Half in Shade: Family, Photography, and Fate.* Coffee House Press, 2012.

Koch, Kenneth. *Rose, Where Did You Get That Red?* Vintage Books, 1990.

Kolosov, Jacqueline. "The Ekphrastic Poem: A Grounded Instance of Seeing." *The Writer's Chronicle.* Oct/Nov, 2012, pp. 125–135.

Krieger, Murray. *Ekphrasis and the Still Movement of Poetry or Laokoon Revisited.* Frederick P.W. McDowell, editor. Northwestern University Press, 1967.

_____. *Ekphrasis: The Illusion of the Natural Sign.* The Johns Hopkins University Press, 1992.

Lampel, Jonathan. Digital Artist. Interview, 24 May 2019.

Lange, Dorothea. *The Evacuation.* www.anchoreditions.com/blog/dorothea-lange-censored-photographs.

Leonardo da Vinci. Translated by J.F. Riguad and John William Brown. *Treatise on Painting.* J.B. Nicols & Son, 1835.

Lightman, Alan. "Symmetrical Universe: Order and Beauty at the Core of Creation." *Orion.* Mar/Apr, 2013, vol. 32, no. 2, pp. 26–35.

Livingstone, Margaret. *Vision and Art: The Biology of Seeing.* Harry N. Abrams, Incorporated, 2002.

Livingstone, Margaret, and Bevil, R. Conway. "View Masters." *Skeptical Inquirer,* vol. 30, no. 6, 2006, pp. 34–37.

Long, Pricilla. *The Writer's Portable Mentor.* University of New Mexico Press, 2018.

"Looking vs. Seeing." *Look, See, Do.* www.lookseedodotorg.wordpress.com/to-look.

Macdonald, Cynthia. *I Can't Remember.* Knopf, 1997.

Macneice, Louis. *Modern Poetry, a Personal Essay.* Haskell House Publishers, Ltd., 1969.

Malcolm, Janet. "Six Glimpses of the Past: Photography and Memory." *The New Yorker,* 29 Oct 2018, pp. 18–26.

Mann, Sally. *Immediate Family.* Aperture, 1992.

Martineau, Kim. "Teaching Machines to Reason about What They See: Researchers Combine Statistical and Symbolic Artificial Intelligence Techniques to Speed Learning and Improve Transparency," *MIT Quest for* Intelligence, 2 April 2019, www.news.mit.edu/2019/teaching-machines-to-reason-about-what-they-see-0402.

Maxwell, William C. *Printmaking, a Beginning Handbook.* Prentice-Hall, 1977.

Mayes, Frances. *The Discovery of Poetry.* Harcourt Brace College Publishers, 1994, pp. 431–435.

McAlister, Elizabeth. "A Sorcerer's Bottle: The Visual Art of Magic in Haiti." *Sacred Arts of Haitian Vodou.* Donald J. Cosentino, editor, UCLA Fowler Museum of Cultural History, 1995, www.wesscholar.wesleyan.edu/cgi/viewcontent.cgi?referer=&httpsredir=1&article=1016&context=div2facpubs.

McCandless, Meghan, Art Conservationist. Interview, 19 Dec 2018.

McClatchy, J.D., editor. *Poets on Painters: Essays on the Art of Painting by Twentieth-Century Poets.* University of California Press, 1989.

McCutcheon, Marc. *Descriptionary: A Thematic Dictionary.* Facts on File, 2000.

McGilchrist, Ian. *The Master and His Emissary: The Divided Brain and the Making of the Western World.* Yale University Press, 2009.

McQuade, Donald, and Christine McQuade. *Seeing & Writing 2.* Bedford/St. Martin's, 2003.

Meinig, D.W. "The Beholding Eye: Ten Versions of the Same Scene." blogs.ubc.ca/thinkingbydesign/files/2016/09/9.22-Meinig-Beholding-Eye-1.pdf.

Michelango's poem, Jan, 2010, www.slate.com/articles/arts/poem/2010/01/labor_pains.html.

Mitchell, W.J.T. *Picture Theory.* The University of Chicago Press, 1994.

Mix, Elizabeth. "The Business of Art: Art Inventory." *Arts Inform, 2006,* www.in.gov/arts/2458.htm.

Moorman, Honor. "Backing into Ekphrasis: Reading and Writing Poetry about Visual Art." *The English Journal,* vol. 96, no. 1, 2006, pp. 46–53.

Mussorgsky, Modest. www.cso.org/uploadedfiles/1_tickets_and_events/program_notes/programnotes_mussorgsky_pictures.pdf.

Myers, David G., and C.N. Dewall. *Psychology in Everyday Life.* Worth Publishers, 2017.

Naqvi-Peters, Fatima. "A Turning Point in Rilke's Evolution: The Experience of El Greco." *The Germanic Review: Literature, Culture, Theory,* vol. 72, no. 4, 1997, 344–362.

Nelson, Maggie. *Bluets*. Wave Books, 2009.

Nims, John Frederick. *Western Wind: An Introduction to Poetry*. McGraw-Hill, 1992.

Orduña, José. *The Weight of Shadows: A Memoir of Immigration & Displacement*. Beacon Press, 2016.

Parms, Jericho. *Lost Wax*. University of Georgia Press, 2016.

Peach, Joe. "Gaudí's Masterpiece-Nature-Inspired Architecture." *Smart Cities Dive*, 2019, www.smartcitiesdive.com/ex/sustainablecitiescollective/gaudis-masterpiece-nature-inspired-architecture/18727/.

Peot, Margaret. *Inkblot: Drip, Splat, and Squish Your Way to Creativity*. Boyds Mill Press, 2011.

Perloff, Marjorie. "The Difference Is Spreading: On Gertrude Stein," *Poets.org*, 11 Oct 2012, www.web.archive.org/web/20121011190719/http://www.poets.org/viewmedia.php/prmMID/19342.

Peterdi, Gabor. *Printmaking: Methods Old and New*. Macmillan, 1959.

Philostratus of Lemnos' *Eikones*. *First example of Ekphrasis in Antiquity*. www.archive.org/stream/imagines00philuoft/imagines00philuoft_djvu.txt.

Plath, Sylvia. *Cross the Water*. Faber & Faber, 1976.

Plato. *Phaedrus*. CreateSpace Independent Publishing Platform, 2012.

Purpura, Lia. *On Looking*. Sarabande Books, 2006.

Rankine, Claudia. *Citizen: An American Lyric*. Graywolf Press, 2014.

Reddy, S.K. *How to Make Neural Networks "Describe" Images*, 13 Sept 2017, www.linkedin.com/pulse/how-make-neural-networks-describe-images-s-k-reddy/.

"The Religious Prohibition Against Images." *The David Collection*. www.davidmus.dk/en/collections/islamic/cultural-history-themes/image-prohibition.

Rilke, Clara, editor. *Letters on Cézanne*. Translated by Joel Agee. International Publishing Corporation, 1985.

Rilke, Rainer Maria. *Auguste Rodin*. Translated by Jessie Lemont & Hans Trausil. Pallas Athese Publishers, 2006.

_____. *The Books of Images*. North Point Press, 1994.

_____. *New Poems: A Bilingual Edition*. Translated by Stephen Cohn. Northwestern University Press, 1992.

_____. *Testament/Das Testament*. Translated by Pierre Joris. www.webdelsol.com/Sulfur/Rilke_text.htm, 1921.

Roberts, Edgar V. *Writing about Literature*. Pearson, 2011.

Rodriquez, George. Ceramic Sculptor/Instructor. Studio visit. 18 Nov and 7 Dec 2018.

Rowling, J.K. *Harvard Commencement Speech*, 2008.

Rusche, Harry. "The Poet Speaks of Art." www.emory.edu.english/classes/paintings&poems/titlepage.

Rushdie, Salman. *The Moor's Last Sigh*. Vintage Books, 1997.

Rusk, Lauren. "The Possibilities and Perils of Writing Poems about Visual Art." *The Writer's Chronicle*. Mar/Apr, 2007, pp. 75–82.

Ruskin, John. *Modern Painters, 1873*. Edited and abridged by David Barrie. Alfred A. Knopf, 1987.

Russell, David L. *Literature for Children: A Short Introduction*. Allyn & Bacon, 2009.

Saff, Donald. *Printmaking: History and Process*. Holt, Rinehart and Winston, 1978.

Saint-Exupéry, Antoine de. *The Little Prince*. Translated by Irene Testot-Ferry. Wordsworth Editions Limited, 1995.

Sandbank, Shimon. "Poetic Speech and the Silence of Art." *Comparative Literature*, vol. 46, no. 3, Summer, 1994, pp. 225–239.

Schjeldahl, Peter. "Artists and Writers." *The New Yorker*, 31 Jan 2011, pp. 80–81.

Scott, Grant F. *The Sculpted Word: Keats, Ekphrasis, and the Visual Arts*. University Press of New England, 1994.

Scruton, Roger. *Beauty: A Very Short Introduction*. Oxford University Press, 2011.

Searls, Damion. *The Inkblots: Hermann Rorschach, His Iconic Test, and the Power of Seeing*. Crown Publishers, 2017.

Shaikh, Faizan. "Automatic Image Captioning using Deep Learning (CNN and LSTM) in PyTorch," *Analytics Vidhya,* 2 Apr 2018, www.analyticsvidhya.cmo/blog/2018/04/solving-an-image-captioning-task-using-deep-learning/.

Shakespeare, William. *Hamlet.* Signet Classic, 1987.

Shakur, Aaminah. "Art, Magic and Pagan Theology." *Patheos Public Square on Religion and Visual Art,* 4 Feb 2015, www.patheos.com/topics/religion-and-visual-art/art-magic-and-pagan-theology-aaminah-shakur-020415.

Sibley, Mike. "Negative Drawing." *Art Instruction,* 2009, www.artinstructionblog.com/an-introduction-to-negative-drawing-with-mike-sibley.

Sills, Leslie. *In Real Life: Six Women Photographers.* Holiday House, 2000.

Simonite, Tom. "Google's Brain-Inspired Software Describes What It Sees in Complex Images." *MIT Technology Review,* 18 Nov 2014, www.technologyreview.com/s/532666/googles-brain-inspired-software-describes-what-it-sees-in-complex-images/.

Smith, Ray. *New Artist's Handbook: Equipment Materials Procedures Techniques.* DK Publishing, 1987.

Snodgrass, W.D. "Four Personal Lectures: Poems About Paintings." *In Radical Pursuit: Critical Essays and Lectures.* Harper & Row, 1975, 3–100.

Sontag, Susan. *On Photography.* Picador, 1977.

Spiegelman, Willard. *How Poets See the World.* Oxford University Press, 2005.

Stafford, William. "A Way of Seeing." *The William E. Stafford Archives Series 1, Sub-Series 4: Prose Drafts.* Lewis & Clark College, Special Collections & Archives, 2000.

Stallabrass, Julian. *Contemporary Art: A Very Short Introduction.* Oxford University Press, 2006.

Starbird, Margaret. *The Woman with the Alabaster Jar.* Bear & Company, 1983.

Stein, Gertrude. *Tender Buttons: Objects, Food, Rooms.* Haskell House Publishers, 1970.

_____. *Three Lives (1909).* CreateSpace Independent Publishing Platform, 2018.

Sterle, Francine. *Every Bird is One Bird.* Tupelo Press, 2001.

Steves, Rick, and Gene Openshaw. *Mona Winks: Self-Guided Tours of Europe's Top Museums.* John Muir Publications, 1993.

Stobart, Jane. *Printmaking for Beginners.* Watson-Guptill, 2001.

Stone, Irving. *The Agony and the Ecstasy: A Biographical Novel of Michelangelo.* New American Library, 2004.

Strand, Mark. *Hopper.* Alfred Knopf, 2001.

Strathausen, Carsten. "Rilke's Stereoscopic Vision." *The Look of Things: Poetry and Vision Around 1900.* University of North Carolina Press, 2003, pp. 190–236.

Stream of Consciousness—Narrative. www.narrative.georgetown.edu, 2008.

Swensen, Cole. "To Writewithize." *American Letters and Commentary, No. 13,* 2001, pp. 122–127.

Switalski, Caitie. "Time Is Running: Museum Curator in Florida Races to Preserve Holocaust Items," *National Public Radio,* 21 Mar 2019, www.npr.org/2019/03/21/688886161/museum-curator-in-florida-races-against-time-to-preserve-holocaust-items.

Talbot, Margaret. "Color Blind." *The New Yorker,* 29 Oct, 2018, pp. 44–51.

Tartt, Donna. *The Goldfinch.* Little, Brown and Company, 2016.

Tolstoy, Leo. *What Is Art?* Translated by Aline Delano. T.Y. Crowell & Co., 1899.

Tourtillott, Suzanne J.E., editor. *The Figure in Clay: Contemporary Sculpting Techniques by Master Artists.* Lark Books, 2007.

Updike, John. "Writers and Artists." *Just Looking: Essays on Art.* Knopf, 1989, pp. 191–200.

von Hagens, Gunther. *Body Worlds: The Anatomical Exhibition of Real Human Bodies.* DVD, 2007.

Vreeland, Susan. *Girl in Hyacinth Blue.* Penguin Group, 1999.

_____. *Life Studies: A Collection of Stories.* Viking, 2005.

_____. *A Penguin Readers Guide to Girl in Hyacinth Blue.* Penguin Group, 1999.

White, Michael. *Travels in Vermeer: A Memoir.* Persea Books, 2015.

Wilde, Oscar. *The Picture of Dorian Gray.* Penguin Classics, 2003.

Williams, Terry Tempest. *Leap.* Pantheon Books, 2000.

Winterson, Jeanette. *Art Objects: Essays on Ecstasy and Effrontery.* Vintage Books, 1995.

Wolf, Bryan. "Confessions of a Closet Ekphrastic: Literature, Painting, and Other Unnatural Relations." *Yale Journal of Criticism,* 1990. pp. 181–204.

Yeganeh, Hamid Naderi. "Drawing Birds in Flight with Mathematics," *Huffpost,* 6 Dec 2017, www.huffpost.com/entry/mathematical-birds_b_8876904.

Index

Numbers in **_bold italics_** indicate pages with illustrations

225